DANGEROUS SUBJECTS

Dangerous Subjects

James D. Saules and the Rise
of Black Exclusion in Oregon

KENNETH R. COLEMAN

Oregon State University Press   Corvallis

Library of Congress Cataloging-in-Publication Data

Names: Coleman, Kenneth R., author.
Title: Dangerous subjects : James D. Saules and the rise of black exclusion in Oregon /
    Kenneth R. Coleman.
Other titles: James D. Saules and the rise of black exclusion in Oregon
Description: Corvallis, OR : Oregon State University Press, [2017] | Includes biblio-
    graphical references and index.
Identifiers: LCCN 2017024582 | ISBN 9780870719042 (trade pbk. : alk. paper)
Subjects: LCSH: Saules, James D., b. 1806?- | African American pioneers—Oregon—
    Biography. | Pioneers—Oregon_Biography. | African American sailors—Biography.
    | United States Exploring Expedition (1838-1842)—Biography. | Frontier and
    pioneer life—Oregon. | Willamette River Valley (Or.)—History—19th century. |
    African Americans—Legal status, laws, etc.—Oregon—History. | Oregon—Race
    relations—History—19th century.
Classification: LCC E185.93.O7 C65 2017 | DDC 305.8009795/09034—dc23
LC record available at https://lccn.loc.gov/2017024582

∞ This paper meets the requirements of ANSI/NISO Z39.48-1992
(Permanence of Paper).

First published in 2017 by Oregon State University Press
Printed in the United States of America

Oregon State University Press
121 The Valley Library
Corvallis OR 97331-4501
541-737-3166 • fax 541-737-3170
www.osupress.oregonstate.edu

Contents

Preface

For as long as I can remember, I have used history as a means to psychically ground myself in a particular place. This was especially important when I was seven years old, and my family moved from California's bustling Bay Area to Aloha, Oregon, then a semi-rural suburb of Portland in the Willamette Valley. I felt as if I had traveled from the center of the universe to a distant and culturally bereft satellite. But as I roamed my new elementary school library, I noticed the omnipresence of something called the Oregon Trail in books, filmstrips, and wall art. I was relieved to learn that something historically "important" had happened in my new home state, something that briefly allowed Oregon to take center stage when schoolchildren around the nation studied something called manifest destiny. Destiny struck me as the crucial word whenever the Oregon Trail periodically emerged as a subject of study. I never once thought about the agency of the overland settlers who risked their lives to come to Oregon. I never pondered whether they were motivated by economic hardship, natural pluck, or the thrill of the unknown. To me, they were sturdy and solemn historical actors who had a part to play in the unfolding drama of American expansion.

The primacy of the Oregon Trail in forging my own sense of local history and heritage required cognitive dissonance. The master narrative of the Oregon Trail was that Anglo-American settlers headed west to populate and improve what had previously been empty space. Except I knew it was never empty. My public school teachers took pains to teach us about prosperous Indians of the Lower Columbia, who lived in communal long houses and worked salmon-choked fisheries. We also learned about the hardy indigenous communities of the Columbia Plateau, particularly the Nez Perces, whose headman, Chief Joseph, had initially resisted and then honorably acquiesced to the US military. Furthermore, I attended several field trips to a nearby replica of Fort Vancouver, a former outpost of the British fur trade where a multi-ethnic workforce, including Native people from throughout the region, acquired and processed animal skins to feed a ravenous world market long before the Anglo-American overlanders arrived.

But if the Oregon Trail's terminus had never been empty, that meant I was living in a colonized space. Did that make the Anglo-American settlers colonial invaders? This contradicted one of the central tenets I learned in high school US History, that American imperialism only began in the 1890s with the Spanish-American War and the US invasion of the Philippines. Once I began my formal study of history several years later, I quickly grasped that this position promoted American exceptionalism by privileging oceans as the chief conduits of empire building. It also recast the nation's later imperialist adventures as anomalies from what was purportedly a tradition of humanitarian intervention. Instead, I embraced the notion that imperialism in North America did not end with the American Revolution, and colonialism— the crucial tactic of American imperialism—continued unabated, if not uncontested, throughout the nation's history. And as I explore in this book, American colonialism is a complex and multifaceted phenomenon that has encompassed sailing ships, military campaigns, religious missionaries, and farm families riding aboard ox-drawn prairie schooners.

Any examination of American colonialism is incomprehensible without a deep discussion of race. Many observers often describe Oregon as a "white" state or Portland as a "white" city. This is an erroneous description, as it erases the fact that people of color have always lived in the region. On the other hand, these populations have been historically small. Even as I child, I noticed the lack of racial diversity in Oregon, particularly in contrast to the Northern California cities where I spent my early childhood. Once I began studying the history of race and colonialism in Oregon, it became clear that Oregon's racial composition was by design and not happenstance. Author and activist Walidah Imarisha occasionally gives a fascinating lecture titled "Why Aren't There More Black People in Oregon?" in which she identifies that Oregon's original American settler colonizers conceived of the region as a white homeland. She then describes how Oregon's long history of institutional racism had made the state an inhospitable place for black people. My goal with this book is to contribute to this discussion in a two-fold manner. First, by examining settler colonialism in Oregon within the larger context of imperialism and race relations in the antebellum United States, and secondly, by providing a more intimate account of how settler colonialism and racist lawmaking affected one specific person.

This leads me to this book's subject, James D. Saules. I was a history undergrad when I first encountered Saules' name in Elizabeth McLagan's 1980 book *Peculiar Paradise: A History of Blacks in Oregon, 1788-1940*. Later, while researching Oregon's racial exclusion laws for a seminar paper, I repeatedly encountered fleeting yet intriguing references to Saules. Once I completed the paper, I continued to collect as much information about Saules as I could. While many historians had treated Saules merely as a peripheral bearer of an issue (black exclusion), I was convinced he was much more than this. As my research led me beyond the Willamette Valley to archives in such places as Astoria, Oregon; Ilwaco, Washington; New Bedford, Massachusetts; and New York City, my initial rough impression of his life acquired an epic scope. By moving Saules from the periphery to the center of Oregon history, I hope to shed light on how racialized colonialism affected a man caught on the wrong side of the color line and his struggle to retain his agency amidst far-reaching and often cataclysmic social changes.

I began the initial work on this project as an undergraduate and later graduate student at Portland State University. This book would not exist without the guidance of several faculty members. I owe a particularly large debt of gratitude to Katrine Barber, who familiarized me with the historiography of the American West, encouraged my work, and eventually served as my thesis advisor. She was also the first person to suggest I turn my research into a book. Patricia Schechter was another crucial mentor at Portland State and an invaluable source of knowledge, wisdom, and support. I was also fortunate to learn much from Darrell Millner, whose vast knowledge of Oregon history is matched only by his penetrating insights.

Many friends, family members, mentors, and colleagues have improved this work immeasurably by taking the time to read all or parts of it. These include Gail Coleman, Robert Coleman, G. Thomas Edwards, David A. Johnson, Gwendolyn Carr, Merritt Linn, Colman Joyce, Natalie Linn, Bennett Gilbert, Laura Robson, Beth Cookler Merrill, Murray Cizon, and Bradley Richardson. I am grateful for their advice and constructive criticism.

Any research project requires the assistance of a far-flung network of archivists, librarians, independent historians, and educators. I am indebted to the following people for generously responding to my frequent queries and providing me with invaluable resources: Liisa Penner at the Clatsop County Historical Society, the entire staff of the Oregon Historical Society Research Library, Wayne E. Lee at the University of North Carolina at Chapel

Hill, Hobe Kytr, Mary Malloy at Harvard University, Jodi Goodman at the New Bedford Free Public Library, and Mai Reitmeyer at the library of the American Museum of Natural History.

Writing a first book is a daunting process, but the staff at the Oregon State University Press was extremely helpful and patient. I am especially thankful to Mary Braun for guiding me through the process of proposing and crafting a manuscript.

Most importantly, I must thank the three people with whom I share a home. They have endured my distracted and often absentminded behavior and a house filled with unwieldy stacks of books, articles, and documents. I cherish my two daughters, Casey and Jane, for their curiosity, good humor, and sensitivity. Finally, no one has contributed to this work more than my wife, Jodi Coleman. She is the greatest partner, friend, sounding board, and editor I have ever known. Without her intelligence, unflappability, and encouragement, I would still be wringing my hands over page one.

Kenneth R. Coleman

DANGEROUS SUBJECTS

Introduction

Though the colored man is no longer subject to be bought and sold, he is still surrounded by an adverse sentiment which fetters all his movements. In his downward course he meets with no resistance, but his course upward is resented and resisted at every step of his progress. . . . The color line meets him everywhere, and in a measure shuts him out from all respectable and profitable trades and callings.

—Frederick Douglass (1883)

We Americans are all cuckoos, —we make our homes in the nests of other birds.

—Oliver Wendell Holmes Jr. (1872)

On March 31, 2016, Washington state senator Pramila Jayapal issued a press release outlining her efforts to review racially offensive geographic names throughout the state.[1] In an earlier newspaper editorial, the Seattle-based Democrat wrote, "We have a responsibility to ensure that we create a welcoming environment for all people in our country to enjoy our public lands and that we honor the contributions of so many people of color who were some of our earliest and most intrepid explorers."[2] Jayapal identified three features in Wahkiakum County in southwestern Washington among her initial targets for potential name changes: Jim Crow Point, Jim Crow Creek, and Jim Crow Hill. *Jim Crow* is a term that originated in the popular minstrel shows of the nineteenth century and referred to a clownish stock character developed by blackface performer T. D. Rice in the 1830s. Jim Crow later became synonymous with the web of segregative laws and customs that state and local governments throughout the United States used to deny citizenship and civil rights to American black people following the end of the Civil War.[3] In an era when many Americans are understandably reluctant to commemorate a

racist system that survived into the late twentieth century (and many argue
still exists), it is obvious why Jayapal sought new names for the sites. Yet in an
April 15, 2016, interview with the *Chinook Observer*, she expressed a more
specific reason to remove the derogatory term from state maps—she believed
the three locations were actually named for a real person, James D. Saules.

Saules was a black sailor who first arrived in the Pacific Northwest in 1841
with the US Navy as part of the United States Exploring Expedition (US Ex.
Ex.). After deserting from the mission, he married a Chinook woman, worked
as a river pilot and ferryman, and operated a freight business on the Columbia
River. At the time of a large influx of Anglo-American immigrants via the
Oregon Trail in 1843, Saules lived with his wife on a plot of land in Oregon's
Willamette Valley near modern-day Oregon City, where he intended to make
his living as a subsistence farmer. One year later, he was peripherally involved
in the 1844 Cockstock Affair, a memorable instance of violence between local
Native people and American settlers. A few weeks later, Saules was arrested
and tried for allegedly inciting local Natives to violence against a white settler.
The district judge handed Saules over to US Indian subagent Elijah White,
who ordered him to leave the Willamette Valley. Saules, however, remained in
the region for the next several years, living north of the mouth of the Columbia
River at Cape Disappointment. Some historians claim he later moved further
west, where he was the first non-Native settler at the aforementioned Jim
Crow Point, ostensibly named in his honor.[4]

Not everyone in Wahkiakum County shared Jayapal's enthusiasm for the
proposed name changes, and neither the state senator nor the Washington
State Committee on Geographic Names had the authority to replace Jim
Crow with James D. Saules on state maps. They instead had to submit their
recommendation to the state's Board on Geographic Names. The board's
policy is to seek input from the public on proposed changes before it alters
any maps. Wahkiakum County Commissioners Blair Brady and Dan Cothren
were among the first to react, and both rejected the idea of any name changes.
Cothren, in particular, objected to a Seattle liberal like Jayapal dictating policy
to rural Washingtonians: "We're getting agencies telling us what we do with
our property. . . . It hasn't hurt anybody, the name. Do we have any colored
people here? I don't see it."[5] Cothren was also skeptical whether the names
were racist or even pertained to Saules. Instead, Cothren offered another
theory for the origin of the name Jim Crow: "I have an issue with it because
we have a lot of crows here."[6]

In the end, Commissioners Brady and Cothren modified their positions once they realized that many of their constituents were embarrassed by the name Jim Crow, and both commissioners eventually voted in favor of changing the names.[7] Yet many Washingtonians were ambivalent about honoring Saules. While at least one local resident, Columbia River kayaking guide Andrew Emlen, already referred to Jim Crow Point as Jim Saules Point when conducting tours of the area, others questioned the appropriateness of the name change once they began researching Saules's life.[8] In 1846 Saules was accused of causing the death of his Chinook wife. Although he was never convicted, Joe Budnick, who grew up in Brookfield, Washington, near Jim Crow Point, was disturbed that the state might honor a man who had allegedly mistreated Native women. He proposed a less controversial alternative: name the places after Brookfield, a defunct former cannery town, and the surnames of notable Brookfield residents. Therefore, Jim Crow Point, Jim Crow Creek, and Jim Crow Hill would be renamed Brookfield Point, Harlow's Creek, and Beare Hill. In May 2016, the Washington State Committee on Geographic Names unanimously approved Budnick's suggestions.[9]

The residents who supported Budnick's proposal were clearly aware of the racist implications of Jim Crow as a place-name but were unwilling to embrace James D. Saules as a worthy alternative. Most place-names in the Pacific Northwest are either indigenous names (or Anglicized variations) that survived colonial contact or Anglo-American names that honor white founding figures, early residents, or settlers' places of origin. The majority of these honorees escaped the kind of scrutiny faced by Senator Jayapal's proposed name change, suggesting that some Washingtonians held Saules and his legacy to a different standard. Furthermore, the removal of Jim Crow from state maps, while laudable, erases possible evidence that black people were among the area's early residents. The Pacific Northwest does boast a handful of schools, parks, and streets named for black people, although most commemorate famous national figures from the black freedom struggle (Rosa Parks, Martin Luther King Jr.) or local activists and political figures (DeNorval Unthank and Charles Jordan in Portland, Edwin T. Pratt and Flo Ware in Seattle). The closest analog to Saules might be George Washington Bush, a mixed-race man after whom an elementary school was named in Tumwater, Washington, a community he helped found. Bush, however, traveled west with his Anglo-American wife and children in 1844 as an overland immigrant on the Oregon Trail. He therefore fit the mold of a Pacific Northwest histori-cal archetype—the rugged and enterprising pioneer.

Saules represents something else. He was a black mariner who came to Oregon as a single man during the height of the fur trade. Yet he became nei-ther fur trader nor trapper. Saules was a well-traveled and intelligent man of considerable talents and daring who attempted to navigate, both literally and figuratively, the shifting cultural landscape of the Pacific Northwest in the mid-nineteenth century. Therefore, Senator Jayapal was correct to describe Saules as among the regions "earliest and most intrepid explorers" if one ignores the fact that most of the places he visited in his life were already inhabited by indigenous people. But Saules was also a protean figure whose life story dis-rupts tidy binary categories such as hero vs. villain; aggressor vs. victim; and most crucially, colonizer vs. colonized.

Regardless of whether he is ever immortalized on a map, Saules has already left his mark on the history of the region. Since the latter half of the nineteenth century, he has made frequent, if fleeting, appearances in numer-ous books and articles about early Oregon history. In one of the earliest examples from 1875, whaleman turned naturalist Charles Melville Scammon wrote a profile for Bret Harte's *Overland Monthly* titled "Pioneer Nig Saul." Scammon's piece was a mélange of minstrel-show stereotypes in which he described Saules as a "son of Africa" who "led a half-civilized, half-savage life" in Oregon.[10] Historian Lucile McDonald wrote a 1964 article about Saules for the *Seattle Times* in which she described him as an "extraordinary charac-ter" who was the first settler to live in Washington's southeast corner.[11] But what made Saules extraordinary in the Pacific Northwest of the 1840s had as much to do with how he appeared to others than any of his exploits. One key reason he appears so often in the historical record is that he was unmistak-ably black in a region where black people were rare. Second, he was a highly mobile sailor in Oregon during a period in which movement across space, either by land or water, was difficult. Finally, he married a Native woman with whom he started a family. While this was common among Euro-American men associated with the fur trade, a black man associating with Native people in this manner carried special and dangerous significance for many American settlers in the 1840s.

In the more scholarly studies of early Oregon history, Saules is most often cited at the chief inspiration for Oregon's first black exclusion law. In some works, Saules's activities are presented as a virtual cause of black exclusion in Oregon. In her 1886 *History of Oregon*, Frances Fuller Victor wrote, "The trouble occasioned by Winslow [Saules's mixed-race friend] and Saules aroused a strong prejudice against persons of African blood."[12] Such claims are reductive and ignore far deeper social and historical structures at work in the region. To suggest that Saules and other free black people somehow caused black exclusion is tantamount to blaming the victims for the crime. Still, Saules's influence on Oregon's first black exclusion law is unmistakable. Immediately following Saules's arrest and exile in June 1844, Indian sub-agent White referred to Saules and all other black people living in the region as "dangerous subjects." White wrote a letter to his immediate superior, the US secretary of war, asking if Oregon could legally remove the dozen or so black people then living in the region. Oregon's provisional government did not wait for a response and quickly passed its infamous Lash Law of 1844, subjecting any black man or woman who dared come to live in the region to public flogging. The provisional government justified the law on grounds that it would prevent slavery from taking root in Oregon. This was disingenu-ous, since the legislature had already banned slavery in an earlier session. Although the whipping provision was removed in December 1844 (and the exclusion law was repealed in 1845), the Lash Law has received much atten-tion in recent years from historians and nonhistorians alike, many of whom cite it as a shocking example of Oregon's racist past.

Despite the demise of the Lash Law, black exclusion remained a hallmark of Oregon lawmaking in the period prior to the Civil War. Oregon passed a similar black exclusion law in 1849 and included a black exclusion clause in its 1857 state constitution. Furthermore, the 1850 Donation Land Act excluded black people in Oregon from receiving generous free land claims from the federal government. The wording of such racist legislation—and the rhetoric Oregon lawmakers used to support it—suggested Saules's lingering influ-ence. In particular, black exclusion supporters focused their attention on pro-scribing the activities of black sailors who might desert their ships. Oregon lawmakers repeatedly raised concerns that worldly and morally suspect black sailors would commingle with Native communities—supposedly their natu-ral allies—and incite them to violence against white settlers.

Black exclusion was not unique to Oregon, and one can find examples of similar laws in other regions of the United States during the eighteenth and nineteenth centuries. In the American South, for example, many states required manumitted slaves to move elsewhere upon gaining freedom. Southern states often passed laws prohibiting free black men—particularly sailors like Saules—from visiting or immigrating.[13] Southern lawmakers feared the presence of free black men would undermine the legitimacy of slavery or that free black men might encourage enslaved people to resist or escape their masters. In addition, some southerners worried that the mere existence of free black people might arouse hopes of freedom among those held in bondage. The proslavery border states generally echoed such sentiments, and in 1820, Missouri's state constitution legalized slavery and banned free black immigration. While many northern states eventually phased out slavery in the late eighteenth and early-to-mid-nineteenth century, racial enmity and exclusion still prevailed. For example, the staunchly antislavery states of Ohio, Indiana, Illinois, and Iowa all passed legislation intended to curtail black people from settling there. In these states, as elsewhere in antebellum America, antislavery sentiment was deeply entwined with racial antipathy. The most common argument against slavery and for black exclusion was to prevent both free and enslaved black people from depressing the wages of white laborers, increasing class divisions, and causing civil unrest.[14] The vast majority of Anglo-American overland settlers who began arriving in Oregon in large numbers in 1843 hailed from the Old Northwest, Iowa, and western Missouri, so perhaps it is not surprising that they imported black exclusion to the region.

But black exclusion took a different course in Oregon, and lawmakers implemented it under different circumstances. The purpose of this study is to examine the life of James D. Saules and the rise of black exclusion in Oregon within the context of the settler colonization of the Pacific Northwest. Settler colonialism emerged as the dominant mode of American imperialism in the nineteenth century. Unlike other forms of colonialism, the intent of the exogenous settler colonizers was not to exploit the indigenous colonized for their labor but rather to remove them from settler society and claim their land. Peter H. Burnett, the architect of Oregon's first black exclusion law and co-leader of the first major wagon train to arrive in the Willamette Valley in 1843, was unequivocal regarding the settlers' colonial purpose: "We came, not to establish trade with the Indians, but to take and settle the country exclusively for ourselves."[15]

The Anglo-American settlers who arrived in the mid-eighteenth century sought to dismantle the preexisting multiethnic social order, privatize and commodify commonly held land, and create a homogenous settler society based on classical republican principles. (Most assumed the indigenous population would disappear on its own.) This presented a quandary because the colonization of Oregon still left a portion of the population that did not comfortably adhere to the categories of settler colonist or indigenous colonized. But most settlers shared a racialist ideology and used race, as opposed to national origin or religion, as shorthand to determine which previous inhabitants would be included and which would be excluded. This set the stage for ethnic cleansing, as settlers forged a color line to separate white from nonwhite, which in turn separated colonizer from colonized. Therefore, a Scottish or French Canadian Catholic fur trader could theoretically join the settler society, but a black sailor turned yeoman farmer born in the United States could not. As for the region's indigenous population, the common assumption among settlers was that they were an inferior race destined for extinction.

Black people, to the consternation of settlers, did not seem preordained to share a similar fate, and the population of both free and enslaved black people in the United States increased significantly between 1830 and 1840. Despite having a minuscule black population of probably no more than fifteen people, black exclusion was among the first preliminary steps that Anglo-American settlers took to claim Oregon as a white homeland and legally enforce the color line. At the time of the first black exclusion law in 1844, Anglo-American settlers were in the earliest stages of conquering the region, which comprised various Native and multiethnic communities. Burnett later framed the Lash Law upon the "settled conviction that Oregon would be the first American State of the Pacific."[16] Therefore, Burnett determined that "each State had the constitutional right to determine who should be citizens, and who residents."[17] Oregon's provisional government decided that black people belonged in neither category. Burnett both despised slavery and feared racial mixing. He never claimed to hate black people but instead associated them— enslaved and free—with "great evils that had so much afflicted the United States and other countries."[18] For Saules and the black people who chose to remain in the Pacific Northwest, however, the Lash Law and subsequent black exclusion legislation firmly placed them in the category of the colonized other. For Saules, this meant harassment, displacement, and dispossession.

But Saules did not come to Oregon in 1841 to be colonized and pushed to the margins of settler society. And neither did any other black person who dared settle there. What made Saules a "dangerous subject" in Oregon is that he continually struggled to maintain his position in settler society as a colonizer despite being racially marked as colonized. Moreover, in spite of his subordinated racial status in antebellum America, Saules was also an agent of empire who came to Oregon as a crew member of a US exploring mission that had specific colonial designs to make the Pacific Northwest a branch of the metropole. Like thousands of American settlers after him, he remained in the region and lived off the abundant resources found on land traditionally used by indigenous peoples. When the Oregon Trail immigrants began arriving in large numbers in 1843, Saules joined the overlanders as a resident of their emerging agrarian settler community.

But Saules encountered an ever-thickening color line every time he tried to retain his place among the colonizers, and he found it increasingly difficult to establish a foothold in a community predicated on white supremacy. In a sense, he had to operate in a liminal space that revealed the instability of constructed categories like colonizer and colonized.[19] And as a free man, Saules violated what many Americans viewed as the natural condition of a black person, as that of slave. Instead, as an intelligent and intrepid sailor with close connections among Native people, Saules and others like him were viewed by Anglo-American settlers in Oregon with great suspicion as a source of potential resistance. There is evidence that Saules, for his part, was willing to join with Native people to oppose settlers if necessary, particularly to resist dislocation and removal. On the other hand, other sources suggest Saules may have participated in violence against indigenous people. Therefore, given his protean and adaptable nature and a nearly complete absence of sources that represent his own point of view, Saules has remained a difficult figure to fully grasp, then and now.

According to historian Roxanne Dunbar-Ortiz, "The history of the United States is a history of settler colonialism," and recent scholarship regarding settler colonialism as a global phenomenon has helped shape this study.[20] In addition, historian James Belich has argued that the early nineteenth century witnessed the emergence of a new "discourse of emigration" or "mass ideology" in which many in the Anglophone world were compelled to travel unprecedented distances to dispossess indigenous peoples and install conservative settler societies modeled on the ones they left.[21] This marked a change from previous forms of colonialism in which colonists usually sought to incorporate indigenous people (often temporarily) into their economic ventures. Much of the success of settler colonialism was due to it being a massive "bottom-up" movement. The American settlers who came to Oregon in the early 1840s were not organized or sponsored by the US government. They were conceived along kinship lines rather than national affiliation. By the time the nation-state stepped in, much of the colonial work of building infrastructure, developing statecraft, and dispossessing Native people was already completed. Because of this, Belich argues, indigenous peoples "could cope with normal European colonization; it was the explosive colonization that proved too much for them."[22]

The settler invasion also proved too much for Saules, demonstrating the strong connection between racial exclusion and settler colonialism. My use of the term *race* refers to a fluctuating social and historical idea or discourse—rather than any kind of biological phenomenon—in which various meanings are attached to different kinds of bodies. According to sociologists Michael Omi and Howard Winant, "The concept of race continues to play a fundamental role in structuring and representing the social world."[23] This is particularly true of social groups, like nineteenth-century Anglo-American settlers, who ascribed racial characteristics onto others as a pretext for domination. Sociologist Collette Guillaumin argues that race emerged as both a scientific and legal status in the post-Enlightenment nineteenth century as a result of the "interaction between the economies of colonialism, industrial growth, and progress in the natural sciences."[24] Therefore, what historian Patrick Wolfe refers to as "the organizing grammar of race" came of age at the same time as modern settlers' colonialism, and race was either a qualification or disqualification for citizenship in most settler societies, Oregon included.[25] Wolfe contends that race, as a means of inclusion and exclusion, "becomes activated in the context of the threat of social space having to be shared with the colonized."[26] But Wolfe also argues that, for many white Americans, free black men like Saules existed in a disturbingly gray area between colonizer and colonized: "The presence of Black people who were not slaves . . . produced all sorts of legal and ideological anomalies for a society that was premised on an equation between blackness and slavery."[27]

Settler colonialism was not the only form of colonialism at work in Oregon, and racial exclusion in the Pacific Northwest is best understood through an examination of the shifting and overlapping modes of colonialism in the region during the mid-nineteenth century. Many historians of black exclusion on the American frontier have focused almost exclusively on the white American immigrants and the values and laws brought with them. This ignores what the Oregon Country and, more specifically, the

Willamette Valley were like prior to Anglo-American settler colonization and who was living there. While many American settlers envisioned the region as containing free land for the taking, it was neither an empty space nor an Arcadian paradise. It was a region thoroughly transformed by colonial contact, both direct and indirect. The preexisting population, although small, was culturally complex, containing not only various indigenous peoples, but also the ethnically diverse workforce of the fur industry and missionaries, both Catholic and Protestant. And when the first American settlers left Independence, Missouri, in 1843, the United States was still a maritime nation. While the Oregon Country was remote from centers of power in United States and Great Britain, sailing ships linked it to the various multiethnic seaports made necessary by the exigencies of merchant capitalism during the Age of Sail, the period from the fifteenth to the mid-nineteenth century. This was the maritime global market network that brought Saules to the region and would presumably continue to bring other people of various ethnicities.

Lawmakers conceived the black exclusion laws of 1844 and 1849 when American settlers in Oregon felt most vulnerable. Most had traveled incredible distances overland to arrive in an ethnically diverse region they did not fully understand. When the first large American wagon train arrived, the overlanders had little leverage in the region and were still largely dependent on the preexisting population for their survival. Yet the settlers also understood that their desire for more land would be met with resistance from those already living on it or those who used it as hunting and gathering grounds. Tensions over competing land claims also emerged between the recently arrived Americans, Methodist missionaries, and the local management of the Hudson's Bay Company (HBC). At the same time, settlers feared that disenfranchised free blacks would cause trouble for settlers or, even worse, collaborate with the Native population to foment an uprising. While this might seem absurd in hindsight, such collaboration was not without precedent. Throughout the first half of the nineteenth century, escaped slaves joined forces with the Seminoles in Florida to resist attempts by the United States to remove the escapees to reservations. This resulted in two wars between the US Army and the Seminole and black fighters. In 1847, in the aftermath of the Whitman Massacre in which a party of Cayuses killed several missionaries, settlers again feared for their safety and legislators called for black exclusion as a means to neutralize potential threats.

Although as a historical concept, Richard White's notion of a "middle ground" has been overused and abused, the term remains useful to describe the dynamics of the lower Columbia River region and Willamette Valley prior to settler colonization. According to White, "The middle ground is the place in between: in between cultures, peoples, and in between empires and the nonstate world of villages. It is a place where many of the North American subjects and allies of empires lived."[28] A middle ground is not a place in which a dominant group absorbs or acculturates a subordinate group. Instead, it is a confusing and often violent place in which, through accommodation and mutual dependence, new cultural meanings, values, and practices are formed.[29] In this study, I stretch the notion of the middle ground to include Saules's entire milieu; that is, the sites fostered by merchant capitalism and economic colonialism during the Age of Sail, including the seaports and deep-sea vessels of the maritime world. It was in these various middle grounds that Saules found something resembling a home. To dismantle the middle ground that existed in Oregon, American settlers had to enforce a color line that divided the included from the excluded. Saules repeatedly found himself on the wrong side of that line.

This work is more microhistory than biography. A proper biography of Saules would require more sources that provide his own perspective on the events that shaped his life. Aside from one letter ostensibly written by Saules, most of my sources come from white authority figures and elites. This suggests one reason why marginalized and nonelite people seldom have biographies written about them. A microhistory, on the other hand, reduces its scale to focus on one person—or a small group of people—in an attempt to resist the tendency to subsume ordinary people within larger groups or cast them as helpless victims to larger historical processes. Microhistory emphasizes the experiences and activities of ordinary and subaltern people, people whom more traditional historians often generalize about or ignore altogether. I am attracted to the methods and reduced scale of microhistory because they vividly reveal both the possibility and limits of human agency in the face of institutional restraints. Therefore, by focusing on what made Saules a dangerous outlier in Oregon, I can connect him to larger social and historical changes. This approach has its risks, as there are long stretches of this study in which Saules seems to disappear from the narrative. But I contend it is necessary to frequently pull the historical lens back to adequately reconstruct the social, cultural, and political context of Saules's life in antebellum America and the maritime world.

One of the purposes of doing a microhistory is to try to gain insight into everyday lives and how various institutions and structures of power affected ordinary people. Yet representatives of these same institutions were responsible for most of my sources. This poses the daunting question of whether it is even possible to recover the voices of nonelites. Throughout this work I have attempted to read my "top-down" sources (government reports, legal documents, public journals, congressional records, etc.) against the grain by approaching them critically and skeptically. I have also tried to address the numerous silences in the historical record through historically informed speculation or by borrowing the macrohistorical techniques of social history. In each of these cases, I have tried to remain transparent when doing so. However despite my best efforts, I recognize that this work, like the work of Lucile McDonald and Charles Melville Scammon before me, will probably reveal as much about my own interests and biases as it will about the life of Saules.

1

James D. Saules and the Black Maritime World

On a cloudy July evening in 1841, a black man named James D. Saules sat shivering on the shore of Baker Bay, located east of Cape Disappointment on the north side of the mouth of the Columbia River. He tried to warm himself by a small spruce bonfire he had helped build, but his damp wool sailors' garments—now his only worldly possessions—made this difficult. While collecting firewood, he and his crew members had failed to find any food, and Saules was now experiencing severe hunger pangs. About two miles away on the opposite side of the cape, ocean breakers were demolishing the USS *Peacock*, his home and worksite of the two previous years. In 1813 New York laborers had built the 114-foot sloop-of-war, which saw major action as a US naval ship during the War of 1812. The vessel later battled piracy in the South Pacific and was briefly decommissioned after a whale strike nearly destroyed it in 1827. Yet the fearsome Columbia bar finally proved insurmountable for the venerable ship. Astonishingly, all of Saules's fellow crew members survived the wreck, due in part to the skillful intervention of local Chinookan boatmen. The need for food later led the crew to the southern banks of the river. There they erected a small tent village and awaited the arrival of a replacement vessel so they could complete their mission and sail back to the United States. Saules, however, had no intention of returning to the nation of his birth.

Saules's experiences and exploits while living in the Pacific Northwest during a period of rapid colonization have earned him a minor but enduring place in the annals of regional history, but his journey to Oregon itself was almost as remarkable. He first appears in the historical record as a crew member of the United States Exploring Expedition (1838–1842), commonly abbreviated as the US Ex. Ex., or the Wilkes Expedition after its commander,

Cape Disappointment at the mouth of Columbia River. Source: Henry J. Warre, *Sketches in North America and the Oregon Territory* (1848). Courtesy of the Oregon Historical Society.

US Navy Lieutenant Charles Wilkes.[1] Saules joined the expedition in its second year during a brief stop in Callao, Peru; he traveled thousands of miles, visited places few Americans even knew existed, and eventually arrived in the ethnically diverse lower Columbia region of the Pacific Northwest. Yet the fact that a black man like Saules participated in a US Navy expedition during the antebellum period was no anomaly. The demand for maritime labor during the Age of Sail provided free black men with an opportunity to earn a living and provide for their families. They contributed to the vibrant, heterogeneous culture aboard ships and at seaports.

But who was James D. Saules and where did he come from? Because he joined the US Ex. Ex. in Peru, many historians have assumed he was Peruvian, but this is highly unlikely. In fact, ample evidence suggests Saules was born in the United States. First of all, Saules probably carried a Seaman's Protection Certificate to prove his national origin and likely had to produce one to join a US Navy expedition.[2] Secondly, in a November 1845 letter from British spy Henry I. Warre to Peter Skene Ogden, Warre referred to Saules as an American.[3] More specifically, Oregon lawyer Silas B. Smith described Saules as a "Virginia negro" who played the fiddle in "plantation style."[4] Smith was a child when he knew Saules in the 1840s and only wrote about him as an adult in 1897, but this remains an important clue to Saules's regional origins.

Saules's exact birth date and place are difficult to determine because free black sailors were seldom included in the US Census due in part to their residential instability. For instance, the federal census of 1850 counted only 9 percent of the free black sailors who shipped out of Philadelphia that year.[5] Fortunately, many nineteenth-century crew lists of oceangoing vessels survive, including one that features Saules. The crew list for the December 1833 whaling voyage of the bark *Winslow* refers to Saules as a twenty-seven-year-old, five feet five man with a black complexion and "wooly" hair residing in New Haven, Connecticut.[6] If this source is reliable, Saules was probably born in 1806. The fact that Saules lived in New Haven in 1833 is less helpful due to the peripatetic nature of a sailor's existence; Saules may have lived there for years or mere weeks.

Saules's surname—often written as "Sauls" or simply "Saul"—might provide a clue to his regional origins, provided it was not an assumed name. Since he was a black person living in the United States, he was, at the very least, a descendant of enslaved people. Enslaved black people were usually referred to only by a first name. After gaining freedom, former slaves often changed or altered the names their owners had forced upon them or raised their names from diminutive to full form. In the antebellum South, it was common for former slaves and their offspring to adopt the surname of their former owner, while other freed women and men, particularly in the North and border states, chose either common Anglo-American surnames like Jackson, Johnson, or Morgan or names that proudly announced their free status, such as Freeman, Liberty, or Newman.[7] Saules, Sauls, and Saul were not common Anglo-American surnames in the early nineteenth century, and the 1810 US Census listed no one named Saules and only a few dozen people with the surname Sauls or Saul in the entire country.[8]

Because the vast majority of men named Sauls in the census were white southern slaveholders in North Carolina and Virginia, Saules or his ancestors may have had a connection to one of these families. The odds of Saules having origins in the Upper South, as Silas B. Smith—an attorney who knew Saules—once suggested, are bolstered by the fact that in 1820, there were nearly as many free black people living in Maryland, Virginia, and North Carolina (91,231) as in all the northern states combined (99,281).[9] In 1870 the US Census finally recorded the full names of black Americans, and data reveals that the majority of black people named Sauls resided in the Upper South, and North Carolina in particular.[10] In the nineteenth century, North

Carolina was a rural state where many white Virginian families relocated to purchase inexpensive land.[11] Many free blacks from Virginia also moved to North Carolina to escape oppressive conditions in the commonwealth.

Another mystery regarding Saules's past is whether he was born an enslaved or free person. Unfortunately, census data sheds little light on this question, as the US Census captured little specific information on enslaved persons until 1850, and even then the census only enumerated slaves as the nameless property of slaveholders. Regrettably, speculation is probably the only available tool to address this question. This is problematic because the varied history of black people in America contains nearly as many exceptions as examples, making any attempt to generalize somewhat futile. For example, some historians have suggested without evidence that Saules was a runaway.[12] But if historians mention Saules's legal status at all, they almost always refer to him as a "free Negro" or "free black." Saules was certainly free by 1833, which would have been confirmed by the seaman's papers he likely carried, and his parents might have been among the small but significant number of free black people living in the North and Upper South around the turn of the nineteenth century.

It is possible that Saules was born into slavery and gained his freedom later in life. If he was born a slave, he may have won his freedom through the limited means available during this period, such as manumission by slave owner, self-purchase, or escape. At the time of Saules's birth during the decades following the Revolutionary War, enslaved people in the Upper South found slightly increased opportunities for gaining freedom than in the decades immediately preceding the Civil War. Revolutionary rhetoric, the rise of evangelical Christianity, and the decline of tobacco as a cash crop led some enslavers to have second thoughts about the "peculiar institution." Saules was a creative and intrepid person who may have seized on one of these openings. Yet even this small window would soon slam shut. The rising number of free black people in the South following the Revolutionary War alarmed many southerners, and the primacy of slave labor for the profitability of the southern cotton economy made enslaved people more valuable than ever to the US economy. These factors contributed to laws throughout the South severely curtailing manumissions.

Even if Saules lived as a free man in the South, he would have faced severe challenges. To be free only meant one was not permanently bound to a slave owner. Free black people in the South were denied citizenship and equal access to economic opportunity. Many white southerners reviled free black people because their presence was a symbolic threat to the institution of slavery, challenging both the racialist idea that black people were naturally predisposed to slavery and the paternalist canard that they preferred bondage to freedom. Many free blacks also posed a tangible danger to the institution by promoting abolitionist ideas and assisting slaves in gaining manumission or escaping from their masters. Therefore, authorities and elites in many southern communities strove to keep contact between free black people and slaves to a minimum.

State and local governments in the South reacted to perceived and real threats by imposing a web of regulations to circumscribe the activities of free black people. For instance, all southern states required them to carry a certificate of freedom; if they didn't have one, they were presumed slaves. Free black people with papers often could not move or relocate throughout the country as many state constitutions contained provisions that restricted or proscribed free black immigration. For example, North Carolina prohibited free blacks from traveling beyond the county adjoining their home county, and in 1827 the state's general assembly passed a law banning free blacks or mulattos from migrating to the state.[13] In many southern states, free black people could not own a gun without a license, and most states barred free blacks from serving in a militia except as servants or musicians. By 1835 southern free blacks had lost their right to assembly and often could not hold church services without the presence of a white minister. In order to conduct any kind of business, free blacks often had to obtain licenses, which added to the difficulty of earning a living. At the same time, free blacks in all states were required to work and demonstrate proof of employment.[14]

If Saules lived in the North, he would have had greater access to education and property ownership, but the region was no paradise for free black people. While some northern and border states allowed blacks to vote in the early nineteenth century, by the mid-1840s free blacks were denied voting rights in New Jersey, Connecticut, Rhode Island, and Pennsylvania. In 1821 New York introduced property and residency requirements for black voters.[15] The federal 1793 Fugitive Slave Law allowed slave owners to retrieve runaways who had escaped to freedom in the North. When authorities asked black people to prove their free status, these blacks were further hamstrung since local courts and magistrates could decide a person's legal status without a trial. In addition, simmering racial prejudice in the North, often against recently arrived free black immigrants from the South, frequently came to a full boil with mob violence and rioting.[16]

Saules, like all ostensibly free black people in antebellum America, knew that even a modicum of freedom was precarious. Because the cotton boom of the nineteenth century increased the profitability of slavery, many free blacks, particularly children, were kidnapped and sold back into bondage. The most famous of such cases was that of New Yorker Solomon Northrup, author of *Twelve Years a Slave* (1853), who was kidnapped in 1841, the same year Saules arrived in the Oregon Country. Unlike most kidnapping victims, Northrup eventually regained his free status, but he was unable to bring his kidnappers to justice.[17] Free black communities attempted to combat the scourge of kidnappings by making warnings a regular feature of church services and forming local organizations like Baltimore's Society for Relief in Case of Seizure.[18]

Although a morass of legal proscriptions and societal pressures restricted social and economic opportunities, free black people like Saules created spaces in which to maneuver and live meaningful lives.[19] Black people married, raised children, started businesses, received educations, and educated others in return. They fought in the Revolutionary War—some for the American colonists, others for the British. They attended church services and political meetings, formed benevolent societies, and found amusement at dances and in various drinking and gambling establishments. They wrote poems, plays, historical works, and newspaper articles. They worked as scientists, mathematicians, and inventors. They composed and performed musical works, painted portraits, made quilts, and created sculptures. Former slaves and free blacks formed the vanguard of the movement to end slavery and provided assistance to runaway slaves. While many were poor, some free blacks owned property and a few became wealthy. Some free blacks even owned slaves themselves. And some, like James D. Saules, went out to sea and traveled the world.

A SAILOR'S LIFE

Saules became a sailor early in life. According to US Navy Lieutenant Neil M. Howison, who met Saules near the mouth of the Columbia River in 1846, Saules claimed he "had followed the sea twenty years prior to arriving in the Oregon Country in 1841."[20] This means he was approximately fifteen years old when he began to work aboard ocean vessels. But if Saules or his family ever lived in North Carolina, it is highly doubtful that he became a sailor there. The state boasted no significant seaports, and most residents, white or black, were engaged in agricultural pursuits. To become a sailor, Saules may have started in a major southern port city like Richmond, Norfolk, Charleston, or

Baltimore. Baltimore was a particularly important city for black sailors, and in 1850 free black people comprised 15 percent of the city's total population. Yet the fact that the 1833 crew list from the bark *Winslow* shows Saules living in New Haven suggests that either Saules had roots there or he, like so many other black mariners, gravitated to a northern port city with a significant free black community.

Although New Haven paled in commercial importance to multiethnic northern seaports like New York, Philadelphia, Providence, or Boston, Saules lived there at a time when the free black community was gaining prominence. By 1820 New Haven's black population officially reached 624 (7.5 percent of the city's entire population), and the state's free black population exceeded 8,000 by 1830.[21] These numbers are probably conservative, since census takers typically undercounted black residents, particularly sailors. Many black New Haveners were the descendants of New England enslaved people, and in 1784 the state passed a gradual emancipation act that freed all children of enslaved women when they reached the age of twenty-one.[22] In addition, a significant portion of Connecticut free black people had emigrated from North Carolina and Virginia, some as fugitive slaves and others as free artisans.[23] Much of the city's black population lived in New Township, an area largely owned and developed by William Lanson, a prominent black entrepreneur, hotelier, and engineer. The city also boasted autonomous black institutions including churches, schools, and political and fraternal organizations. The majority of New Haven free black people worked as artisans, domestics, and in various service industry positions. And despite New Haven's somewhat isolated harbor, many black men like Saules worked as mariners.[24]

While Saules lived much or all his life free from bondage, the idea that he was truly free in New Haven was inaccurate. While Connecticut's 1818 state constitution expanded white male suffrage to nonproperty holders, it also denied voting rights to black residents. Furthermore, New Haven was a highly segregated city, which was one of the major reasons it boasted so many autonomous black institutions. Many white New Haveners viewed black neighborhoods as dens of vice and depravity and were loathe to grant free black people the rights of citizenship. New Haven was also home to an active chapter of the American Colonization Society (ACS), an organization whose members sought to solve the nation's black "problem" by repatriating free black people to Africa, Central America, Canada, or the Caribbean. White mobs also rioted and targeted black New Haveners in the early 1830s.[25]

By 1833 Saules had left New Haven and traveled to New Bedford, Massachusetts, to seek work in the town's burgeoning whaling industry. At that time, whaling was the fifth-largest industry in the United States, and New Bedford was on its way to eclipsing Nantucket as the nation's preeminent whaling hub.[26] On December 18, the twenty-seven-year-old seaman presented his Seaman's Protection Certificate and joined the twenty-two-man crew of the bark *Winslow* for a four-year whaling voyage around Cape Horn to the offshore grounds of the Pacific Ocean. By the early nineteenth century, the onshore grounds of the Atlantic were mostly depleted, and many whalers were drawn to an area of the equatorial Pacific known for its impressive population of sperm whales. Saules's captain, thirty-four-year-old Edward C. Barnard, had recently commanded the ill-fated and well-publicized 1832 voyage of the *Mentor*. The *Mentor* was wrecked on a reef north of the Palau chain in the South Pacific, and a group of Palauan islanders captured Barnard and the surviving crew members and held them hostage in exchange for muskets. In February 1833, after escaping to the island of Tobi, a passing ship rescued Barnard and one other crew member. Although Barnard's exploits received wide publicity, the financially strapped captain commanded the *Winslow* a mere three months after returning to New Bedford.[27]

Although racism certainly existed among whaling crews, the *Winslow*'s crew list shows that Saules served in the officer class as a mate, a rank just below captain. Black mates aboard whaling vessels were somewhat rare during this period but not unheard of, and at least 80 black men served as mates on 105 different voyages during the peak years of the whaling industry from 1803 to 1860.[28] According to historian Stuart M. Frank, due to "the enthusiastically abolitionist atmosphere of the whale fishery, with its origin in Quaker Nantucket and its prosecution necessarily meritocratic, opportunities for people of color abounded disproportionately to the norms in other industries."[29] Yet for a black man like Saules to reach the rank of mate, he would have demonstrated advanced skills as a seaman to overcome racial prejudice. Luckily for Saules, he was a seasoned mariner with over ten years' experience. He would have worked directly under Barnard along with two or three other mates, each commanding his own whaleboat. Most whale crews were multiethnic, meaning Saules probably commanded white men in addition to black, Native, Cape Verdean, and Pacific Islander sailors.

Herman Melville captured the multiethnic milieu of New Bedford and its whaling vessels in his 1851 novel *Moby-Dick*. In the late 1830s, Melville, barely out of his teens, went to the city to work as a greenhand (an inexperienced seaman) on whale hunts. Although they came from very different backgrounds, Melville and Saules would have shared many experiences and seen similar sights. In fact, Melville shipped out on a whaling ship in the 1840s that traveled a similar route as Saules did with the US Ex. Ex., and he later used Wilkes's narrative of the expedition as research material when writing his most famous novel.[30] While his description of the *Pequod* and its crew is fictional, Melville's writing remains useful because, unlike most officer's journals, Melville was interested in both the more quotidian aspects of maritime life and the social interactions of the entire crew. And whereas earlier readers embraced *Moby-Dick* for its psychological and philosophical symbolism, contemporary literary critics are as likely to focus on the novel's depiction of antebellum race relations.[31] One chapter, "Midnight, Forecastle," presents an American whaling crew that included New England, Dutch, French, Sicilian, Pacific Islander, black, Chinese, American Indian, Irish, and East Indian sailors.[32] Another chapter, "Stubb's Supper," concerns an abusive second mate who harasses Fleece, an elderly black sea cook from Roanoke, Virginia.[33] Finally, Pip, a tambourine-playing black greenhand turned Shakespearean fool is the subject of one the novel's most memorable chapters, "The Castaway."

Despite the exceedingly dangerous (yet often tedious) life of a whale man, Saules was motivated by the potential for financial gains rare for a black man in the antebellum United States. Furthermore, when he worked aboard the *Winslow*, he received payment equal to white crew members. Whalers, however, did not earn conventional wages for their labor. Instead, each sailor received a share, or "lay," of the voyage's profits. Customary lays for New England whalers in the 1830s and 1840s were assigned by berth: 1/185 for greenhands and 1/150 for seamen like Saules. This arrangement had an obvious catch: an unsuccessful voyage could yield meager or even zero profits. Therefore, crew members assumed considerable financial risk when they agreed to work on a whaling vessel. On the other hand, a four-year voyage with room and board promised almost unheard of job security for black sailors.[34]

On July 7, 1837, the *Winslow* returned to New Bedford after four years at sea, but Saules was probably not on board when the bark arrived in the harbor. Desertion rates on whaling ships hovered between 50 and 75 percent, and voyages almost never returned with their original crew.[35] Because Saules joined the US Ex. Ex. approximately two years later in Peru, it is plausible that he deserted and remained in the Pacific. Desertions were particularly common if whale hunts yielded meager results and sailors realized their lays would be correspondingly low. The report of the Commissioner of Fish and Fisheries shows that *Winslow* returned to the United States with 1,001 barrels of sperm oil. This was not a disastrous result, but it was certainly below average for a four-year voyage to the Pacific during the golden age of American whaling.[36]

Saules may have had other reasons to desert besides paltry earnings. According to Henry J. Dally, who shipped with Saules aboard the *Winslow* as an eighteen-year-old greenhand, the first leg of the voyage was an unbridled disaster. After ten months at sea, the bark's supply of salted meat was putrid, and the entire malnourished crew was stricken with scurvy. When the troubled vessel arrived at Paita, a seaport in the northwest corner of Peru, Dally and four other crew members took advantage of a few days' shore leave by abandoning the voyage. The five men traveled as far as the Peruvian town of Sechura, where local authorities arrested them for desertion and transported them back to Paita. Dally and his co-conspirators spent five days in the stocks before returning to the *Winslow*. Dally did not mention any of his companions by name, but he did describe one man as a "darkey," an ethnic slur for a black person typical of the era. This may have been Saules; but given the typical racial composition of whaling crews, it is unlikely that Saules was the *Winslow's* only black crew member. Dally wrote that the unnamed black man was the only crew member who did not return to the vessel. Instead, he apparently threatened the life of Captain Barnard, who chose to leave the disgruntled black seaman in Paita.

Conditions did not improve once the *Winslow* returned to open waters. With supplies again depleted, Barnard took the vessel to the uninhabited Cocos Island—located 342 miles off the coast of Costa Rica—to obtain wood and fresh water. Dally and eight crew members again responded to ongoing privations by deserting. Nine men constituted a large percentage of the now twenty-one-man crew, and there is a strong chance Saules was among them if Barnard had not already left him behind in Paita. The nine deserters loaded up on provisions from the bark and defiantly climbed to the top of a mountain in full view of Barnard. The alarmed captain rushed to the base of the mountain and ordered the men to return to the ship. The men laughed, refused to budge, and instead threatened to crush the captain with falling boulders if he attempted to take them by force. Barnard waited two days for the men to reconsider; then he and his depleted crew departed without them. The men survived for two weeks on a diet of shellfish and seagulls until a passing whaling vessel, the *Almira* out of Edgartown, Massachusetts, picked them up and transported them back to Paita. Some of the men, including Dally, chose to remain working aboard the *Almira* while others remained in Peru.[37]

BLACK MARINERS AND A SEA OF POSSIBILITY

Saules lived during a period in which many black men in the antebellum United States earned a living for themselves and their families on a seafaring vessel or in a seaport town. This was particularly true of the whaling industry, and in 1822 the schooner *Industry* sailed to the whaling grounds of the Pacific with an all-black crew.[38] Although the image of the nineteenth-century black sailor may be unfamiliar to modern observers, the maritime industry was the largest employer of black men by the early part of century.[39] So many young black men signed on to work on deep sea voyages that women often significantly outnumbered men in the urban free black communities of the North and Upper South.[40] The black sailors involved in overseas commerce and exploration in the Age of Sail stood apart from the rest of the US population; many traveled remarkable distances and experienced a variety of cultures in an era in which most Americans never ventured far from their hometowns. The fact that Saules was living, if only temporarily, on the west coast of South America when he signed on the US Ex. Ex. suggests how far the black maritime world extended by the late 1830s.

The rise of the black maritime world was inextricably tied to the development of merchant capitalism following the European colonization of the Americas beginning in the late fifteenth century. Merchant capitalism is a system in which investors earn profits by adhering to the maxim "buy low, sell high." Merchant capitalists earn the most profits by investing in projects in which laborers extract resources from places where the resources are plentiful and transport them to places they are scarce. The American whaling industry is one clear example of merchant capitalism, particularly since the whaling grounds of the Atlantic Ocean were largely depleted by the early nineteenth century. At the height of merchant capitalism during the Age of Sail, European and American investors earned the most dramatic profits by financing sea voyages to remote places where resources were obtained through a variety of means, including purchase, trade, or outright theft. Such "resources" included enslaved human beings, and in 1526 Portuguese traders first began transporting captured Africans to the Americas. Conversely, traders could also employ sailing ships to locate and open new markets for European trade goods. The infamous Atlantic triangular slave trade route was a dramatic example of merchant capitalism in action, circulating manufactured trade goods, raw materials, and enslaved human beings between Europe, Africa, and the Americas.

In Europe and Great Britain, the evolution of merchant capitalism led to revolutions in nautical technology and finance, which in turn fueled a dramatic expansion of imperialism and its chief tactic, colonialism. At the same time, people from wide-ranging corners of the globe began encountering each other with increasing frequency, resulting in transformative—and often violent—cultural transmissions. Maritime imperialism fueled the economies of the nations of Europe, and by the late seventeenth century, inchoate notions of geographic and ethnic superiority began to solidify into Manichean notions of whiteness and blackness. White supremacy emerged as a rationale for the dispossession of land, wealth, and resources. The rise of maritime colonialism also meant that many people—both elite and subaltern—lived and worked in places far from where they were born. Yet unlike the industrial form of capitalism that later arose in England during the eighteenth century, merchant capitalism was not predicated on revolutions in production or the rationalization of the labor process. Merchant capitalists obtained labor by any means necessary, the cheaper the better. Of course, this labor often included enslaved people—both indigenous and imported—and indentured servants. But in instances in which enslavement or servitude was not practical or possible, merchants, traders, cultivators, and sea captains had to find laborers willing to perform backbreaking work for relatively low wages or trade goods. Therefore, the movement of various people around the world and merchant capitalism's insatiable appetite for labor combined to encourage the rise of multiethnic labor forces in extraction colonies, seaports, and on board ships.

This voracious demand for labor made black sailors like Saules ubiquitous in the Age of Sail. Despite the pervasive white supremacism of the antebellum period, it was not feasible for either American or British ships to meet the demand for maritime labor with all-white crews. The exigencies of imperialist wars and the expansion of maritime commerce resulted in employment opportunities aboard whaling ships, merchant ships, naval boats, and vessels commanded by privateers and pirates. For laborers in the nineteenth century, toiling aboard a deep-sea vessel was among the most difficult, dangerous, and least remunerative type of work available. White seamen had to surrender their freedom for the duration of a voyage and were among the most impoverished and marginalized white laborers of the nineteenth century.[41] Many sailors often abandoned their ships when they reached a habitable seaport, and desertion was one of the few forms of resistance available to maritime laborers. Moreover, frequent desertion and disciplinary problems on deep-sea voyages created job opportunities for sailors located in various seaports. For instance, Saules later joined the US Ex. Ex. following the desertion of eight men during its brief stop in Callao, including the ship's cook whom Saules likely replaced.[42] This was not an unusual number for an expedition that ultimately lost over a half of its original crew of 346 to desertion, death, and dismissal.[43]

For free black men in the North and South—and even some enslaved men—the sea afforded some of the best opportunities for economic compensation and independence in a deeply racist society. In the antebellum North, black men suffered discrimination in most trades and had difficulty procuring productive land.[44] The maritime industry, on the other hand, provided black men with a wider range of economic activity and mobility. Black sailors were integral to the development of a coherent black community in antebellum America, and as historian Jeffrey Bolster observed, "Maritime wages provided crucial support for black families and underwrote organizations such as churches and benevolent societies through which black America established an institutional presence and a voice."[45] While all sailors' pay was typically low, black sailors working on ships, particularly those working out of northern ports, often earned the same amount as whites with the same job title.[46] Maritime work, particularly the rigorous tasks associated with whaling, afforded black men the opportunity to assert their masculinity and equality with whites, in contrast with more demeaning work they often performed on land.[47] While racial boundaries and the color line certainly existed aboard ships, such categories often took a back seat to the nonracial hierarchies established by the ship and other maritime institutions.

It is difficult to determine an accurate percentage of how many black men of Saules's generation served on sailing ships, since most crew lists in the eighteenth and early-to mid-nineteenth century made no specific mention of race or ethnicity. However, many lists had categories for complexion and hair. Historian Martha S. Putney delved into nineteenth-century crew lists and sought out terms such as "African," "colored," "black," "wooly," and "negro" to determine the presence of black crew members sailing out of various

American cities.[48] She found that the percentage of black sailors was lowest in the South and highest in the North. For example, in 1838, 8.4 percent of crew members sailing from New Orleans were identifiably black, although that is a conservative estimate.[49] In 1836, 30 percent of crew members working out of Providence, Rhode Island, were black.[50] The percentages were nearly as high in New York City, Boston, and New Bedford.

While social class, knowledge, and ability may have trumped race aboard many ships during the Age of Sail, Saules still encountered a rigid social order that was often racially encoded. Many white sailors disliked blacks, and even extremely skilled and experienced black sailors had difficulty ascending to the officers' class. Less skilled black sailors often served as ordinary seamen—called "boys," as opposed to skilled sailors known as "men"—and suffered a disproportionate amount of hazing.[51] And while a majority of black sailors did not work as cooks or stewards, black men filled these positions almost exclusively. These positions existed outside the ranking system of officers, men, and boys and were often gendered feminine by other sailors, who placed a premium on masculinity.[52] Furthermore, seamen commonly referred to cooks, stewards, and boys as "idlers" because unlike the rest of crew members who alternated between four-hour shifts, the so-called idlers worked in the daytime and slept at night.[53] These "idlers" were still called upon to perform a variety of tasks on board ships, particularly during times of crisis or emergency.

ANCHORS AWEIGH: SAULES SHIPS WITH THE US NAVY

By July 1839, Saules was in Callao, Peru, seeking new job opportunities. He first boarded the ill-fated US Navy sloop-of-war *Peacock* of the US Ex. Ex. on a summer day while its crew made a month-long stop in the town to resupply and restaff the ship. Callao, located about nine miles from Lima, was an active seaport in the 1830s. George Musalas Colvocoresses, a midshipman with the expedition, spotted six American merchant ships and one naval vessel when he arrived at the port in the summer of 1839.[54] Whether or not Saules deserted from the *Winslow* or came there aboard the *Almira*, it is almost certain he arrived aboard a whaling ship. Saules may have later found employment in the harbor or perhaps he sought to profit from conflict taking place between newly independent Latin American nation-states. When the *Peacock* sailed into Callao's harbor in June 1839, Chile had defeated Peru six months earlier in the War of Confederation (1836–1839). Callao was teeming with idle and inebriated American soldiers of fortune, and Saules may have fought among their ranks.[55] Regardless of his reason for being there, Saules probably felt comfortable in Callao, a cosmopolitan seaport typical of the maritime world. The cosmopolitan quality of seaports like Callao was a reflection of the multiethnic composition of most sailing ships during the period from 1812 to 1860 when the United States dominated maritime commerce in the South Pacific. For instance, Charles Erskine, who served with the US Ex. Ex. as a teenager, later wrote about a St. John's Day celebration he witnessed during the expedition's brief stop in the coastal town: "Several nationalities were present—Peruvians, Chileans, Indians, negroes, half-breeds, and others of both sexes."[56]

Regardless of how comfortable Saules had become amidst the multiethnic atmosphere of Callao, he was clearly eager for a change—even if it meant signing on with the US Ex. Ex. as a cook rather than a mate. The expedition had already been at sea for nearly a year and crew members were beginning to desert. One in particular was ship's cook Elias Russel, whom Saules signed on to replace. Despite this apparent demotion, Saules had much to gain by taking an ostensibly lower position. By the 1830s, a heightened demand for maritime labor meant that black cooks and stewards frequently earned as much or more than white sailors.[57] This also resulted in an improvement of their image. For instance, in his 1875 profile of Saules for the *Overland Monthly*, Charles Melville Scammon referred to Saules as having held "the important position of cook aboard the Peacock."[58] As Saules's whaling experience demonstrates, serving as a cook or steward did not mean that one was not a capable seaman or had never held other maritime positions. Saules, who worked for two years as a cook for the expedition, would later demonstrate his nautical skills when he commanded a schooner on the Columbia River, at that time one of the most dangerous rivers in North America. Saules may have also longed for a position less tied to the ship's chain of command. Cooks like Saules could also enjoy a sense of independence while working in their galleys, even if this meant they were often isolated from the rest of the crew.

For Saules, the opportunity to work on a US Navy vessel in particular was probably too good to refuse. Beginning with a labor shortage during the War of 1812, a small but significant number of free black men and foreign black nationals were able to enlist in the US Navy and receive the same wages, privileges, and opportunities for promotion as white sailors.[59] Racism in the US Navy still prevailed, however, and many black men served as waiters, barbers, bakers, and cooks. Still, naval ships, both British and American, provided better food and easier work than whaling or merchant ships and some positions offered health care and pensions.[60] Saules was probably also drawn by the inherent prestige of serving with the US Ex. Ex., even if only as a ship's cook. He may also have received news that the expedition was about to attempt the discovery and first reconnoitering of the continent of Antarctica in recorded history.

In addition to serving as a cook, Saules played the violin, or fiddle, and likely worked as a musician on the US Ex. Ex., although "musician" was not an official capacity noted on the crew list. According to Silas B. Smith, Saules and his fiddle were later fixtures at social events in Clatsop County in the late 1840s.[61] The journal of Lieutenant William Reynolds, an officer with the US Ex. Ex., reveals that there was a fiddler aboard the Peacock, the ship on which Saules served. On January 23, 1840, when the Peacock's anchor first struck land in Antarctica, an unnamed fiddler played for the elated crew as they coiled the mud-coated sounding line.[62] In addition to fiddlers, naval ships and privateers frequently hired drummers, trumpeters, french horn players, and fife players. On sailing ships, music was used not only to entertain but also to recruit unemployed sailors in seaports, call men to their posts, and provide rhythmic accompaniment for drills and tedious collective labor. Music also had a diplomatic function. For example, when the expedition reached the Fiji Islands, Charles Erskine, one of the few nonofficers to write about the US Ex. Ex., recalled an event in which unidentified crew members of the Peacock "treated the natives to a regular, old-fashioned negro entertainment."[63] This does not necessarily mean that the performers were black, as minstrel shows featuring white performers in blackface were already popular by the 1830s, but Erksine does not mention the race of the performers, and it is possible that Saules was involved in this musical and theatrical presentation.

Saules was part of a tradition of black fiddlers in the United States stretching back to the late seventeenth century, and on the plantations of the antebellum South, enslaved fiddlers were a common sight at both white and black social events. They brandished homemade and store-bought instruments and provided crucial accompaniment for the popular dances of the period. Although musical ability seldom excused enslaved musicians from their primary tasks on the plantation, they could use the money they earned from performing to supplement their rations. Such earnings may have also helped fund self-purchases or escape attempts.[64] The importance of black musicians in plantation life fueled the common racist trope that people of African descent were "natural" musicians, belying the fact that mastery of the violin without the luxury of formal training was extremely difficult and required countless hours of practice. But despite the mendacious claims of slavery apologists that enslaved peoples' love of music proved they were happy in bondage, music did provide solace for both free and enslaved black people. In *Twelve Years a Slave*, Solomon Northrup wrote, "I was indebted to my violin, my constant companion, the source of profit and soother of my sorrows during years of servitude."[65] Northrup used his instrumental prowess to earn additional income and local renown as both a slave and freeman. Yet mastery of an instrument did not always make black fiddlers esteemed members of the community. Musicologist Dena J. Epstein has noted that "black fiddlers in the North were regarded as marginal vagabonds outside the bounds of respectable society."[66]

While not every maritime musician was black, it was a stereotypical role for black sailors. In 1808 a naval surgeon wrote, "There will be no difficulty procuring a 'fiddler,' especially among the coloured men, in every American frigate, who can play most of the common dancing tunes."[67] Black sailors also left their mark on the kind of music performed on ships. This included the African American–derived music of minstrel shows, then the most widely known music in the United States. Black sailor-musicians who traveled north on cotton boats first inspired working-class white men living along the Mississippi and Ohio Rivers—many of whom were sailors themselves—to imitate and appropriate their songs, dances, and physical appearances.[68] Black sailors also contributed a famous musical form to emerge during the Age of Sail: the sea shantey. The shantey is an example of the "chanter-response performance" form common to African and African American musical forms.[69] The shantey also first emerged in the late eighteenth century concomitant with a marked increase of black sailors in the maritime world, and its development mirrored the participation of black men in forging maritime culture.[70]

Music was only one example of what made ships and seaports such important sites of cultural transmission. Paul Gilroy refers to a ship as "a living, micro-cultural, micro-political system in motion."[71] Maritime exploration and commerce created countless middle grounds on both land and sea, sites where diverse peoples encountered and interacted with each other, forging new hybridic cultural practices and meanings. Maritime labor brought sailors from varied backgrounds together. The mutual needs of sailors and the absence of a strict racial hierarchy bridged cultural gaps and helped forge a more egalitarian social order than what was found in the cities of the northeastern and southern United States. According to Bolster, "Sailors constantly crossed cultural and geographic boundaries as they maneuvered between white and black societies ashore and maritime society afloat."[72] Sailors of various races wore similar fashions, such as baggy trousers and earrings and had similar images tattooed on their skin. Because black sailors, who were often multilingual and deeply cosmopolitan, were such a large presence on ships and in seaports, their impact on maritime culture was considerable. For example, black and white seafarers also shared in the oral storytelling tradition of "yarning," a practice likely influenced by African folk traditions.[73] And because maritime culture did not exist in a vacuum and had a reciprocal relationship with culture on the mainland, black sailors were a major factor in the development of an American culture inseparable from African American cultural forms and practices.

According to those who either knew or wrote about him, Saules fit the profile of the worldly, versatile, and independent black sailor. He was capable of traversing various communities and cultures while employing various means of survival. According to early Oregon settler Silas B. Smith, "From his associations with cultured people [Saules] had acquired considerable knowledge of things in general and could sustain a very interesting conversation on a variety of subjects."[74] Writer and naturalist Charles Melville Scammon noted Saules's "shrewdness" and "aptness for picking up a language."[75] Scammon also mentioned Saules's gift for yarning, in either English or Chinook Jargon.[76] In the Pacific Northwest, Saules also earned a reputation for hard living common to seaman. According to English overland settler John Minto, who met Saules in Astoria in 1844, "I do not believe [Astoria resident] Indian Cooper carried one tenth the vice about with him than J.D. Sauls [sic] did."[77] Although sailors were notorious for heavy drinking, alcohol was, as with most working-class people, also a means to numb the pain caused by physically strenuous labor.

THE BLACK ATLANTIC

While Saules's ability to earn his livelihood as a sailor was due in part to the nature of maritime America in the mid-nineteenth century, the rise of the black maritime world was a transnational phenomenon. Sailing ships were the connective tissue between the far-flung ports of the Atlantic and Pacific

Oceans and the plantations of the American South, West Indies, and South America. Black sailors served as essential lines of communication for the black diaspora, much of which was highly subversive. For instance, black sailors carried the news of the successful Haitian Revolution and the establishment of the world's first independent black republic. Black sailors also read and distributed abolitionist literature throughout the black maritime world.

Because black sailors so often moved beyond national borders, it is useful to consider Saules's life within the context of the Black Atlantic, a hybridic cultural formation—cultural theorist Paul Gilroy describes it as a "counterculture"—that encompasses the black diaspora in Africa, Europe, the Americas, and the Caribbean while transcending specific national and ethnic origins.[78] This framework draws attention to the crucial role Africans and their descendants played in the social, cultural, economic, and biological exchanges that shaped the Atlantic Basin and the modern world. At the heart of the Black Atlantic is the trauma of the Middle Passage, the forced migration and enslavement of twelve million Africans from the fifteenth to nineteenth centuries. The Middle Passage involved many of the transnational elements that gave rise to a new colonial economy: the development of sophisticated nautical technology and multifaceted relationships that involved traders, rulers (European and African), financiers, and numerous other agents. At the same time, the forced migrants and their progeny became engaged in struggles, both large and small, against domination, exploitation, and the enforcement of racial categories and exclusion.[79] For free and enslaved black people during the eighteenth and nineteenth centuries, sailing ships and seaports were among the Black Atlantic's most important contact zones, sites of cultural transmission and resistance. Black sailors also formed a communication network that extended to enslaved people working at or near seaports.

Black maritime workers played a vital role in the struggle against slavery in antebellum America. Among the most widely known was Denmark Vesey, a free black Charleston preacher and carpenter who had sailed the Atlantic as an enslaved youth. In the summer of 1822, Vesey conspired with one hundred enslaved and free black people—many of whom were mariners—to coordinate what would have been the largest slave rebellion in US history. South Carolinian authorities, however, learned of the plot and captured, tried, and executed Vesey and many of his co-conspirators. During this process, investigators became aware of the extensive involvement of black sailors in various stages of the plan.[80] Even in death, Vesey became a potent symbol of the black freedom struggle. Many black sailors carried and distributed David Walker's *Appeal to the Colored Citizens of the World* (1830), a work that systematically decimated arguments for white supremacy and colonialism. Walker was a free black Boston clothier who recruited local black sailors to spread his message. In 1838 an unknown black sailor gave future abolitionist and author Frederick Douglass his Seaman's Protection Certificate, which the enslaved Douglass carried when he disguised himself as a sailor to escape to freedom.[81] In 1842 Harriet Jacobs, an enslaved woman, also disguised herself as a sailor to travel to the North. With the help of her seafaring uncle, she escaped slavery and eventually emerged as a major abolitionist and writer.[82]

Not all black sailors were political dissidents, but southern lawmakers in the early to mid-nineteenth century increasingly looked to the black maritime world as a source of antislavery agitation. Immediately following Vesey's execution in 1822, the South Carolina legislature passed the Act for the Better Regulation and Government of Free Negroes and Persons of Color. The law stipulated that any "free negroes or persons of color" arriving in a South Carolina harbor or port be "confined in jail until said vessel shall clear out and depart from the State."[83] In 1823 Charleston attorney Benjamin Hunt defended the incarceration of black sailors by likening them to an infectious disease: "We have much more reason to believe in the moral contagion they introduce, than in the importation of yellow-fever. . . . In South Carolina, we think the presence of a free negro, fresh from the lectures of an Abolition Society equally dangerous."[84] Several other southern states, including Georgia, Alabama, North Carolina, Florida, Louisiana, Mississippi, and Texas, soon followed suit with a series of similar laws known collectively as the Negro Seaman Acts. These laws affected the ability of at least ten thousand black sailors to earn a living, and some northern black sailors who were also US citizens, such as Amos Daley of Rhode Island, challenged the laws on constitutional grounds.[85] Northern and southern white merchants, who relied on the labor of black sailors for profits, also objected to the statutes and their impact on commerce. The British government also repeatedly protested the incarceration of its black subjects. But although such challenges led some states to revise their statutes, most of the Negro Seaman Acts—aided by the 1857 *Dred Scott* decision of the US Supreme Court—persisted until the end of the American Civil War.

It is impossible to know Saules's exact feelings about slavery or whether he was involved in the sort of subversive activities that frightened and enraged southern elites. Saules, however, did willingly join the US Ex. Ex., a mission conceived and conducted by a US government that openly endorsed white supremacy and condoned chattel slavery. The voyage was also the most audacious exploration and surveying project in human history, and its backers hoped it would extend US political and economic power. The US Ex. Ex. transported its multiethnic crew around the world and eventually to the Pacific Northwest, where Saules would encounter a culturally complex contact zone already transformed by the colonialism that provided his livelihood. Saules would spend the rest of his life there, witness the ascent of American colonialism in the region, and struggle to maintain his place in the new order.

2
The United States Exploring Expedition and American Imperialism in the Age of Sail

As a marginalized black man in antebellum America, Saules had little personal stake in the success of the US Ex. Ex. This should not obscure the fact that Saules himself was an agent of empire, and his labor power directly contributed to the goals of American colonialism. Because he served as a cook, the white officers and midshipmen of the expedition likely considered Saules to occupy the lowest rung of the mission's hierarchy. But Saules served a crucial function for the expedition. If the adage is true that an army marches on its stomach, it is also true that a naval crew sails on its stomach. And regardless of his specific reasons for participating, there is no indication that Saules ever resisted any of the colonial aspects of the mission. Instead, evidence suggests that Saules participated in some of the expedition's more unsavory projections of imperialist power in the South Pacific. Once the expedition arrived in the Oregon Country, Saules, a bold and protean man, continued to exploit the forces of colonialism to his advantage.

Saules was doubtless aware of the US Ex. Ex.'s purpose and why the *Peacock's* commander, Lieutenant William L. Hudson, was eager to brave the entrance to the Columbia River. Like the Lewis and Clark Expedition but on a much larger scale, the US Ex. Ex.'s federal supporters envisioned it as a voyage of discovery to collect scientific data, reconnoiter remote places, and project US power. Although such aims were obviously imperialistic, the backers were initially more focused on the expansion of commerce rather than the immediate colonization and resettlement of distant lands. But whereas Americans eventually came to celebrate Lewis and Clark's Corps of Discovery as a harbinger of overland expansion and Manifest Destiny, the US Ex. Ex. is less well-known today. Perhaps this is because the expedition belonged to an era in which many US elites expressed anxiety over the prospect of rapid continental expansion and hoped the United States would remain a geographically modest maritime nation that could complete economically with the great imperialist powers of Europe. As the nineteenth century progressed with its transportation revolution and resource extraction booms, this notion, like the US Ex. Ex. itself, receded into the mists of history. Indeed, the arrival of the US Ex. Ex. in the Oregon Country in 1841 signaled a shift in the mission's objective, as many of the expedition's supporters—and Saules himself—coveted the Pacific Northwest as not only a site for resource extraction but also as an ideal place for Americans to settle.

Saules joined the US Ex. Ex. in the summer of 1839, but the mission had embarked from the US naval base at Norfolk, Virginia, nearly one year earlier on August 18, 1838. The US government–authorized voyage was unprecedented in both scope and objective. It lasted four years, traveled over eighty thousand miles, and consisted of six vessels (*Vincennes, Peacock, Relief, Porpoise, Sea Gull*, and *Flying Fish*) and over four hundred crew members, including naturalists, botanists, mineralogists, sketch artists, a taxidermist, and a philologist. Expedition commander Lieutenant Charles Wilkes's assignment included attempting to reach the then-undiscovered continent of Antarctica (it was generally assumed there was a landmass beneath the ice), a thorough survey of the islands of the South Pacific, and an exhaustive reconnoitering of the Pacific Northwest.

The historical background of the US Ex. Ex. reveals fluctuations in the nature of American foreign policy and imperialism in the first half of the nineteenth century. The expedition occurred at a point in which the United States was transitioning from a maritime nation that relied primarily on overseas commerce to a continental nation in which resources could be extracted from North America's vast interior. During this same period, the nation underwent concomitant political changes. President John Quincy Adams, a New Englander and former diplomat with strong support from the northeastern commercial class of bankers, manufacturers, and land speculators, first conceived of the mission in the mid-1820s. As he tried to rally support for the venture, Adams was also enduring a long and ultimately successful challenge from his political rival, Andrew Jackson. Unlike Adams, Jackson often depicted himself as a westerner, frontiersman, and opponent of northern elites. A former war hero and Tennessee judge, he insisted that his political sensibility was forged far from northeastern corridors of power. In 1828 his newly minted Democratic Party drew impressive support from Anglo-American farmers, artisans, laborers, and slaveholders in the West and South. Jacksonian Democracy became synonymous with a new American egalitarianism and expanded notion of citizenship, although suffrage and the ability to hold elected office remained exclusive to white men. Jackson attacked the Adams administration for alleged corruption and cited the Second National Bank of the United States as a threat to agrarian republicanism.

Although Lieutenant Wilkes himself later described the US Ex. Ex. as the first naval mission "fitted by national munificence for scientific objects," the expedition's chief aims during its first phase were commercial. It fit squarely in the same long tradition of merchant capitalism that brought workers of disparate backgrounds together and provided Saules with an occupation. The first sentence of US secretary of the navy James Kirke Palding's instructions to Wilkes referred to "the important interests of our commerce embarked in the whale-fisheries, and other adventures in the great southern ocean."[1] The United States had the largest whaling fleet in the world, and information gathered from the mission would provide American whalers like Saules with reliable maps of the Pacific Ocean. Its backers also hoped the expedition would unearth ample sources to supply burgeoning markets in fish, seals, sandalwood, and feathers.[2]

Like Lewis and Clark, Wilkes was charged with the task of collecting data and samples pertaining to flora, fauna, and indigenous peoples.[3] However, Paulding's instructions to Wilkes forbade him and his crew from harming Native people or interfering with indigenous cultures. Paulding insisted that the expedition "is not for conquest, but discovery."[4] Wilkes and the crew were instead encouraged to promote national interests by leaving a positive impression of the United States. Paulding's instructions strike a somewhat dissonant note considering the expedition's assignment to accumulate data regarding the Pacific Northwest, an area long since "discovered." And many Americans made no secret of the fact that they had long coveted the Oregon Country as a future site of American expansion.

Despite pleas for restraint, the expedition's backers understood its imperialist implications. According to Paulding, its primary objective was "to extend the empire of commerce and science."[5] President John Quincy Adams first proposed a maritime expedition in 1825, claiming that if the United States failed to match the maritime exploits of Great Britain, France, and Russia, the former would be doomed to "perpetual inferiority."[6] Adams was a passionate nationalist and chief architect of the Monroe Doctrine. He insisted a strong central government was crucial to promoting US interests in commerce, military power, manufacturing, and science. Adams was also an early proponent of westward expansion, and he was central to the crafting of the Convention of 1818, which established the joint occupation of the Oregon Country by the United States and Great Britain. He later made his reasons clear in an 1846 address to Congress: "I want the Oregon country for our western pioneers."[7] However, Adams did not initially envision the Pacific Northwest as part of the United States but instead as an independent republic with strong diplomatic and trade ties to his nation.[8] The idea of overland expansion was controversial in the early nineteenth century, since the United States remained primarily a maritime nation dependent on overseas trade. It was also only beginning to make the necessary internal improvements to tap the wealth of its interior, such as the 1825 completion of the Erie Canal. Therefore, Adams intended the expedition as an audacious demonstration of US military and commercial power.

The election of Andrew Jackson as president in 1828 sounded the death knell for this early version of US Ex. Ex. The new chief executive quickly abandoned the idea of a major voyage of discovery. Jackson rode a populist wave of antipathy toward northeastern elites and Adams's vision of a robust federal government. Such ire was directed toward politicians like Daniel Webster, who urged the federal government to develop overseas commerce and once derided agrarian republicans for seeing the United States as "as a great land animal . . . who has nothing to do with the ocean, but to drink at its shores or sooth its slumbers by the noise of its waves."[9] US representative Albert Gallatin Hawes, a Jacksonian Democrat, referred to the proposed expedition as a "chimerical and hairbrained notion" that required vast sums of money to be "wrested from the hands of the American people."[10] Democratic senator Robert Y. Hayne of North Carolina, the chairman of the Committee on Naval Affairs, attacked the expedition on the grounds that government funds were better spent on developing agriculture and that commerce and science could be "safely left to the enterprise of individuals."[11] Haynes also feared the expedition would lead the United States to develop "unnecessary connections abroad" or the establishment of an overseas colony requiring massive amounts of government spending to defend.[12]

Jackson, like many Americans in the early nineteenth century, shared similar isolationist instincts regarding overseas exploration. During the 1828 presidential campaign, he portrayed Adams as an educated, Old World–style aristocrat with diplomatic and cultural ties to Europe. Instead, Jackson, the first president not born and raised on the Eastern Seaboard, saw America's future in the West. He largely rejected the notion of an American economy fueled by federally financed industrialization and overseas commerce. According to historian Richard Hofstadter, "Jackson's politics chiefly resembled the agrarian republicanism of the old school, which was opposed to banks, public debts, paper money, high tariffs, and federal internal improvements." Jackson was deeply influenced by Thomas Jefferson's Empire of Liberty concept and believed the nation should be dominated by Anglo-Protestant farmers, small merchants, and artisans working in its interior. This world was diametrically opposed to the cosmopolitan maritime world Saules had long inhabited. According to agrarian republican logic, the seemingly limitless expanse of inexpensive land to the west would check the power of elites and preserve American democracy and egalitarian social relations.

Yet Saules would live his entire life at the knife's edge of what the economist and sociologist Gunnar Myrdal once called "an American Dilemma." Myrdal was referring to a seeming contradiction at the core of US history, that the universalistic values unleashed by American Revolution and Thomas Jefferson's Declaration of Independence—equality, liberty, justice, and natural rights—existed alongside a rising tide of virulent white supremacy. What this actually reveals is the extent to which many Americans sought to overlook class divisions in the United States and reconceive of them as racial divisions. Indeed, whiteness as a legal category is a relatively new phenomenon in human history and can be traced to the late seventeenth century—a period in which many American colonists, who had begun to think of themselves as something other than mere British subjects, first started moving into the multiethnic North American interior. Yet the inheritors of these values saw nothing contradictory about their desire to expand Jefferson's egalitarian Empire of Liberty and preserve the United States as a white man's country. Indeed, in the Age of Jackson, it was often those Americans most committed to egalitarianism who were the strongest advocates for the legal enshrinement of the color line. For them, the subordination of black people—both enslaved and nominally free—and removal of Native people from their traditional lands were essential preconditions for white freedom and a society without social divisions and class struggle.

Indeed, Jackson and most of his supporters espoused white supremacy and believed that a racially homogenous citizenry was necessary to avoid internal division, sectional strife, and lopsided social relations. As such, Jacksonian Democrats were likely uncomfortable with the multiethnic composition of most sea crews and ports during the Age of Sail. At the same time, Jackson also urged aggressive westward expansion regardless of preexisting federal treaties with Native groups and made Indian removal—particularly from cotton-growing Georgia—the top priority of his presidency. In addition, Jackson, a staunch supporter of slavery, supported the extension of the institution into the West despite its attendant political volatility. Many of Jackson's political foes in the Northeast attacked both positions on moral and political grounds, since Jackson threatened to undermine federal power. Indeed, the Jacksonian embrace of states' rights was largely a means to limit federal interference with frontier settlers and slaveholders. Still, many Americans living on the western frontier or the slave societies of the South believed northeastern elites harbored antiquated and naïve notions of race relations based on residual Enlightenment ideas of natural rights and the equality of human beings. Many of Jackson's supporters inherited a hatred of Native people based on generations of struggle with Native groups that resisted Anglo-American encroachment and dispossession. Furthermore, the intractability of the institution of slavery in the South encouraged the conventional view that black people were inherently different and inferior.[13] Such racial views later informed the overland emigrants who traveled to the Pacific Northwest on the Oregon Trail in the 1840s.

By the end of his second term in 1836, Jackson had warmed to the idea of an overseas exploring expedition. Despite his earlier isolationist tendencies, Jackson was as nationalistic as Adams and believed that the United States should be at least the equal of European nations in terms of scientific knowledge.[14] And in spite of his professed distaste for federal internal improvements, his administration's spending on federal transportation projects significantly outstripped Adams's—although Jackson was careful to apply a states' rights gloss to such endeavors. Jackson also saw the economic value of exploration and surveying for the United States and resigned himself to the fact that the United States continued to rely on overseas commerce, particularly its thriving whaling industry. Some of the infrastructure projects he supported included dredging harbors and building lighthouses. Furthermore, in 1832 he restored trade with the British West Indies, and he sent two naval ships—one of which, the USS *Peacock*, was later Saules's home for two years—to the Far East to make treaties benefiting US commercial and shipping interests.[15]

Jackson also became increasingly interested in the Pacific Coast of North America and tried to purchase San Francisco Bay from Mexico in 1835.[16] In addition, he was acutely aware that his idol, Jefferson, coveted the Pacific Northwest as part of a future Empire of Liberty and sent Lewis and Clark to the lower Columbia region as a prelude to possible colonization. On May 14, 1836, the US Congress, after a contentious debate, passed an amendment to the Naval Appropriations Bill authorizing Jackson to "send out a surveying and exploring expedition to the Pacific Ocean and South Seas."[17]

Two US Democratic senators from Missouri, Thomas Hart Benton and Lewis F. Linn, voted for the bill. Benton and Linn were architects of the settler colonialist wave Saules later encountered in the Pacific Northwest, and both senators were extremely passionate about westward expansion and establishing American settlements in the Oregon Country. They were eager to support a bill that included a thorough exploration of the Pacific Northwest coastline and interior. Benton, unlike many other Democrats, was also keenly interested in overseas trade. But he worried that Atlantic maritime trade forced the United States to defer to European powers. Instead, Benton promoted the overland settlement of the Pacific Coast as a conduit to direct trade with Asia.[18] Both Benton and Lewis shared a vision that government land grants would encourage settlers to venture to the Far West, where they could market their surplus via the maritime trade of the Pacific Ocean. Earlier, Benton had supported the temporary preemption acts of the 1830s, as well as the permanent Log Cabin bill of 1841, which gave squatters the first right to purchase western lands for cultivation. This was a notable move away from the land policy of Adams and his fellow National Republicans, who had planned to use the sale of federal land to fund internal improvements. Benton, however, was not averse to spending federal dollars on scientific and commercial exploration. In 1842 Benton secured the passage of a bill authorizing his son-in-law, John Charles Frémont, to explore, survey, and map the Oregon Trail as far as the South Pass of the Rocky Mountains.[19] The support of such influential Democrats was necessary if the expedition was to have any chance of winning congressional approval.

In August 1838, following two years of grueling preparations, the US Ex. Ex. was finally underway under the command of Lieutenant Wilkes, an expert surveyor with an avid interest in astronomy and natural science. Unfortunately, Wilkes, who was forty years old at the time, was less experienced as a seaman and military leader. According to historian Constance

Bordwell, "Even Wilkes supporters found him arrogant, suspicious, secretive, sardonic, and unduly exacting."[20] His assignment also led to tensions between Wilkes and his fellow officers on the expedition. His second-in-command, Lieutenant William Hudson, held slight seniority over Wilkes and initially refused to serve under him. The US Navy resolved this dilemma by removing all military trappings from the voyage and promoted the expedition as a purely civil mission.[21] However, the mission retained much of its military purpose and character, and the intimidation of the potentially rebellious indigenous peoples of the South Pacific was implicit to Wilkes's instructions to "diminish the hazards of the ocean."[22] Furthermore, Wilkes's surveying and cartographical activities incorporated the synchronized nautical maneuvers of naval warfare, making frequent use of cannons and landing craft.[23]

Given the concurrent rise of the nation-state, merchant capitalism, empire building, and scientific inquiry, Wilkes's assignment to survey and map foreign territories must be seen as part of a larger colonialist project. Before lands or people can be conquered or exploited, they must first be known. While various cartographic practices have existed in many cultures since ancient times, the European powers of the eighteenth and nineteenth centuries seized on technological advances in mapmaking, such as the chronometer in 1761, to extend the reach of their empires beyond their own coasts.[24] The increasingly accurate maps of the nineteenth century provided European and American elites with new ways to imagine their position in a shrinking world. According to historian Greg Dening, "The map-readers in bureaus and salons needed to make the globe a real world and the real world a map for the strategies of empire."[25] For these elite readers, abstract spatial knowledge of faraway places served as a rationale for concrete action.

Cartography also embodied the uneven power dynamics necessary for imperial domination. The abstract knowledge embedded in a map can be understood as a form of what Michel Foucault called "power/knowledge." For Foucault, geography is one of many disciplines in which acts of measurement, examination, inquiry, and surveillance are inextricably intertwined with normative judgments and deployments of force on bodies and spaces.[26] The maps produced by the US Ex. Ex. were made for the benefit of the United States and its commercial and military interests, not the indigenous peoples who inhabited the surveyed territories. In most cases, conquered and exploited peoples were not granted access to cartographic information. This was a crucial aspect of American expansion, since surveying was the primary means to inscribe property, the essential precursor to the privatization of land previously held in common. In mid-nineteenth-century Oregon as elsewhere, the measurement and privatization of land became an essential means of racial exclusion and domination, directly affecting Saules and numerous other nonwhite people.

SAULES TOURS ANTARCTICA AND THE SOUTH PACIFIC

Saules served with the US Ex. Ex. from July 1839 to October 1, 1841. Since he had previously worked aboard at least one whaling voyage to the Pacific, Saules had already seen much of the world. Yet the scope of the expedition would have far exceeded any of his previous experiences. Prior to Saules's signing on, the expedition had already visited Madeira, the Cape Verde Islands, Rio de Janeiro, Cape Horn, and the South Shetland Islands near the Antarctic Peninsula. Immediately after disembarking from Callao, the expedition collected specimens and surveyed lands in the South Pacific to help American whalemen find crucial provisions. During this stretch, Saules visited the Tuamotu Archipelago, Tahiti, and Samoa.

In December the expedition again ventured southward, engaged in an imperial competition with Great Britain and France to be the first nation to reach the rumored continent at the South Pole. On January 16, 1840, midshipman Henry Eld and Lieutenant William Reynolds of the *Peacock*, Saules's ship, spotted the mountains of Antarctica. Unfortunately, this detail was not captured in the ship's official log, and the crew of Wilkes's flagship, the USS *Vincennes*, claimed discovery of the continent on January 19, 1840. This was after Wilkes had already surveyed fifteen hundred miles of Antarctic coastline, later known as Wilkes Land. This administrative oversight complicated the United States's claim, since a competing French exploring expedition also recorded landfall on the continent the same day.

On February 21, 1840, the *Peacock* ended its ice exploration and sailed to Sydney, Australia, for extensive repairs. Prior to the British founding of Sydney as a convicts' colony in 1788, the area was home to the Eora aboriginal people, most of whom had perished by the early nineteenth century due to exogenous diseases brought by the British. By the time Saules arrived there, Sydney was a notoriously rowdy seaport that exemplified the heterogeneity of maritime culture. According to crew member Charles Erskine, "Here you find all nations mixed up together, eating, drinking, singing, dancing, gambling, quarreling, and fighting."[27] Erskine, a young Bostonian, was particularly struck by what he perceived as a disregard for racial norms in Sydney: "It was a curious, but not an uncommon sight, to see a big, burly, thick-lipped negro, black as a coal, walking on the street, arm in arm, with a beautiful English lady, both neatly dressed."[28] After the grueling and perilous exploration of Antarctica, Saules probably enjoyed the familiar cosmopolitan and earthy milieu of Sydney. It is worth noting that the attractions of Sydney, however, were not enough to lure Saules away from the expedition.

On May 1, 1840, the *Peacock*, with Saules aboard, rejoined the other ships of the US Ex. Ex. for an extensive survey of the Fiji Islands. Europeans first reached the Fiji Islands in 1789, although surveyors had only charted a small portion of its hundreds of islands. While those islands had a reputation among European and American sailors for endemic warfare and cannibalism, the verdant islands had long held appeal for potential deserters, many of whom abandoned their ships to live among the indigenous inhabitants. However, due to earlier and presumably negative interactions, many islanders took a dim view of colonial interlopers. For example, Wilkes expressed astonishment upon meeting a group of Fiji children who ran away from him in terror, suggesting their previous contact with American or European sailors was far from benign.[29]

Regardless of initial claims that the expedition's goals were peaceful, at this point in the mission Wilkes intended to inform Fiji's indigenous population that they must now acquiesce to US power. The US Navy assigned Wilkes to investigate the alleged 1834 murder of ten American sailors by a Fiji headman named Veidovi. On May 20, 1840, Wilkes dispatched the *Peacock* to Rewa, where the crew was instructed to apprehend the chief. On May 21, Lieutenant William L. Hudson of the *Peacock* took Veidovi's brother, the current king of Rewa, hostage aboard the ship as ransom for the delivery of Veidovi.

It is possible that Saules played a role in the scheme to kidnap Veidovi. In his journal, Lieutenant Reynolds referenced a sham ceremony that Lieutenant Hudson ordered to lure the king on board the *Peacock*. He described a musical fanfare in which Reynolds's black steward played a drum roll accompanied by "several abortive squeaks of the fife breathed by the Ship's Cook."[30] Since Saules was later among the survivors of the wreck of the *Peacock*, it is highly likely he was the fife-playing cook. And if Saules was complicit in the ruse, it demonstrates his role in the expedition's attempts to overawe the indigenous people the crew encountered. Once aboard, Hudson greeted the king warmly,

VENDOVI.

Sketch of Veidovi by Alfred T. Agate.
Source: Charles Wilkes, *Narrative of
the United States Exploring Expedition*
(1858). Courtesy of the Oregon
Historical Society.

but he was flanked by several highly armed crew members to demonstrate the
expedition's power.

On May 21, Hudson invited the king and about one hundred islanders
to return to the *Peacock* for another reception. Shortly following another fanfare and ceremony, Hudson separated the king from his people and held him
ransom. On May 22, the crew captured Veidovi, and Lieutenant Reynolds
informed him he would be brought to the United States where he would
"become a better man . . . with the Knowledge, that to kill a white person was
the very worst thing a Feegee man could do."[31] While the officers promised
Veidovi that he could eventually return to Rewa, he died in New York City in
1842, mere hours after the expedition reached its final destination.

Such heavy-handed treatment of Fiji Islanders increased in brutality over
the next three months. By mid-July, a boat of a surveying crew in Solevu Bay
was claimed by local inhabitants when it washed ashore during a gale. Wilkes
ordered his flagship, the *Vincennes*, to return to the bay and retrieve the boat
by force if necessary. When the village headman returned the boat, Wilkes
realized the villagers had kept the surveyors' personal belongings. On July
14, Wilkes vowed to "make an example of these natives" and ordered his men
to burn the village of Tye to the ground.[32] Luckily for the villagers, they had
already abandoned the village to the safety of nearby hills.

Less than two weeks later, Saules would have noticed that provisions in
the galley were running dangerously low, and he likely heard crew members

grumble over their dwindling rations. In response to this crisis, a small surveying crew from the *Porpoise* went ashore to the island of Malolo to bargain
with Native people for food. When negotiations broke down, a melee ensued
that resulted in the death of two officers, including Wilkes's nephew. In retaliation Wilkes sent seventy men to the southern tip of Malolo where they were
instructed to kill as many warriors as possible and raze their villages. In the
end, two villages were completely destroyed and eighty Native people were
killed. When a handful of survivors presented Wilkes with a peace offering he
refused, insisting that all survivors must appear before him, bring all the food
they could muster, and recognize that the United States was "a great Nation,
a powerful people."[33] According to Wilkes, had he not ordered this act, the
Malalo islanders would "never acknowledge themselves conquered."[34] While
Saules's ship, the *Peacock*, was not involved in the massacre, Wilkes ordered
the crew of the *Peacock* to bring him Veidovi, the Rewan prisoner taken two
months earlier. An enraged Wilkes put Veidovi in solitary confinement and
had his head shaved. This was a particularly brutal act, since Rewan headmen
took immense pride in their prodigious locks.

The survey of Fiji ended in August 1840, although the US Ex. Ex. continued to combine the gathering of scientific knowledge with more punitive
activities. In late September, the expedition reached the Hawaiian Islands and
dropped anchor near Honolulu, another of the Pacific Ocean's boisterous
multiethnic seaports. Saules and the rest of the expedition's crew enjoyed two
weeks of rest while Wilkes led a scientific mission to the summit of Mauna
Loa. By this point, Wilkes believed it was too late in the year to begin surveying the Pacific Northwest and abruptly added another year to the expedition. Several crew members responded to this news by deserting. Wilkes also
assigned the *Peacock,* on which Saules still served, to both survey the Gilbert,
Marshall, and Caroline Island groups and punish specific Native persons for
past offenses. Their first order of business was to visit the Samoan village of
Saluafata and capture two recalcitrant tribal chiefs wanted in connection with
the murder of an American seaman fifteen months earlier.[35]

· In April, Saules and the *Peacock* arrived at Utiroa in the Drummond
Islands, where the crew committed another massacre of Native people.
Apparently, the *Peacock*'s commander, Lieutenant Hudson, and some crew
members went ashore to have dalliances with several Native women. They
soon grew suspicious that the women were luring them into a trap. The
crew members returned to the ship with the exception of crew member

John Anderson, whom they presumed Natives had killed. In retaliation, the Peacock sent eighty-seven men ashore; they destroyed the village and killed approximately twenty Native people.[36] Since the eighty-seven constituted virtually the entire crew, Saules's participation in the massacre is highly likely. When Lieutenant Reynolds, now the commander of the expedition vessel the USS *Flying Fish*, heard of the latest carnage, he wrote, "It seems to me, that our path through the Pacific is to be marked in blood."[37] The *Peacock* returned to Oahu on June 14 with its provisions depleted, and the crew prepared for its ill-fated voyage to the Oregon Country.

The image of Saules and other black sailors assisting in the kidnapping or massacring of indigenous people is a stark reminder of the indispensability of black labor to furthering the objectives of American colonialism in the Age of Sail. It also established that Saules identified and aligned himself with the colonizers over the colonized. His labors supported the surveying, claiming, and naming of geographic spaces, and he was apparently involved in brutally violent expressions of imperial power. Unfortunately, because Saules and other black sailors' voices are not found among the surviving documents of the US Ex. Ex., it is impossible to know how Saules felt about such activities. Saules worked on behalf of a nation that boasted a slave-based economy and offered few legal protections for free black people. On the other hand, Saules and other black sailors would have understood that when they chose to join a US Navy expedition, they were also compelled to follow their commanding officer's orders. It is also possible that despite their marginalization, Saules and his fellow black sailors had developed some degree of camaraderie with the other crew members and that he simply worked in earnest for the success of the mission. Within a matter of weeks, however, Saules's dedication to the US Ex. Ex. would be sorely tested and eventually broken.

THE US EX. EX. REACHES THE OREGON COUNTRY

Wilkes knew his survey of the Pacific Northwest would be the crowning achievement of the US Ex. Ex. Although the sponsors of the expedition were interested in exhibiting US might throughout the world, the United States had yet to develop any serious designs on territories in the South Pacific. Oregon Country, however, was a far different case. Wilkes understood his survey as a prelude to US claims and wrote that he was "fully satisfied [Oregon] was to be full part and parcel of our country."[38] The region, which encompassed all of present-day Oregon, Washington, Idaho, and British Columbia, was still under joint occupation by the United States and Great Britain, a delicate arrangement first established by the Convention of 1818 and extended in 1827. Many in the United States believed that Robert Gray's 1792 discovery of the Columbia River, as well as the Lewis and Clark Expedition, granted them sole rights to the territory below the 49th parallel, the site of the current border between the United States and Canada. The British, on the other hand, had a far more pronounced presence in the region due to the activities of the Hudson's Bay Company (HBC), a joint stock company chartered by the British crown to extract valuable furs from North America.

In 1824 the HBC established a major base of operation at Fort Vancouver near the confluence of the Columbia and Willamette Rivers. Eleven years earlier, during the War of 1812, British fur traders from the North West Company (NWC)—the HBC's chief rival and regional predecessor—strong-armed the representatives of John Astor, an American fur magnate, into selling them his Pacific Fur Company, based near present-day Astoria, Oregon. This act cemented Britain's domination of the fur trade in the region for nearly thirty years. In 1821, after years of bitter competition that veered into violence, the British government forced the NWC to merge with the HBC, granting the latter a monopoly over fur extraction in Oregon. And although the fur trade was in decline by 1841, Fort Vancouver's chief factor, John McLoughlin, had diversified its operations to export timber, grain, and various foodstuffs to other outposts and settlements throughout the Pacific Slope.

Born in 1784 to a French Canadian mother and Scottish father, McLoughlin originally joined the NWC as a surgeon and apprentice clerk and rose to the rank of chief factor following the company's merger with the HBC. He was a physically imposing figure who stood six feet four with flowing white locks and piercing blue eyes. Notwithstanding his reputation as quick-tempered, he was a pragmatic merchant capitalist who usually adjusted his tactics to suit the particular situation. This is probably attributable to his history with the NWC, whose leadership was less conservative than the HBC and sought to adapt to the realities of fur trade culture. And unlike the HBC, the NWC encouraged its employees to forge relationships with Native or mixed-race women. This was true at the highest ranks of the Fort Vancouver hierarchy, as McLoughlin was married to Marguerite McLoughlin, a Cree-Swiss woman who emerged as a highly respected figure at the fort in her own right.[39]

On April 28, 1841, Lieutenant Wilkes and his flagship, the *Vincennes,* arrived at Cape Disappointment. The cape was a foggy headway marked by steep sea cliffs located at the north side of the mouth of the Columbia. Saules would later live on the eastern side of the cape overlooking Baker Bay, a longtime calm rendezvous point for indigenous and fur trade boats.[40] He eventually built a cabin less than two miles from a Chinookan village that had long played a major role in regional trade. Point Adams was situated at the southern side of the mouth and comprised the western side of Young's Bay, the future site of the city of Astoria. Between Cape Disappointment and Point Adams was the loathsome Columbia bar, where river currents collided with ocean tides to create a frenzied swirl atop a succession of sandbars hidden beneath the churning water.

Wilkes originally planned to quickly cross the Columbia bar and continue up river. Upon arrival, however, he found conditions too treacherous. Wilkes later wrote, "Mere description can give little idea of the terrors of the bar of the Columbia: all who have seen it have spoken of the wildness of the scene."[41] The Columbia bar remains one of the most perilous river entrances in the world and is the only one in the United States where officials require vessels to use a bar pilot. Wilkes opted to avoid crossing the bar and instead sailed northward to begin his survey of the Puget Sound, which he found far more to his liking. "Nothing can exceed the beauty of these waters, and their safety,"[42] he said. While Wilkes found the region's Nisqually Indians "vicious and exceedingly lazy,"[43] he treaded far more lightly among the indigenous peoples of the Pacific Northwest than those of the South Pacific. He even forbade his crew from purchasing the valuable pelts offered by local Native people. One reason for this was that Wilkes did not want to alarm the region's major players in the fur trade, such as those located nearby at the HBC's Fort Nisqually. Wilkes believed that if they detected his imperial designs, they would be less willing to provide shelter and provisions for his crew. Once Wilkes completed the first part of his reconnaissance, he led an overland expedition back to the mouth of the Columbia River to rendezvous with the *Peacock* and begin the survey of the river. On May 23, when Wilkes reached the Columbia, he discovered that the *Peacock* had still not arrived. After spending some time at Fort Vancouver, where John McLoughlin hosted him with typical hospitality, Wilkes headed up the Willamette River.

Because Saules left behind no writings about his experience with the US Ex. Ex., we must rely on Wilkes's journals for insight on what Oregon was like when Saules arrived. Wilkes's writings on the Willamette Valley vividly depict the multifaceted nature of colonialism in Oregon in the decades following initial face-to-face colonial contact. He provided a guided tour of a region on the cusp of major changes. Much like Lewis and Clark's Corps of Discovery journal, his observations regarding the Pacific Northwest and its inhabitants circa 1841 are a rich source of environmental and demographic information. But Wilkes's observations are far from definitive and have contributed to the lopsided account of colonial encounters written mostly by Euro-American elites, missionaries, and traders. Literacy was rare among the region's indigenous people and French Canadian trappers, and source materials such as Wilkes's journals favor a colonial gaze and minimize other crucial perspectives. Still, Wilkes offers a glimpse of the social and cultural complexity Saules encountered when he first arrived in the region.

During Wilkes's overland exploration of the lower Columbia and Willamette Valley, he witnessed three distinct if, at times, overlapping forms of colonialism in the region. The first was the merchant capitalist colonialism, sometimes called exploitation colonialism, practiced by the British-backed HBC—the others were religious and settler colonialism. At various times, Saules would ally himself with each form to maintain or improve his social standing in Oregon.

Wilkes was impressed by the bustling merchant colonialist operation of the HBC at Fort Vancouver. For the British government, joint stock companies like the HBC were a cost-effective means of establishing colonies since investors were the sole source of funding. Such companies often functioned as de facto governments in foreign territories and were not bound by any higher authority. Theoretically, this meant that the governor and council of a company could enslave or annihilate indigenous inhabitants with impunity. But although joint-stock companies engaged in similar practices in the plantation colonies of the Caribbean, South America, and the southern United States, the most common tactic employed by fur trade colonizers was to forge economic dependence among indigenous peoples. The powers behind the fur trade were then able to extract the natural resources and labor of Native peoples and convert them into profit.[44] In exchange, Native people received items they could not necessarily produce for themselves, such as firearms, ammunition, imported foodstuffs, and clothing.

Nevertheless, it is a mistake to assume that the HBC was the dominant power in the region. Because the employees of Fort Vancouver never consisted of more than a few hundred people, the profitability of the fur trade in the Pacific Northwest was entirely contingent on obtaining the cooperation

Fort Vancouver, ca 1846. Source: Henry J. Warre, *Sketches in North America and the Oregon Territory* (1848). Courtesy of the Oregon Historical Society.

and labor of local Native groups, who despite the devastation of imported diseases, still outnumbered Euro-Americans in the region. For example, Chinook-speaking peoples had controlled trade on the lower Columbia long before colonial contact with Europeans due to their geographic position between coastal Native groups and those living on the Columbia Plateau. Therefore, the cooperation of Native people could not be attained through violent coercion. And although McLoughlin held a monopoly on firearms in the region and was known to launch brutal punitive expeditions against local Native people who undermined the fur trade, Fort Vancouver had no army or police force. Indeed, when Wilkes visited Fort Vancouver, he observed that the two large cannons on display were strictly ornamental.[45] But McLoughlin and the HBC never faced significant resistance, since many local Native groups were interested and active participants in the fur trade. This meant that the HBC could forge alliances with powerful Native groups through intermarriage or other forms of mutually beneficial collaborations.

The British and their surrogates among the HBC were also more interested in using the Pacific Northwest as an extraction colony than in establishing a permanent British settlement, which would have necessitated the importation of families as opposed to male laborers. Instead, McLoughlin oversaw a heterogeneous and cosmopolitan culture at Fort Vancouver, a place not unlike the various seaports Saules visited with the US Ex. Ex. Residents included Britons, French Canadians, and American citizens as well as the Native or mixed-race wives of managers and employees. Other employees and laborers, including Pacific Islanders, black men, Métis, and Iroquois from the East Coast, lived in a village of log huts located immediately outside the fort. When Wilkes toured this village, he noticed the preponderance of mixed-race children "of all shades of colour, from the pure Indian to that of the white."[46]

Such cultural and ethnic diversity should not obscure the fact that a definite color line existed in Oregon during the height of the fur trade. The HBC's organizational hierarchy recognized ethnic, national, and class distinctions. Educated Anglo-Celtic Canadians with roots in England and Scotland dominated the fur trade officer class in the Oregon Country. They presided over the aforementioned multiethnic workers, some of whom were affiliated with the company and others who worked as independent contractors. Although he was married to a Cree-Swiss woman, McLoughlin viewed race in binary terms and believed the mixed race children of workers should be raised either as Natives or, preferably in his mind, whites.[47]

The color line in Oregon prior to Americanization was somewhat permeable, and the elites at Fort Vancouver never introduced legal mechanisms to enforce racial segregation. In fact, James Douglas, the chief trader at the fort in the 1830s and later the governor of British Columbia, would have been considered black according to the "one-drop" rule codified into law in the southern United States in the early twentieth century. He was born in Guyana to a "free coloured" woman from Barbados and a Scottish merchant father. He, in turn, married and had a large family with a half-Cree woman.[48] Similarly, the mixed-raced sons of the fur trade elite, such as John McLoughlin Jr., were also poised to assume plum positions with the HBC.

On June 9, 1841, Wilkes visited the multiethnic French-Indian community at Champoeg—later known as French Prairie. This was a significant and influential community in the region, consisting of about sixty families and numbering around six hundred people in the 1840s.[49] Although many fur trade workers in the Oregon Country were migratory and never intended to stay permanently, this was not the case with the French Canadian men who settled in the Willamette Valley, most of whom had been contractors rather than HBC employees. French Canadian fur trappers typically retired from strenuous work as they approached their forties, and many turned to subsistence farming. According to Melinda Marie Jetté, a number of factors likely drew these men and women to Champoeg, including access to the Willamette

River, prairie land primed for cultivation, and the area's role as a trading hub. Yet Jetté stresses that the Native wives likely played a role in choosing the location, since it was on Kalapuyan land and many had kinship connections there. The location also meant the women could continue their traditional subsistence practices of gathering plants and roots.[50] The women themselves came from ethnically and linguistically-diverse backgrounds, and in addition to Kalapuyans and many others, the community included women with ties to Chinook, Cayuse, Spokane, Iroquois, Cree, Shasta, and Nisqually peoples.[51]

Although the residents of Champoeg exemplified the emerging trend toward permanent agrarian settlement in the Willamette Valley, the French-Indian community also epitomized the accommodating and adaptable culture of Oregon Country during this period. For instance, while many residents practiced Catholicism, they later forged generally warm relationships with their neighboring Methodists and the handful of Anglo-American settlers in the Willamette Valley. They also did not isolate themselves from more worldly matters. As the number of American settlers in the valley increased and proposed American-style governance, the French-Indians willingly participated in community meetings to establish and protect their own interests.[52]

Protestant and Catholic missionaries began arriving in the Oregon Country after the fur trade established a foothold in the region, and Wilkes noted the presence of religious colonialism during his exploration of the Pacific Northwest. After returning from Fort Nisqually in late May 1841, Wilkes visited the Methodist's Oregon Mission located near the French-Indian settlement at Champoeg. In 1834 the Reverend Jason Lee, a Canadian-born Methodist missionary, was inspired by written accounts of the journey of four Native men who traveled from the Columbia Plateau to St. Louis and asked William Clark, who was now superintendent of Indian Affairs, for the "book." Clark quickly realized the book in question was the Christian Bible. News of this event galvanized Protestant evangelicals in the Northeast, who perceived it as an invitation to send missionaries to the Pacific Northwest to convert Native people to Christianity.[53] Lee's generation of Methodists played a major role in the Second Great Awakening of 1790–1840, in which Protestant sects held revivals in then-western frontier cities preaching an optimistic and egalitarian Christian message. The Second Great Awakening accompanied the rise of industrial capitalism in the Northwest, and innovations in transportation and communication bolstered its reach to western emigrants and the "unchurched" in the American interior. Lee responded to the request of the so-called Flathead Delegation and sought to establish a permanent Oregon colony where whites and Native people would live in "civilized" harmony. Lee failed at that goal, but the Methodists played a major role in the Americanization of Oregon Country. Upon arrival in Oregon, Saules himself gravitated to the Methodist community, which employed him in various tasks.

Unlike Jacksonian Americans, who favored removal or extermination, many Methodists included Christianized indigenous people in their vision of the nation's future. In fact, in the nineteenth century, Methodist missionaries were among the most outspoken opponents of Indian removal in the United States. Yet the Methodist vision of peaceful coexistence was colonialist and predicated on unequal power relations; their conversion project required submission, assimilation, and a complete transformation of Native people and their lifeways. In 1833 Wesleyan University president Wilbur Fisk, among those most committed to sending missionaries to the Oregon Country, articulated his plan: "Let two suitable men, unencumbered with families, and possessing the spirit of martyrs, throw themselves into the nation. Live with them—learn their language—preach Christ to them and, as the way opens, introduce schools, agriculture, and the arts of civilized life."[54] Fisk's proposal highlights how his notion of Christianization intersected with Anglo-American republican values.

At Fisk's urging, the Missionary Board of the Methodist Church agreed to back Lee and his nephew Daniel's mission to the Pacific Northwest. On September 15, 1834, the pair arrived at Fort Vancouver, where McLoughlin met them with typical conviviality. Curiously, McLoughlin recommended that Lee install his mission in the fertile Willamette Valley instead of the more rugged and remote environs of the Columbia Plateau. Lee listened carefully and chose a site about sixty miles southwest of Fort Vancouver on the Willamette River, where he was soon joined by a handful of missionaries and their families. This move has puzzled observers then and now, as Lee built the mission several hundred miles from the actual homelands of the Nez Perces and Flatheads, the people he ostensibly traveled across the country to convert. Furthermore, the local population of Kalapuyan Natives living near the Oregon Mission had experienced widespread death and depopulation in the 1830s due to an outbreak of what was likely malaria brought to the region aboard an American vessel.[55] This epidemic and its aftermath reduced the indigenous population in the entire Willamette Valley from over seven thousand to fewer than one thousand people at the time of Wilkes's visit in 1841.[56] The surviving Kalapuyans, still coping with this traumatic loss of life, were at best indifferent to Christianization. McLoughlin later justified the advice he gave Lee by insisting that the Native groups of the Columbia Plateau were too dangerous and intractable. And if Lee hoped to convert Native people to Christianity through a combination of religious instruction and agricultural training, McLoughlin contended that the Willamette Valley was a preferable base from which to extol the virtues of a settled agrarian lifestyle.[57]

For the next ten years, Lee struggled to fulfill the mission's original purpose, and many historians have questioned his commitment to Native people. Prior to erecting the Oregon Mission on their land, Lee never met with any Kalapuyans to discuss his plans and most remained aloof toward the missionaries. For their part, the Methodist missionaries were continually frustrated by the fluid and syncretic spiritual practices of a heterogeneous Native population. Two years after his arrival, Lee lamented, "The truth is we have no evidence that we have been instrumental in the conversion of one soul."[58] Notwithstanding this lack of success, in 1839 over fifty Methodist adults and children traveled from New York to Oregon aboard the *Lausanne* as part of the Great Reinforcement. The Methodists in Oregon soon created new mission stations at Willamette Falls, The Dalles (Wascopam), Clatsop Plains, and Nisqually.[59]

When Wilkes visited the Oregon Mission, he immediately recognized that the Methodists had abandoned their initial conversion project and focused almost exclusively on agriculture, tilling two hundred acres of farmland and raising herds of livestock. By 1841 the Methodists were posing a serious challenge to HBC hegemony by creating a significant and growing American community. In 1875 James W. Nesmith, a US senator from Oregon who arrived in the region in 1843, summed up the Methodist's contributions to the Americanization of Oregon: "It is my opinion that the Methodist missionaries conferred no benefit upon the natives. They were however, of some advantage to the early pioneers in forming a nucleus for settlement and trade by which both parties were benefited."[60] Wilkes himself was struck by the scarcity of Native people at the mission and expressed disgust that the Methodists had neglected their initial project while still collecting large sums of money from their backers on the East Coast.[61] He lamented, "We had the expectation of getting a sight of the Indians on whom they were inculcating good habits and teaching the word of God; but with the exception of four Indian servants, we saw none."[62] But Wilkes also observed a notable shift in the Methodist's religious colonialist aims: "On inquiring, I was informed . . . that their intention and principal hope was to establish a colony, and by their example to induce the white settlers to locate near those over whom they trusted to exercise a moral and religious influence."[63] Three years later, the Mission Board learned of Lee's shift in priorities and withdrew its support.

Prior to visiting French Prairie and the Methodist mission, Wilkes traveled near Willamette Falls, where he encountered a small group of Anglo-American settler colonists with little interest in furs or converting Indians. In 1841 this group comprised a tiny minority of the region's population at probably fewer than fifty people.[64] Despite their small numbers, the restlessness and impatience of his fellow countrymen made a strong impression on Wilkes, who contrasted them with the residents of French Prairie: "While those of French descent appeared the most contented, happy, and comfortable, those of the Anglo-Saxon race showed more of the appearance of business, and the 'go-ahead' principle so much in vogue at home."[65] Hall Jackson Kelly, a passionate supporter of an American settlement in Oregon, was among the earliest Anglo-American settlers in the Oregon Country. Kelly came to the Willamette Valley in 1834 accompanied by Ewing Young, an American cattleman. Kelly soon fell ill and returned to his native Boston, while Young remained in the area and became one of the richest men in the region when he broke Fort Vancouver's cattle monopoly.

Wilkes's meeting with the settlers occurred mere months after Young's death in February 1841, which sparked a crisis over how best to divide his estate in a region without any coherent system of law. At the gathering, Wilkes noted the presence of George Gay, Young's business partner and traveling companion on an 1837 cattle drive, whom Wilkes described as "as much Indian as a white can be."[66] The group also included Robert Moore, an original member of the Peoria Party, who later presided as justice of the peace in the trial that led to Saules's 1844 expulsion from the Willamette Valley.[67] In 1840 a nine-man overland party led by Thomas Jefferson Farnham arrived in Oregon from Peoria, Illinois; they were inspired by Reverend Lee's national speaking tour in which he extolled the agricultural virtues of the region. According to Wilkes, these "idle people" were "all agog about laws & legislatures, with governors, judges, & minor offices all in embryo."[68] They were also frustrated by McLoughlin's power and their economic dependence on Fort

Vancouver; many hoped the arrival of Wilkes and the US Ex. Ex. signaled the end of British control in the region. Wilkes warned them that establishing their own government too soon would only antagonize the HBC. Instead, he advised them to wait "until the government of the United States should throw its mantle over them."[69]

THE WRECK OF THE PEACOCK

Saules finally reached the mouth of the Columbia River aboard the *Peacock* on July 18, 1841. Like Wilkes before him, the *Peacock's* Lieutenant Hudson found the conditions at the bar unfavorable. Unfortunately, Hudson was reluctant to fall further behind schedule and decided to brave the high breakers of the bar. He soon had second thoughts and tried to steer the ship back to more tranquil waters. This act was futile, as the ship's keel had hit bottom, and its bow was permanently submerged in the sand of what later became known as Peacock Spit. The high waves at the bar meant that although the ship was filling with water, the *Peacock's* crew was trapped aboard the ship until river conditions subsided. By evening a crowd of onlookers formed— most of them local Chinook Natives—and watched as the waves began to break the ship apart. Luckily for the *Peacock's* crew, John Dean, a black steward from Wilkes's *Vincennes,* was among the eyewitnesses. Although the *Vincennes* had sailed north weeks earlier, Dean was asked to remain at the Columbia to watch for the arrival of the *Peacock.* Dean organized a rescue party comprised of Chinooks—including two highly skilled bar pilots—who rowed out to the beleaguered ship the following morning and began bringing the crew and important materials to shore. Once the high waves subsided, Lieutenant Hudson ordered the release of the *Peacock's* own boats, and eventually all 133 crew members were safely off the ship. Hudson never mentioned his black and Chinookan rescuers, or their racial identity, in his official report of the wreck.[70] Through this omission, Hudson boosted his own role in the rescue and downplayed the nautical expertise of local Native people.

Following the wreck, the *Peacock's* crew showed little motivation to participate in the ongoing survey of the Columbia. They were likely traumatized by their watery ordeal, and some blamed Lieutenant Hudson's lack of surveying skill and experience.[71] Except for the forty men Wilkes sent to Fort Vancouver to help harvest crops, most of the crew remained idle for the next several weeks. During this time they established a makeshift village at Fort

Fort George, ca. 1841. Source: Charles Wilkes, *Narrative of the United States Exploring Expedition* (1858). Courtesy of the Oregon Historical Society.

George, near present-day Astoria, and dubbed it Peacockville. In 1841 Fort George was a modest trading post operated by HBC official James Birnie, who generously offered provisions to the Peacock's crew. Peacockville, which began as a row of crude huts crafted from pine branches and old planks, soon resembled a miniature seaport town replete with street signs, gambling dens, a bowling alley, a barbershop, and a bakery.[72] Chinook and Clatsop Indians visited Peacockville to sell crew members fresh venison and salmon and try their luck in Peacockville's gaming establishments.[73]

The remaining months of the US Ex. Ex. were comparatively placid. On August 10, 1841, Lieutenant Wilkes interrupted the idyllic scene at Peacockville by negotiating the purchase of a brig from John McLoughlin, the *Thomas H. Perkins*, to replace the *Peacock*. On October 15 the vessel, rechristened the *Oregon*, joined the other ships of the expedition on a voyage south to Mexican California and the tiny seaport of San Francisco. While Wilkes wrote that California "was not calculated to produce a favorable impression either of its beauty or fertility," he was extremely impressed by the size and safety of San Francisco's harbor.[74] Wilkes believed this harbor, combined with Puget Sound, made the Pacific Coast "admirably situated to become a powerful maritime nation, with two of the finest ports in the world."[75] The expedition then again traveled west to the Hawaiian Islands, the Philippines,

Singapore, and South Africa. On early June 10, 1842, the surviving ships of the US Ex. Ex. finally arrived in New York City.

The immediate outcome of the US Ex. Ex. was not what its backers or Wilkes anticipated. While Wilkes's excellent charts remained in use by mariners well into the twentieth century and the expedition's specimens would form the basis for the Smithsonian Institution, the expedition was mired in controversy. Upon his return to the United States, the Navy court-martialed Wilkes and several of his officers. The Navy charged Wilkes with mistreating his subordinate officers, losing the *Peacock* at the Columbia bar, and illegally flogging sailors and marines. Although he was cleared of all but the flogging charge, his reputation was tarnished. Wilkes also discovered to his dismay that John Tyler, a political opponent of both Jackson and Martin Van Buren, now occupied the White House. Not only did President Tyler want to distance himself from previous administrations, but in addition, his secretary of state, Daniel Webster, was involved in precarious negotiations with Great Britain regarding the border between Maine and Canada. Tyler hoped the resulting agreement might provide the impetus for settling the boundary question for the Oregon Country; he did not want to tip his hand regarding the importance of Oregon to the interests of the United States and, therefore, issued a news blackout regarding the expedition's exploits.[76] Even former political allies turned against the US Ex. Ex. Senator Thomas Hart Benton, perhaps the most prominent supporter of claiming and settling the Oregon Country, expressed frustration that Wilkes's survey of the mouth of the Columbia River did not conform to his own vision as an ideal site for a major international seaport. Benton later came to view the US Ex. Ex. as a rival venture to his son-in-law John C. Frémont's overland expeditions to the Far West. In 1846 Benton published a pamphlet in which he attacked the expedition and its scientific findings.[77]

SAULES'S NEW LIFE

Saules never joined the *Oregon* on its journey to California. He and two other black crew members— officers' cook Henry Evans and officers' steward Warren Johnson—deserted on October 1, 1841, the same day the rest of the crew boarded the ship to leave Oregon. Evans seems to have disappeared from the historical record, but Johnson was included in US Indian subagent Elijah White's 1842 census of settlers living south of the Columbia River.[78] While some historians have cited Saules's desertion as proof of his status as a "troublemaker," desertions were common during the troubled mission.[79] For example, according to Wilkes's official report, 125 seamen deserted over the course of the expedition.[80] Saules was one of three sailors who deserted at Fort George, a lower number than usual since most desertions occurred at established seaports, such as Rio de Janeiro, Callao, Honolulu, and Sydney, where a sailor could easily join another voyage. One explanation for why Saules deserted in Oregon was that two years spent on a grueling and often violent maritime voyage was enough, especially one that culminated in a catastrophic shipwreck. Also, Saules was nearing middle age, and sea voyages and their accompanying backbreaking labor were notoriously brutal on the human frame. Given the conditions aboard deep-sea vessels, in some ways it is surprising he lasted that long. Jeffery Bolster has provided a succinct distillation of the challenges seaman faced on long voyages: "Sailors were debilitated by vitamin-deficient food, blazing sun, and wet accommodations; threatened by their own ship's equipment and the sea's perils; and answerable to tyrannical captains backed by harsh admiralty laws."[81] This might also explain why Saules, who had made his living on the sea for twenty years, never participated in another deep-sea mission.

Another explanation for Saules's desertion is that he never intended to continue on to New York City. In the antebellum United States, black men like Saules still faced harsh racial discrimination and scant job prospects in the free northern states, particularly if he intended to retire from maritime life. Many sailors racked up significant debts in eastern boarding houses, and perhaps Saules was eager to avoid any such entanglements. And if Saules had indeed deserted the *Winslow*, his reputation as a whale man may have been tarnished. Southern slave societies were even more perilous for a free black man. As mentioned previously, white southerners reviled free black sailors for flaunting racial conventions, and it was not unheard of for southern authorities to arrest black men and sell them into slavery.[82] If Saules returned to working in southern ports, he would have had to contend with the aforementioned Negro Seaman Acts, which President Jackson's attorney general, John Berrien, had earlier affirmed as constitutional exercises of state power ten years earlier.[83]

Perhaps Saules weighed his options and chose the Pacific Northwest as an ideal place to settle and begin a new life—the same decision thousands of other American settler colonists later made in the 1840s and 1850s. But Saules's reasons were probably somewhat different than those of the Anglo-American settlers who followed. In the first half of the nineteenth century, it was not uncommon for black sailors to desert their ships on the Pacific Coast and start over in places where racial caste systems had not yet ossified. Desertions of this kind were especially common in California, where a black man could become a Mexican citizen. For example, Allen Light was a black sailor who jumped ship at Santa Barbara, acquired Mexican citizenship, and later became the first US-born black man to serve as a Mexican official.[84] While such lofty positions were unavailable to black men in the Oregon Country in 1841, the HBC had no strict racial hiring policy beyond the officer class. And since there was no formal government in the region, there could be no racist laws.

In his journal, Lieutenant Hudson, the commanding officer of the *Peacock*, offered another plausible explanation for why Saules, Evans, and Johnson deserted: "[They] had no doubt fell in love with some of the Indian women."[85] This was not without precedent, as the Oregon Country boasted several legends of shipwrecked black sailors who joined coastal Native communities.[86] Hudson also decided not to pursue the men once the *Oregon* was prepared to disembark for California.[87] Charles Melville Scammon supported this theory in his 1875 profile of Saules, although the piece is weighed down by Scammon's indulgence in ethnic stereotypes: "[O]n the day of sailing of the brig *Thomas H. Perkins*, Saul was missing from among his shipmates. Scarcely, however, had the ship cleared the land before he made his appearance, accompanied by an Indian bride, decked out in all the geegaw glories of her tribe."[88] Scammon claimed that Saules quickly learned the Chinook jargon—the trade language of the lower Columbia River area—and gained his vast knowledge of the river and its tributaries from his time spent among the Chinookan people.

Saules did not live exclusively among the Indians. According to Scammon, he "led a half-civilized, half-savage life for the first few years after coming on shore; sometimes living with the Indians, at other times with the Whites."[89] In her 1964 profile of Saules for the *Seattle Times*, historian Lucile McDonald referred to Saules as "Cape Disappointment's first settler," and it appears that Saules built a cabin facing Baker Bay on the north side of the Columbia soon after deserting."[90] According to John E. Pickernell, an early Euro-American settler in what is now Pacific County, Saules lived near the present location of Fort Canby as early as 1842 and was Pickernell's only English-speaking neighbor.[91] It is possible that Saules developed kinship ties with the nearby Chinook village at the site of the present-day town of Ilwaco.

The identity of Saules's wife is unknown. One questionable source, a 1901 article in the *Pacific Monthly*, suggests he was married to a Chinookan woman whose sister married John McClure, an early Astoria settler who arrived in 1843. The article refers to McClure's brother-in-law as "a colored man, who lived at or near the cape, as a pilot."[92] The article clearly referenced a later incident involving Saules and the *USS Shark*, but it confused the *Shark* for the *Peacock* and misidentified the *Shark's* commander as Wilkes. Furthermore, the article refers to the "colored man" in question as George Washington. There was a sailor named George Washington who worked at Fort Vancouver as a cook and pilot in the 1830s, but sources seem divided on whether he was black or Hawaiian. In 1840 Washington served as a pilot aboard the *Lausanne*, a ship carrying the Methodist missionaries Daniel Lee and Joseph E. Frost, but ran the ship aground.[93] However, there is no evidence Washington ever lived on Cape Disappointment. Instead, he moved to the Willamette Valley in 1839 and, according to the 1850 census, was still living there with his wife, a Quinault woman.[94]

One year after he deserted, Saules established a boat service between Astoria and Cathlamet.[95] Approximately thirty miles from Astoria, Cathlamet was once the site of the largest Indian village on the lower Columbia and in 1842 was still home to as many as four hundred Cathlamet, Wahkiakum, Chinook, and Cowlitz people.[96] Saules's business made him an important part of the region's trade network, which circulated goods and resources between Indian communities and HBC outposts. Saules's craft was a small fore-and-aft schooner in which he carried passengers, livestock, and miscellaneous freight. Traveling between these locations was not an easy task in 1842, as the Columbia had no channel improvements, dams, or levees. Therefore, Saules must have been a skilled and knowledgeable navigator. For Saules the rewards were apparently worth the risk, and he earned a solid living as a river man for several years.[97] Saules's business increased when, in 1846, James Birnie, the HBC employee who had helped the crew of the *Peacock* at Fort George, moved his family from Fort George and established a trading post at Cathlamet.

Not only did Saules travel to the Pacific Northwest as part of a colonizing mission, he was a colonizer himself. He came to the lower Columbia to claim land and resources for his own use. And although he seemingly developed warmer and closer ties to local indigenous communities than the Anglo-American settlers who succeeded him, Saules's later actions show that he did not come to live with the Chinook on their own terms. Instead, Saules threw his lot in with the colonizers of Oregon's middle ground, earning his living by transporting the goods and services that were crucial for the expansion of Euro-American economic power in the region. Furthermore, while there is no reason to doubt the sincerity of Saules's intentions when he married a Chinook woman, Native women were forced to cope with shifting power relations in the region following the arrival of the fur trade. Many Native women entered into marriages and even sex work with colonial men to ensure their survival and prestige in a changing world. Many colonial men exploited this situation to their advantage.[98]

Demonstrating the flexibility and creativity common to sailors, Saules adapted quickly to life in the Oregon Country. The region, like the ships and seaports of the maritime world, offered him ample room to maneuver, both physically and socially. In the following year, however, Saules's very presence would test the racial tolerance of Oregon's newest residents. He and his wife would leave their home at Cape Disappointment and relocate to the Willamette Valley during the same period in which hundreds of Anglo-American immigrants arrived in the region. Saules would attempt to stake his claim for a share of the settler colonialist dream of economic independence. These newcomers, however, imported a very different vision for the Oregon Country, one that provided little room for Saules, his wife, or the other inhabitants of the lower Columbia and Willamette Valley. They would also lay the groundwork for the United States to eventually claim and redistribute nearly three hundred thousand square miles of Oregon land, thus overwhelming a region that once boasted a surprising degree of social and cultural fluidity.

3

The Settler Invasion

Sometime prior to the spring of 1843, James D. Saules and his wife sailed up the Columbia and Willamette Rivers to their new home in Oregon's loamy Willamette Valley. The immense agricultural potential of the area likely appealed to Saules since he could support a young family through the sheer fecundity of the soil. But Saules was not alone. At around the same time he starting tilling his land, nearly one thousand Anglo-Americans began their six-month overland journey west. Unlike Saules, most hailed from the nation's interior and probably had never set foot aboard a deep-sea vessel. Instead, they loaded up their wagons with whatever possessions they deemed necessary and traveled several thousand miles along the Oregon Trail, a grueling route initially developed by fur trappers. The new immigrants conceived of themselves as white, and their sheer numbers disrupted the delicate balance of power that had existed between indigenous peoples and Euro-Americans in the Pacific Northwest. They imported a distinct ideology that had a dramatic effect on regional laws, notions of property rights, and race relations. Saules and the other inhabitants of the Oregon Country were forced to cope with this settler invasion. At various times, Saules either cooperated with these new arrivals or resisted them. Yet the ultimate outcome for Saules, as well as many previous inhabitants of the region, was displacement and dispossession.

The Willamette Valley is a 3,500 square-mile region lying between the Cascade Mountains and Oregon Coast Range. At its heart is the Willamette River, which has its source in the mountains south of modern-day Eugene (est. 1862) and extends nearly 150 miles to the river's mouth at the Columbia River north of Portland (est. 1851). The valley's mild climate is characterized by a long rainy season lasting from late fall to early spring followed by a dry

summer. The heavy rains nourish rich alluvial soil from which lush vegeta-
tion emerges. While dense riparian forests lined the Willamette River at the
time Saules settled in the region, much of the landscape was dominated by
savannah-like grasslands and prairies advanced by Native peoples' incendiary
practices. Natives had long burned fields and forests to create more productive hunting and gathering grounds. These grasslands served as a food source
for the population of elk, deer, and waterfowl that Native hunters relied on
to feed their families. Beginning in the 1830s, French-Indian families and
Anglo-American settlers used European methods to cultivate the soil. These
settlers also introduced foreign crops and livestock, such as wheat, cattle, pigs,
and sheep, a trend that eventually transformed the flora and fauna of the valley and altered the economic base of the region. Wheat, in particular, later
emerged as the Willamette Valley's major cash crop. But even in 1842, valley
farmers—many of them Methodist missionaries—cultivated 31,698 bushels
of wheat in one year on 6,284 acres.[1]

Saules and his wife relocated to an area six miles south of Oregon City,
where he purchased a farm and horse. Formerly known as Willamette Falls,
Oregon City was the original site of an HBC sawmill and later a Methodist
mission. It was less than thirty miles from the confluence of the Columbia
and Willamette Rivers and ideally situated for staging and transporting
goods and produce throughout the region. Saules's reasons for leaving Cape
Disappointment are as unclear as his decision to desert the US Ex. Ex. But
Oregon City provided superior prospects for both growing and marketing
produce. He may have viewed the growing indigenous and American settlements near Willamette Falls as an opportune place to expand his freight business, especially as the decline of the fur trade in the early 1840s would have
lowered demand for his services. Saules also may have obtained additional
work from the Methodists, for whom he later worked as a cook.

Saules purchased the land claim, farm, and horse from a man named
Winslow Anderson, also known as George Winslow. Anderson was a
Bostonian who first arrived in the Oregon Country as part of the 1834
California cattle drive that included Hall Jackson Kelly and Ewing Young.[2]
Early Oregon historian William Gray referred to Anderson as "colored,"[3]
while Methodist missionary Elijah White, who first came to the region in
1837, identified him as "mulatto."[4] Like Saules, Anderson probably came to
the West Coast as a sailor, as evidenced by the fact that a black New Englander
named George Winslow received a US Seaman's Protective Certificate in

The Willamette Valley, ca. 1846. Source: Henry J. Warre, *Sketches in North America and the Oregon Territory* (1848). Courtesy of the Oregon Historical Society.

1833.[5] While other black men had undoubtedly visited the region, Anderson was probably the first to settle permanently in the Willamette Valley. He initially lived among the French-Indian families in French Prairie, married a Native woman, and started a family. He eventually moved his family north to a farm on Clackamas Prairie. Embodying the versatility typical of sailors, Anderson also worked as a physician until the 1840 arrival of HBC surgeon Dr. Forbes Barclay, who drew away his patients.[6]

Anderson had a long-standing relationship with the Methodist missionaries in the region and may have helped build the original Oregon Mission. In January 1837, Anderson joined the Methodists' Oregon Temperance Society and signed its petition protesting the creation of a local distillery.[7] Anderson also entered into a long-term labor agreement with Methodist missionary Elijah White, who hired him out to fellow missionary Henry Perkins for a one-year period in 1838. That year Anderson and his family traveled with Perkins to Wascopam near The Dalles, where he spent a year helping Perkins build his mission. Perkins also had Anderson supervise four Native workers. Anderson made a strong impression on Perkins's wife, Elmira, who wrote, "Our hired man, an American by birth, but not all White blood, appears to be deeply anxious about his spiritual welfare, and I

The Oregon Institute, ca. 1845. Source: Henry J. Warre, *Sketches in North America and the Oregon Territory* (1970). Courtesy of the Oregon Historical Society.

hope we shall soon see him rejoicing in God."[8] Anderson remained attached to the Methodists, although his later actions bring his piety into question. In the October 14, 1847, edition of the *Oregon Spectator*, Anderson was accused of visiting Native dwellings in Oregon City and furnishing the residents with alcohol. The writer describes him as "a mulatto man from the Institute," referring to the Oregon Institute, a Methodist school for children built in Salem in 1844.[9] Unfortunately, the article does not mention Anderson's role at the school.

American Methodists had a long and complex history with black people in the United States, and Saules and Anderson's association with the Oregon missionaries suggest they were willing to involve black people in their day-to-day operations. Methodists were for the most part antislavery, and the Second Great Awakening coincided with an increase in northern abolitionist sentiment in in the early and mid-nineteenth century. Methodists in the eighteenth century often encouraged enslaved people in the South to create informal Methodist societies on their enslavers' plantations. Free and enslaved black people developed their own scriptural interpretations and emphasized the emancipatory aspects of Christian texts. By the beginning of the nineteenth century, black Methodists eventually comprised a substantial minority of mixed-race congregations and outnumbered whites in many southern churches.[10] The Methodists also involved free and enslaved members in church governance and practices. For instance, Henry Evans, a free black Methodist preacher from North Carolina, preached to a mixed-raced congregation until his death in 1810.[11] In 1819 the Methodist Episcopal Church licensed John Stewart, a Virginia freeman of mixed ancestry, as a minister. Stewart helped found the first permanent Methodist mission in the United States in Ohio, where he preached to Wyandot Natives.[12]

The Methodists in Oregon were willing to embrace Saules as an employee and a soul worth saving, and Saules, in turn, may have already been a member of an eastern congregation as Methodist revivalism swept through the Northeast in the 1830s. But the Methodists' acceptance of black people had its limits, and racial prejudice lingered in their institutions. Most mixed-raced congregations, even those that allowed black preachers like Evans, had separate seating areas in corners and galleries for black members. Unsurprisingly, many black Methodists found such segregation intolerable and created their own independent and autonomous institutions. In 1816 the Philadelphia-based Methodist minister Richard Allen brought together black Methodist congregations in the mid-Atlantic states and broke with the Methodist Episcopal Church to form an entirely separate denomination, the African Methodist Episcopal (AME) Church. As for the original Methodist Episcopal Church, some prominent members, like Jason Lee's mentor Wilbur Fisk, took a soft-line stance toward slavery, and at least one southern bishop owned a slave. By 1844 the issue of slavery had grown so contentious that the church separated into distinct northern and southern denominations, foreshadowing sectional differences that later severed the nation.[13]

THE GREAT MIGRATION OF 1843

In October 1843, as Saules was settling into life on his new farm, an event took place that drastically altered the social, cultural, political, and ethnic landscape of the Pacific Northwest. A group of nearly one thousand Anglo-American men, women, and children—known to historians as the Great Migration of 1843—arrived in the Willamette Valley from Independence, Missouri, via the overland Oregon Trail.[14] About a third of the new immigrants settled near Saules's residence in Oregon City, and the town grew from one building in 1840 to seventy-five structures by the end of 1843.[15] Those overlanders who did not settle in Oregon City fanned out all over the

Willamette Valley. Within a matter of months, these newcomers assumed prominent positions in a nascent local government that unmistakably imposed a legal color line in the region.

The sudden Americanization of the Willamette Valley resulted in a momentous shift in regional demographics. Two years earlier, in 1841, Lieutenant Charles Wilkes estimated that there were between 700 and 900 mostly male people whom he classified as "white, Canadians, and half breeds" in the Oregon Country. However, only about 150 of these were Americans; the rest were connected with the fur trade and the HBC.[16] Regarding indigenous people, he estimated that 19,204 Natives lived in the entire Oregon Country, although indigenous people living closest to Euro-American settlements had suffered dramatic population losses due to exogenous diseases. In fact, Wilkes contended that there were fewer than two thousand Native people living in the lower Columbia and Willamette Valley regions combined in 1841.[17]

The Great Migration was not an isolated occurrence; it was an early and dramatic product of a deeper imperialist movement later known as Manifest Destiny. The shared objective of the majority of settlers was to impose its collective will and create a self-contained agrarian settlement with little regard for the region's indigenous population. Unlike some other American colonialist excursions, the Great Migration was not a state-sponsored mission. Prominent politicians and pamphleteers had floated the idea for years, but primarily the settlers themselves conceived and organized the mass exodus. Another notable difference between this Anglo-American invasion and earlier, smaller population movements is that many of the fur trade laborers who came to live and work in the Pacific Northwest were sojourners who did not necessarily intend to remain permanently. The Anglo-Americans who comprised the Great Migration were both colonists *and* colonizers, urging settlement in a region that was not officially part of the United States.

The Great Migration was an unparalleled undertaking that rightfully has captured the imagination of Americans past and present. Overland journeys were still relatively rare and impractical in the early 1840s, and the previous wagon train that arrived in 1842—the largest up to that point—consisted of approximately one hundred people. Like Saules, the vast majority of non-Natives in the Oregon Country prior to the Great Migration arrived on ships. In addition, most previous overland American migrations were incremental, with settlers traveling much shorter distances from established communities.

But few living on the nation's western frontier saw the vast and arid Great Plains as a promising site for future American resettlement; they were instead intrigued by reports of a distant agrarian Eden across the Rocky Mountains. Most of the 1843 overlanders were young people in their twenties who originated from either the Old Northwest (Iowa, Illinois, Indiana, and Ohio) or the so-called border states between the North and South (Kentucky, Tennessee, and Missouri).[18] Although the Missouri attorney Peter H. Burnett was instrumental in organizing the wagon train, its cohesion was not based on top-down authority. Burnett conceived of a wagon train divided into two large administrative units, but in reality, the migration cohered according to kinship and neighborhood groupings.[19] This emphasis on kinship is an essential component of settler colonialism and differentiates the Great Migration from earlier overland emigrations, which were composed mostly of male travelers. Such relations likely helped sustain the travelers as they endured an arduous six-month journey, traveling nearly two thousand miles to start over in a region most had only read about.

A group as large as the Great Migration resists generalization, but historians have identified several key reasons why the participants embarked on such a difficult journey. Agrarian republicanism and the Jeffersonian ideal of an Empire of Liberty, a vision of a United States populated by Anglo-Protestant self-sufficient yeoman farmers, was still very influential in the 1840s. Its proponents imagined a self-sufficient society distinct from the Northeast, one free from the evils of wage labor, industrialization, and northeastern banking interests. The agrarian republic would also be devoid of the stultifying social relations of aristocratic southern slave societies. Even Saules likely felt the pull of this agrarian ideal, and it may have led him to abandon the galley and forecastle for a patch of land and a log cabin.

The Anglo-Americans of the Great Migration were not anachronistic throwbacks to an earlier age; they were part of a nation transitioning from a society with capitalism to a capitalist society. Most American agricultural families in the nineteenth century engaged in composite farming: they consumed a portion of their produce and traded or bartered the rest in local markets. By the 1830s, local markets had become inextricably linked to national and international markets via improved communication and transportation technology, and whether or not they would have admitted it, the farm families who arrived in Oregon were products of a modernizing and increasingly market-oriented society. According to historian David Alan Johnson, the settlers who traveled to the Willamette Valley sought their own middle ground, "a rural place somewhere between the isolated and self-sufficient household order of yeoman myth and a world of commercialized agriculture dependent on uncertain markets."[20] Many hoped the Columbia River would grant settlers access to foreign markets in the Far East that would absorb their agricultural surplus. In other words, Anglo-American overlanders sought the benefits of a market economy—competitive pricing, a diverse array of products, access to financing—without creating a wholly capitalist society in which wage laborers, now alienated from the means of production, subsisted by purchasing items produced by other wage laborers.

Yet the US market economy was also in turmoil in the early 1840s, which likely added to the lure of landed independence in the West. In 1843 the nation was still wracked by an economic depression brought on by the Panic of 1837. The Panic occurred following President Andrew Jackson's shuttering of Second Bank of the United States in favor of less regulated state-chartered banks. Some of these state banks issued paper money to fund internal improvements and fuel the activities of land speculators, while others issued massive amounts of credit to southern planters, much of it funded by European investors who purchased securities backed by the value of enslaved labor. This meant that the nation's booming economy was overly reliant on foreign capital, and by the beginning of President Van Buren's first term, the boom turned to bust. Economic problems in Britain resulted in falling cotton prices and the Bank of England tightening its money supply. Such problems were exacerbated by Jackson's hard money policy, which encouraged widespread distrust of paper currency in favor of specie, or hard coin. State banks, the federal government, and the American people all began to hoard gold and silver, starving the nation's money supply and leading to a decline in economic activity. In 1839, following a short recovery, the Bank of England again raised interest rates and cotton (and slave) prices fell. This lead to widespread deflation; plunging crop prices hit Mississippi Valley and Old Northwest farmers hard, many of whom had already suffered years of flooding. Farm families who relied on credit throughout the nation lost their land when they were unable to meet mortgage payments.

It was not merely economic hardship that drove emigrants to leave the life they had known. For instance, better health was probably a key motivation for moving westward as various diseases, particularly cholera and malaria, were prevalent in the Mississippi Valley in the 1830s.[21] Furthermore, during this period disputes over religion, slavery, and race erupted in mob violence in various American towns and cities, likely increasing the appeal of migration. In particular, residents of both Missouri and Illinois had witnessed mob violence toward abolitionists like Elijah Parish Lovejoy and the brutal expulsion of Joseph Smith and the Mormons.

Many of the overland settlers of the 1840s hoped to sidestep the most divisive political issue of the mid-nineteenth century: slavery. Most Anglo-American immigrants were supporters of the Democratic Party, and the majority were members of its antislavery wing. This was not necessarily good news for Saules, since the immigrants objected to slavery on economic rather than moral grounds. And while these Democrats differed with their southern counterparts over slavery, they still shared the vision of the United States as a white man's country. Indeed, during the period of the second party system, one's position on Indian removal—and not slavery—was the best predictor of party affiliation.[22] In the states of the Old Northwest, where the majority of overlanders originated, the influential "free soil" ideology was taking shape. Adherents of free soil believed that slavery impeded the ability of white laborers to compete in a free labor system. They contended that slavery drove down the wages of white workers and reinforced the stratified social relations of the plantation economy. Robert Wilson Morrison invoked this idea to explain why he wanted to emigrate from Missouri to Oregon in 1844: "I am not satisfied here . . . unless a man keeps niggers—and I won't—he has no even chance with the man who owns slaves. . . . I'm going to Oregon, where there'll be no slaves, and we'll all start even."[23]

Morrison came from a border state where although slavery was legal, residents were bitterly divided over its existence. Like their northern neighbors, many in the border states resented the political power of pro-slavery factions. Lindsey Applegate claimed he resolved to leave Missouri for Oregon in 1843 because a proslavery mob had prevented him from entering a polling place.[24] Other settlers had less noble but more visceral objections to slavery. According to Colonel George B. Currey, who relocated to Oregon in 1853, "Several persons from the old slave states told me they came to Oregon to escape the constant dread of a negro insurrection."[25] Such fears betrayed the awareness that a slave economy predicated on racial subordination and labor exploitation seemed destined to erupt into the kind of violent racial and class struggles that would affect more than just slaveholders. In the early 1840s, Nat Turner's rebellion of 1831 was only the latest in a series of insurrections that included Denmark Vesey's thwarted revolt of 1820, the German Coast uprising of 1811, and the Haitian Revolution itself.

By the late 1830s and early 1840s, high-circulation newspapers and periodicals found an audience among an increasingly literate American public. Many of Saules's eventual rivals in the Willamette Valley devoured the published letters and articles of missionaries in Christian newspapers that extolled the virtues of the Oregon Country. These items, combined with the Reverend Jason Lee's regular trips to the East to encourage support for his mission, led to a word of mouth campaign that eventually erupted into a phenomenon called Oregon Fever. Soon emigrant guidebooks provided those afflicted with Oregon Fever with intelligence regarding the region's agricultural potential and the state of the Native population. Would-be settlers carefully perused articles, letters, and guidebooks before deciding to embark on their journey to the West. Most of the missionary texts assured settlers that that the Native population was destined for extinction. In 1844 missionaries Daniel Lee and John Frost wrote the following in regard to Natives in the Willamette Valley: "These Indians are the most degraded human beings that we have met in all our journeying . . . and the time is not far distant when the last deathwail will proclaim their universal extermination."[26] These writings suggest how little remained of Rev. Jason Lee's original vision of whites and Christianized Natives sharing Oregon's future.

Oregon Fever did not just seduce struggling young agriculturalists; it also attracted established and successful Americans with an unquenchable thirst for adventure. In his 1886 memoirs, Samuel T. McKean—who arrived in Oregon with his family in the late 1840s and briefly knew Saules—recalled his aging father hearing "rumors of a wonderful country called Oregon, where anyone could get all the land he wanted for the taking."[27] Reports trickling east from missionaries and recent immigrants described a perfect climate and absence of disease. The elder McKean soon sold everything he owned, abandoned a prosperous family farm near Peoria, Illinois, and took his wife and children on the hazardous six-month overland trek. Forty years after his family arrived in Oregon, the younger McKean remained mystified by his father's rash decision:

> To see a man comfortably fixed, over fifty, deliberately pull up stakes
> and starting for an almost unknown country two thousand miles
> distant over an unknown road, to encounter unknown difficulties,

traverse trackless and arid plains, over almost impassable mountain
ranges, through nations of savages, who though peaceable at times,
are like a keg of powder . . . is a question that I have never been able to
answer satisfactorily to myself.[28]

The McKean family hardly encountered a bonanza when they arrived
in Oregon and settled in Linnton, near modern-day Portland. According to
McKean, who contracted a severe case of measles upon arrival in the supposedly disease-free Willamette Valley, Linnton's chief industry was "fighting
mosquitos."[29] The family eventually relocated to Astoria, where they continued to struggle to make ends meet.

Although the Great Migration was not exactly a state-sanctioned event,
some key American politicians laid the groundwork and offered passionate
support for a venture that would reclaim Oregon as an Anglo-Protestant
homeland. The two Democratic senators from Missouri, Thomas Hart
Benton and Lewis F. Linn, were particularly forceful in their expansionist
rhetoric and legislative actions; both were frustrated that the US government
had done little to promote American settlement in Oregon. The two senators
seemed to endorse a strategy of expansion akin to the original definition of
filibusterism: allow uninvited settlers to force their way onto foreign land and
the US. government would eventually follow. Many future overlanders were
heartened by Linn's 1841 Oregon Territorial Bill, which urged an immediate
resolution of the Oregon boundary question with Great Britain and would
have granted 640 acres of Oregon land to every white male willing to cultivate it. Linn was also responding to the Farnham Memorial, a petition signed
by sixty-seven Oregon settlers who requested that the United States protect
them from Indian violence, British economic interests, and Methodist over-
reach.[30] This kind of rapid and disruptive expansion, however, was still controversial in the early 1840s, and in 1843 the bill failed to pass in the House
of Representatives. Whig president John Tyler also vehemently opposed it,
insisting that land titles could not be granted before the United States reached
a permanent territorial agreement with Great Britain.[31] Still, the terms of
Linn's bill, including its racial component, would be echoed in subsequent
successful legislation.

This marked a swing away from the racial regime of the previous Euro-
American inhabitants of the Pacific Northwest, namely fur industry workers
and missionaries, whose colonial project at least initially involved close contact

and cooperation with Native people and nonwhite residents like Saules. Two major aspects of this involvement were sexual relationships and marriages between Euro-American men and Native or mixed-race women. Such intimate contact not only provided comfort and companionship but was also part of the alliance-building process of fur trade society. Like them, Saules developed marital bonds with local Native people very soon after arriving in Oregon. On the other hand, the married male immigrants of the Great Migration brought their wives with them, making interracial relationships unnecessary for the reproduction of the community. Single male Anglo-American settlers also tended to avoid interracial marriages, resulting in low marrying ages among young Anglo-American girls and various efforts to import white women to the region. Such changes in demographics and economics meant that the era of accommodation and interdependency between Native people and Euro-Americans was drawing to a close. Unlike immigrants such as Saules and those associated with the fur industry, the overlanders sought to remake the existing social order in their own image rather than adapt to it.

Unlike economic colonialism and religious colonialism, settler colonialism involves an outside group attempting to permanently transform and claim sovereignty over a region by displacing or disposing of its previous inhabitants. While in Oregon this current would eventually engulf Saules, indigenous peoples were the primary concern for the immigrants. Many of the overland settlers who arrived in the 1840s shared the missionaries' assumption that Natives were a vanishing race, conveniently clearing the way for white settlers. This mentality allowed Peter H. Burnett to write of conquest as a fait accompli: "We came, not to establish trade with the Indians, but to take and settle the country exclusively for ourselves. . . . They instinctively saw annihilation before them."[32] Although colonialism is defined by external domination and uneven power dynamics, settler colonialism is quite distinct from other forms. Historian Lorenzo Veracini describes this difference in simple terms: "If I come and say: 'you, work for me,' it's not the same as saying 'you, go away.'"[33] If economic colonialists like the HBC saw Native people as a valuable source of labor, and religious colonialists like the Methodists initially saw them as subjects requiring redemption, the settler colonists hoped for their eventual disappearance. This form of colonization as removal could be accomplished through various historically tested means, including relocation, assimilation, and even extermination.

The Anglo-American immigrants of the 1840s also imported the Jacksonian vision of an Americanized Oregon as a white man's country, ironically establishing their own indigeneity while recasting Native people as outsiders.[34] American expansionist ideology in the mid-nineteenth century usually made claims for settler indigeneity predicated on geographical inevitability, arguing that Oregon belonged to the United States since no ocean separated the two. This continentalism was evident in columnist John L. O'Sullivan's famous 1845 pronouncement of the United States's "manifest destiny to overspread the continent allotted by Providence for the free development of our yearly multiplying millions."[35] Thomas Hart Benton insisted that American ownership of the continent was so natural and preordained that it was intuitively understood by all: "The heart of the Indian sickens when he hears the crowing of the cock, the barking of the dog, the sound of the axe, and the crack of the rifle. These are the true evidences of the dominion of the white man; these are the proofs that the owner has come and means to stay, and then the Indians feel it to be time for them to go." Benton's use of the term *white man* is crucial, as it demonstrates the prevalent notion in antebellum America that only whites could be considered American. Because of this, a black man like Saules, who was almost certainly born in the United States, was unable to establish his own indigeneity anywhere on the continent.

Racialism, the notion that race determines inherent traits or abilities, was a significant characteristic of expansionist ideology. It was also likely the main reason why the American immigrants denied Saules and most nonwhites a place in settler society. The settlers' interpretation of Jefferson's Empire of Liberty was essentially racialist, as it was predicated on yeoman farmers being white freemen. The theory also implied that an ethnically homogenous agrarian society would be free from the class distinctions of European and American urban centers and the racial caste system of the southern slave economy. Jefferson himself held explicitly racialist views: "I advance it, therefore, as a suspicion only, that the blacks, whether originally a distinct race, or made distinct by time and circumstance, are inferior to the whites in the endowment both of body and mind."[36] He also insisted that unlike other racial strains, the American descendants of the Europe's Anglo-Saxon tribes were naturally predisposed to democracy. This suggests the degree to which the notion of race had subsumed social class in the collective consciousness of antebellum America, as well as the accompanying notion that only a racially homogenous society could be devoid of class distinctions. Jefferson was not alone among the nation's founders, as the 1790 Naturalization Act reserved American citizenship for white males only. And although many Americans living outside of the Deep South were opposed to slavery, most were also opposed to civil rights for freed slaves and believed blacks could not be incorporated into white society.[37] Also, while Jefferson initially thought Indians could assimilate into American society over the course of hundreds of years through intermarriage and the adoption of sedentary agriculture, by the Jacksonian Age white settlers encroaching on Indian lands in the Southeast and Old Northwest held mostly contempt for Native peoples.[38] Racialism was also bolstered in the 1830s by the post-Enlightenment advent of race science. Many writers and intellectuals of the period began offering pseudoscientific theories as proof of white supremacy, many of which remained influential well into the twentieth century.[39]

For many prominent American proponents of westward expansion, the future of the white race often seemed more important than the future of the nation. For example, in an 1846 speech before Congress, Senator Benton employed racialist rather than nationalist terminology to promote the settlement of the Pacific Coast by whites: "I know of no human event, past or present, which promises a greater, a more beneficent change upon earth than the arrival of the van of the Caucasian race (the Celtic-Anglo-Saxon division) upon the border of the sea which washes the shore of eastern Asia."[40] He proceeded to delineate a racial hierarchy, insisting that the Caucasian and "Mongolian" races were "far above the Ethiopian, or Black—above the Malay, or Brown . . . and above the American Indian, or Red."[41] Yet Benton was also among those who conceived of race in binary terms. During the Second Seminole War (1835–1842), in which Florida Seminole warriors fought alongside black allies against the US Army, Benton claimed, "It is his own white race which has been the sufferer in Florida; and that the colored races have exulted in the slaughter and destruction of [those] descended . . . from the white branch of the human race."[42] Many settlers would later view Saules and other black people in Oregon as having an innate and potentially dangerous affinity with indigenous people, presumably based on skin tone.

THE CREATION OF THE PROVISIONAL GOVERNMENT
AND A LEGAL COLOR LINE

Anglo-American settlers enshrined their notions of sovereignty and racial homogenization in the Pacific Northwest and identified territorial insiders

and outsiders through the creation and enforcement of various legal mechanisms. And although the web of legal codes they imposed would affect the
lives of Saules and other residents of the Willamette Valley whom settlers
considered nonwhite, the latter were excluded from the codes' actual creation.[43] While settlers in Oregon had created small governmental institutions
as early as 1839, the most transformative was the establishment of a provisional government on May 2, 1843, six months before the arrival of the Great
Migration.[44] Lansford Hastings, an attorney who led the 1842 wagon train to
Oregon, urged the formation of a government to "take into the consideration
the propriety for taking measures for civil and military protection of this colony."[45] This was also the body that established a framework for expropriating
Native land. Although the 102 residents who voted on whether to create an
American-style provisional government included several French Canadians
opposed to the idea, the American faction narrowly won.[46] The settlers initially created a relatively decentralized government with a three-person executive committee instead of a governor and strove to establish a middle ground
between establishing independence from the United States and obvious align-
ment with it. Even so, HBC chief factor John McLoughlin and most residents
associated with the fur trade correctly identified the nascent government as a
bold move in that direction.[47] American settlers insisted the government was
necessary to protect their land claims. And while the Oregon Country would
not officially become part of the United States until the boundary question
was settled in 1846, the influence of US policy on the provisional government
was undeniable. For example, its laws were heavily influenced by American
republicanism and based almost verbatim on the territorial statutes of Iowa,
which included the 1787 Northwest Ordinance.[48]

　　Private ownership of land was a central facet of American republicanism,
and the provisional government's chief function was to legitimate land claims.
For the Anglo-American immigrants, land ownership represented autonomy
and economic opportunity, but it also required a state apparatus to levy property taxes and provide protection and security through law enforcement.
While the commodification of land in Oregon would, in theory, protect the
property of yeoman farmers, it also paved the way for commercial agriculture
and rampant land speculation. In the centuries before direct colonial contact, the region's various Native groups practiced communal ownership, but
even the idea of ownership is a misnomer since any notion of commodified
land was unknown. Prior to the provisional government, land in the Oregon

Country—whether held by the HBC, retired fur trappers, Methodist missionaries, or American settlers—was held through simple preemption and use.[49] Winslow Anderson, the man who sold Saules his farm, would have established his property in this manner, and the transaction between them probably occurred outside the purview of any legal body. Even after the new land law, several residents did not register their claims with the government, perhaps in an attempt to avoid the accompanying tax burden. According to Peter H. Burnett, who became a member of the legislative branch of the provisional government shortly after arriving in the region in the fall of 1843, this was an unacceptable situation: "Our commercial and business transactions were considerable. Difficulties were daily occurring between individuals in relation to their 'claims.'"[50] The Organic Code of 1843 restricted land claims to 640 acres and restricted settlers from holding more than one claim at a time.[51] These terms were actually far more generous than existing US laws pertaining to the public domain. As such, the potential of legal systems like the Organic Code was one of the main factors that inspired over ten thousand midwesterners to emigrate between 1844 and 1849, thus further hastening the Americanization of the region.[52]

To create a white man's country, one must first establish a white man's government, and the provisional government made the color line a legal reality. The Organic Code limited citizenship to "every free male descendant of a white man who has resided in the territory for 6 months," which resulted in a racialized definition of citizenship that disenfranchised many residents who had lived in the region long before the overlanders arrived.[53] This included not just Saules and Anderson, but also all indigenous people, Hawaiians, and women of any race. This raises the question of whether a noncitizen like Saules could even have his land claim recognized by the government. The Organic Code did include the mixed-race male offspring of white fathers, a concession to prominent settlers who had married Native women. On the other hand, the government denied citizenship to the several thousand Natives who still outnumbered Euro-American settlers in the region. The citizenship rule signaled to nonwhites that an Americanized Oregon would be a white Oregon.

The provisional government also failed to protect the traditional lands of indigenous peoples. The official position of the provisional government toward Native-owned land still adhered to the Northwest Ordinance of 1787; it promised not to seize Native lands without permission or remuneration.[54]

However, in practice the provisional government disregarded any notion of "Indian Country" and honored settlers' land claims that obviously preempted Native land. In 1845 the government created a provisional land office to record claims and sales. Because the land office lacked the scientific knowledge and equipment to formally survey the land, land office staff often used Native villages and resource sites as shorthand to mark their claims.[55] In addition, many white settlers completely ignored Native land claims, likely assuming that Indian removal and disease would clear the way for the inevitable white settlement of the Oregon Country.

ELIJAH WHITE'S LAWS FOR NATIVE PEOPLE

At roughly the same time, American settlers were providing new rules and regulations for the Euro-American settlers in the Willamette Valley, Dr. Elijah White—the newly appointed US Indian subagent—was doing the same for the various Native groups living east of the Cascade Range. And although the legitimacy of his power was questionable, Saules and many others living on the margins of Anglo-American settler society came to recognize White as the major authority figure in the region, and his reentry into the Oregon Country marked a new era in Native-settler relations. Fur trade representatives like John McLoughlin and George Simpson had earlier worked with local Native leaders to establish a framework of acceptable behavior to protect their interests, but such rules were loose and situational. In general, McLoughlin's policy was to respect Native governance and customs, and he made few attempts to alter them. But if Native people attacked HBC property or personnel, he pledged rapid and brutal retaliation. The Natives of the Columbia Plateau, however, seemed to respect this position, since quick retaliation against offending parties was consistent with long-established traditions in the region.[56] White, on the other hand, strove to introduce a more rigid and delineated code of conduct. This added to the existing burdens settlers placed on Native people such as encroachment, depletion of resources, and disease. These pressures later erupted into violent exchanges, at least two of which affected Saules personally.

White was a medical doctor from New York who first traveled to the Oregon Country in 1837 with his wife aboard an ocean vessel. The Methodist Mission Board had earlier assigned White to join Jason Lee at the Methodist Mission and serve as a medical missionary. By 1840 White and Lee were at the focal point of a major schism within the missionary community in Oregon.

During the previous year, Lee and a group of Methodists held a trial and found White guilty of "imprudent conduct" during a medical examination of Julie Gervais, a French-Indian woman.[57] The Methodists also charged White with appropriating mission funds for his personal use while Lee was back east pleading his case with the Mission Board to continue financial support for the mission. At a later public meeting with Methodist and French-Indian settlers, White vehemently and, by all accounts, impressively denied all wrongdoing and severed ties with the Methodists in September 1840. In 1841 White returned to the United States and testified against Lee before the Mission Board in New England. His testimony later contributed to the board's decision to suspend Lee and replace him with the Reverend George Gary in 1843.

In September 1842, White returned to the Oregon Country, although by this time he had reinvented himself as an agent of state power rather than an evangelical worker. His new role was a vivid illustration of how religious colonialism in Oregon served as a harbinger of settler colonialism. White traveled west the second time as the leader of the same contentious 105-person wagon train that brought the adventurer Lansford Hastings.[58] Upon his reappearance in the Willamette Valley, White informed settlers that the US secretary of war had personally summoned him, appointed him subagent to the Native people of the region, and imbued him with general powers of law enforcement. This was an unusual assignment, since typically an Indian subagent served under a governor, and the Oregon Country had no such office.[59] This appointment made him the sole representative of the US government in the region, although his purported authority was tempered by the reality that the Pacific Northwest was not officially part of the United States. Moreover, the US War Department had selected White as subagent in anticipation of the passage of Senator Linn's 1841 bill pushing to absorb a large section of the Oregon Country into the United States.[60] Because the bill failed to pass, the legality of White's authority was dubious. Moreover, because the Oregon Country was a neutral territory, the treaty of joint occupancy forbade the US War Department from establishing a military presence. American settlers in Oregon would not learn of the bill's failure until 1843, and White managed to cling to the position until 1845.

White's return to the region as subagent was celebrated by some and dreaded by others. The Anglo-American settlers with whom Charles Wilkes met in 1841 on his tour of the Willamette Valley were ecstatic that White's appointment signaled the success of their petition and that the US government was taking an active interest in the Americanization of the region. On the other hand, many in the missionary community were chagrined that the former missionary was now intruding on their autonomy. Lee and the Methodists faced a one-time ally turned disgruntled adversary, and when White appeared at a political meeting in Champoeg, their influence helped deny him the gubernatorial powers he sought.[61] The HBC governor George Simpson and chief factor McLoughlin, who arguably wielded the most power and influence of any Euro-Americans in the Pacific Northwest, interpreted White's reappearance as a violation of the policy of joint occupation and an ominous sign of impending conflict between the United States and Great Britain. Simpson advised McLoughlin to not extend any courtesy or assistance to White or anyone else claiming such authority until the boundary question was settled.[62]

Considering White's self-proclaimed clout, it is worthwhile to consider into which camp Saules fell. Saules was not a missionary nor was he officially aligned with the fur trade, although his transportation services on the Columbia and Willamette Rivers contributed to the viability of a local economy that benefited both missionaries and traders. Because he was married to a Chinookan woman and had strong social ties with Native villages along the Columbia, Saules would have been aware of the potential impact an American Indian agent would make in the region. But by the early 1840s, Saules had started farming in the Willamette Valley and probably shared concerns with his Anglo-American neighbors. He would have wanted protection for his land and surrounding community from potentially hostile Native people. Saules's later actions would reflect that he recognized and accepted White's authority, but he also displayed hints of skepticism toward the subagent's ability to convert his purported authority into effective action.

White's first major act as subagent was his introduction of a "civil compact" to the Nez Perces. His rules addressed genuine fears among settlers that Natives would not respect their property rights and might even attack their settlements. For their part, Natives were justifiably suspicious that the newly arrived settlers would appropriate their lands.[63] White was especially concerned about the Native groups living on the Columbia Plateau, such as the Nez Perces, Cayuses, and Walla Wallas. These groups remained relatively strong since they had been less affected by exogenous diseases than the Natives of the Willamette Valley. In particular, White responded to recent news of disorder at the Presbyterian mission at Waiilatpu, which included the suspected arson of the Whitman's gristmill. Several Nez Perces had also alleg-edly accosted the missionaries at the Lapwai station.[64]

On November 15, 1842, White rode to the Columbia Plateau with six armed men and two interpreters to meet with various Nez Perce, Cayuse, and Walla Walla leaders and other interested Native parties. White hoped that if he convinced the elders to accept his new laws, he could discourage future incidents, protect the settlers already present in the Willamette Valley, and encourage other Anglo-Americans to relocate to Oregon. White also intended the meeting to announce to the Native people of the region that he, and not McLoughlin, was now the major Euro-American authority in the Oregon Country. Furthermore, while many of the Native leaders would have likened White to the Euro-American missionaries who had resided in the area for the past several years, the subagent came to extend the power of US federal government, not to preserve and encourage their spiritual welfare. When he arrived in Waiilatpu and then Lapwai stations, he found mostly Nez Perces and a few Cayuses. He proceeded to pitch the laws to the Nez Perces with reciprocity in mind, claiming that if they accepted his code, White would protect them from American settlers who might steal from Natives, ply them with liquor, or murder them.[65]

In an effort to ensure the Nez Perces that they still maintained some autonomy, he informed tribal leaders that they, and not representatives of American law enforcement, would enforce the laws and mete out punish-ments to their own people. This aspect of the civil compact actually betrays White's inability to marshal any significant legal or military muscle and dem-onstrates his reluctance to completely abandon the HBC's tendency to pre-serve order by not overriding local Native authority and customs. White also planned to simplify his relationship with the numerous and diverse Native people of the Columbia Plateau by asking the Nez Perces, Cayuse, and Walla Walla to each select a single headman—a chief of chiefs—to represent their respective groups. Therefore, White could communicate directly with one supreme headman, who would then delegate power and punitive action to a group of subchiefs representing smaller village units.

The following is the civil compact White asked tribal leaders to recognize and enforce:

1. Whoever willfully takes life shall be hung.
2. Whoever burns a dwelling house shall be hung.

3. Whoever burns an outbuilding shall be imprisoned six months, receive fifty lashes, and pay all damages.

4. Whoever carelessly burns a house, or any property, shall pay damages.

5. If any one enter a dwelling, without permission of the occupant, the chiefs shall punish him as they think proper. Public rooms are excepted.

6. If any one steal he shall pay back two fold; and if it be the value of beaver skin or less, he shall receive twenty-five lashes; and if the value is over a beaver skin he shall pay back two fold, and received fifty lashes.

7. If any one take a horse, and ride it, without permission, or take any article and use it, without liberty, he shall pay for the use of it, and receive from twenty to fifty lashes, as the chief shall direct.

8. If any one enter a field, and injure the crops, or throw down the fence so that cattle or horse go in and do damage, he shall pay all damages, and receive twenty-five lashes for every offence.

9. Those only may keep dogs who travel or live among the game; if a dog kill a lamb, calf, or any domestic animal, the owner shall pay the damage, and kill the dog.

10. If an Indian raise a gun or other weapon against a white man, it shall be reported to the chiefs, and they shall punish him. If a white do the same to an Indian, it shall be reported to Dr. White, and he shall redress it.

11. If an Indian break these laws, he shall be punished by his chiefs; if a white man break them, he shall be reported to the agent, and be punished at his instance.[66]

Notwithstanding White's claims to the contrary, his laws tilted power in favor of settler colonists and were obviously designed to protect settlers' homes, building, livestock, and personal property. And while the Native groups of the Pacific Northwest had always observed laws, moral codes, and systems of governance, White's laws dealt with property and violent crimes in ways alien to most Natives. For instance, article two stipulated, "Whoever burns a dwelling house shall be hung."[67] Hanging was a practice unknown to Natives; a more typical punishment for such property damage was retaliation in kind or payment to the victim. Furthermore, the proscription on burning structures is likely an attempt to curb the Native practice of clearing areas through burning. While this was an essential feature of Native agriculture and subsistence, it was also an activity that threatened the hundreds of new buildings that would spring up over the next few years. White's laws also made it a crime to enter homes without knocking or peer through windows, neither of which most Native people considered improper conduct.

White's use of supreme head chiefs to impose order over large populations also ran counter to traditional practices. In a disastrous move echoed by many other policy makers, White mapped Anglo-American notions of leadership and social control onto Nez Perce communities and assumed that elders spoke for the majority of tribal members. He presupposed that Nez Perce headmen and councils exercised authority over their people, when in reality, power among the Nez Perces was highly decentralized. Nez Perce country boasted over one hundred villages, each with its own headman. But headmen served the role of advisors and had little power to coerce villagers. In fact, some historians have suggested that by accepting White's laws, Nez Perce leaders were attempting to extend their influence and prestige.[68] Indeed, many tribal leaders told White they sympathized with his aims and some even argued for harsher punishments.[69] Yet many younger and nonelite Native people in the region did not recognize White's laws and resented his intrusion. Ultimately, whether he realized it or not, in addition to acrimonious relations between Native groups and Anglo-American settlers, White laid the groundwork for internal power struggles within Native groups,

By early 1843, White's presence on the Columbia Plateau sparked rumors among local Native groups that White planned to bring soldiers to the region so the United States could enslave Natives and steal their land. The Cayuses, in particular, resented White's laws and many refused to plant crops for fear they would only benefit white settlers. Presbyterian missionary Narcissa Whitman wrote a letter to her husband Marcus in which she reiterated the Cayuses's case: "They say the laws in themselves are good, they do not object to them— but do not wish to be compelled to adopt them."[70] In May, amid rumors among settlers that the Cayuses planned to attack the nascent community in the Willamette Valley, White held another council with the Cayuses, Nez Perces, and Walla Wallas at the Presbyterian mission at Waiilatpu. The reports were apparently well founded, as some younger Cayuse leaders insisted a preemptive strike would chasten the Anglo-American invaders.[71] Presbyterian missionary Henry Perkins also claimed a Nez Perce chief had traveled east of present-day Idaho to enlist other Native people in this cause. White again promised the assembly that he intended to protect them from settlers and reiterated the importance of following his laws.[72] Following the two-day convocation, the Cayuses agreed to accept his laws, and White left feeling satisfied he had averted a catastrophe. However, McLoughlin, who met with Walla Walla leader Piupiumaksmaks to discuss the potential uprising, may have actually been more instrumental in averting bloodshed by convincing Piupiumaksmaks that claims regarding White's nefarious intentions were unfounded.[73]

White's civil compact was enormously significant in the relations in the Pacific Northwest, as it recognized and enshrined the color line in a legal code. His laws established a rigid binary distinction between "Indian" and "white" people. Whereas White once served as a Methodist missionary who sought Native conversions as part of an assimilationist project; as an Indian agent he now dealt with Native and settler societies as two separate spheres. The sub-agent devised specific and severe punishments for Native people but left all punishments of offending white settlers to his own discretion. For instance, White's laws left open the question of whether white settlers would be hanged for burning a Nez Perce dwelling, or if they would be punished for squatting on Native land. Piupiumaksmaks, for one, was skeptical that White's code offered Native people anything resembling reciprocity. He once asked Jason Lee, "If white men sleep with our women by stealth, is it right for us to tie them up and whip them? If they steal our wood, as they are coming through our country, is it right for us to whip them?"[74]

The racial system White imposed also demonstrated that he conflated "white" with "settler," placing nonwhite settlers like Saules in a liminal legal position between colonizer and colonized. This begs the question of how these laws would affect a black settler like Saules. Would a black American man with a Chinookan wife be tried and convicted by a tribal headman or by White's discretion? If a Native man stole Saules's horse, would White come to Saules's aid? This is not a hypothetical question, as a Native man named Cockstock actually stole Saules's horse approximately one year after White introduced his legal code, and the result of Saules's appeal to White nearly plunged the region into full-scale war.

4

The Cockstock Affair, the Saules-Pickett Dispute, and the Banishment of Saules

By late 1843, Saules, like John McLoughlin, realized that the Anglo-American settlers represented the Willamette Valley's future. And for a man whose livelihood revolved around commerce, the arrival of the Oregon Trail immigrants may have even portended an uptick in his freight business. Perhaps he even thought he and his wife might blend in as yet another local farm family raising its own food and bringing the surplus to market. Less than one year later, however, Saules faced the grim reality of his dwindling position in the new settler society. At the same time, many of the new settlers also realized that Oregon was not exactly the Eden they had envisioned. Furthermore, their attempts to refashion the region into an American agrarian republic put them at odds not only with Native groups that had lived in the area for hundreds of years, but also with many of the economic and religious colonists who had preceded them. These settlers knew they would have to diminish their rivals' power and push them to the margins of settler society. But the settlers' adversaries showed no sign of surrendering without a struggle. As such, Saules's fellow Willamette Valley agriculturalists found themselves living in a community gripped by apprehension and paranoia.

In late 1843 and early 1844, tensions between the new arrivals and the previous inhabitants made the Willamette Valley feel like a very dangerous place. In November 1843, Indian subagent Elijah White wrote to his benefactors in Washington, DC, that the Native people of the Oregon Country "are becoming considerably enlightened on the subject of the white man's policy, and begin to quake in view of their future doom."[1] Many recently arrived overlanders were also disappointed that the lofty promises of Oregon boosters had yet to materialize. According to Frances Fuller Victor, the actual author of Hubert Howe Bancroft's 1886 *History of Oregon*, "They found themselves more than two thousand miles from the land of their birth, without houses to shelter them, destitute of the means of farming, without provisions or clothing, surrounded by unfriendly natives, and without the protection of their government."[2]

The following dispatch from the Willamette Valley, published in the December 14, 1843, edition of the *Missouri Republican*, captures the ominous mood: "The Indians on the Columbia are expected to be troublesome to these newcomers. It is supposed they are induced to acts of violence by some persons as yet unknown."[3] The article also suggested that the HBC was preparing to use Natives to attack American settlers: "We have always believed that the Indians, backed and incited as they will be by agents and emissaries of the Hudson's Bay Co., and furnished as they doubtless will be, with arms and means of warfare from some source, would oppose the emigrants in making their settlements."[4] This last statement appears to be pure paranoia, as the HBC's McLoughlin, by all accounts, treated American settlers with undue kindness and generosity because he saw them as potential customers and debtors. But it was also common for antebellum Americans to view Natives—and to some extent black people—as natural British allies determined to circumvent US interests.[5] The article closes by explicitly reminding settlers of their imperialist mission: "That the country must be conquered before it is attained, we hardly entertain a doubt."[6]

In the early months of 1844, Saules was involved in a series of events that ultimately erupted in a riot between the Native man Cockstock, his five Molalla traveling companions, and several white settlers in Oregon City. The incident, known as the Cockstock Affair, was a result of rising anxieties and ethnic tensions in the region, largely brought on by the imposition of Elijah White's foreign laws. It caused a sensation among Anglo-American settlers in the Willamette Valley and was the most significant case of violence between settlers and Natives prior to the Whitman Massacre of 1847. Cockstock is most often referred to as a Molalla, a Native group that lived east of Oregon City, although he also had familial relations and tribal loyalties to the Wascos of the Columbia Plateau. The Cockstock Affair was particularly noteworthy since relations between American immigrants and the region's various indigenous groups had been mostly peaceful—if uneasy and circumspect—up to that point. The response of the American settlers in the aftermath of the Cockstock Affair demonstrated how much relations had changed between Euro-American settlers and the region's indigenous people, especially once the settlers began to undo the middle ground that existed between them.

According to Elijah White's full account of Cockstock's activities, in April 1843 Cockstock rode to Saules's farm near the outskirts of Oregon City and demanded he relinquish his horse to him. Saules was dumbstruck by this request and understandably reluctant to surrender an animal he had only recently purchased from his neighbor, the "mulatto" man Winslow Anderson. Saules almost certainly recognized him, as White claimed Cockstock had performed various tasks on the farm even after Anderson sold the plot to Saules. And although Cockstock's people lived dozens of miles from Oregon City, he was related to the Clackamas people of the Willamette Valley through marriage and had considerable notoriety in the area. On this particular visit to the farm, Cockstock seized the horse and for the next several months continued to harass both Saules and Anderson.

In the spring of 1843, news of the recalcitrant horse thief sent shockwaves through the small community of settlers living nearby, as it coincided with aforementioned rumors of Cayuse unrest on the Columbia Plateau. The Reverend Gustavus Hines, a Methodist missionary who came to the region in 1840, provided an account of the alleged theft in his 1850 memoir. In his entry for April 14, 1843, Hines wrote that a group of Clackamas Natives rode to his settlement and told him a Molalla related to the Clackamas by marriage had stolen a horse from Saules.[7] According to Hines, Saules questioned Cockstock, who supposedly replied, "Yes, I stole your horse, and when I want another one I shall steal him also."[8] When Saules demanded payment, Cockstock offered him what Hines described as a horse with a missing eye and sore back. He refused the proposition and replied, "That is a very poor horse, and mine is a good one; I shall not take him, and if you don't bring him back I will report you to Dr. White."[9] Cockstock then assured him he was not afraid of the subagent: "Let him come if he wants to, and bring the Boston people with him; he will find me prepared for him."[10]

Saules's neighbor Anderson had hired Cockstock earlier to clear the land claim he later sold to Saules. Hiring Native people as laborers and servants was a common practice among American and French Canadian settlers despite any pretensions regarding self-sufficiency. White's 1842 census counted over 70 such servants among only 431 adults.[11] In fact, Cockstock continued performing various tasks on the farm even after it was sold to

Saules. Apparently, Anderson had promised to compensate Cockstock with the same horse he later sold to Saules.

After he received Saules's complaint regarding his horse, Subagent White sent an armed party of six men to apprehend Cockstock at his camp early in the morning. According to Hines, when the men arrived at the camp, they found Cockstock accompanied by "thirty or forty Indians painted in the most hideous manner, and armed with muskets, bows and arrows, tomahawks and scalping-knives, and determined at all events to protect the horse thief, and drive back those that should come to take him." The party wisely withdrew and rode back to Willamette Falls to update White on the current situation. White then recruited provisional government member George LeBreton to help him search for Cockstock. Neither man was successful, but on April 17, Le Breton learned that the armed group of Native people they earlier encountered at the camp had been alarmed by the visit and vacated the area. Before they left, however, they visited Saules's residence and, according to Hines, tied a "good horse" to a tree near his house and told him "he must take that and be satisfied."[12] In this same April 17 entry, Hines added, "The colony is indeed in a most defenseless condition; two hundred Indians, divided into four bands, might destroy the whole settlement in one night."[13]

On a November afternoon in 1843, Cockstock and his slave rode to Subagent White's house near Oregon City intending to shoot and kill him. Cockstock was retaliating against White's actions in the previous month. The subagent had personally flogged a Wasco headman named Skiats for disobeying White's civil compact and trespassing and threatening a white man, the Presbyterian missionary Henry Perkins. White clearly violated his own laws by flogging the headman himself instead of finding a Native chief to administer the lashes, but he later claimed he could not locate a suitable candidate. Prior to the flogging, Skiats had always willingly enforced White's laws. But like most of the Native people of the region, Skiats and his fellow Wascos held enslaved people, which aroused the abolitionist tendencies of Protestant missionaries. When the missionary Perkins forbade Skiats from conducting a slave raid of Klamath country, Skiats allegedly entered Perkins's house and bound him with ropes in punishment for interfering with a practice the headman deemed necessary to support his people. In addition to being Cockstock's headman, Skiats was also his relative. When Cockstock arrived at White's residence, he could not find the subagent. He conducted a thorough search of the house and allegedly smashed every window in with the breech of his gun.[14] When White returned home that evening, he formed a party to pursue and capture Cockstock but was unsuccessful.

White was justifiably alarmed by this assassination attempt and the realization that Cockstock was conducting a bitter campaign against his civil compact. Therefore, he was highly suspicious when, in December 1843, fifteen Molallas and Klamaths gathered near White's residence to visit with a Kalapuyan headman named Caleb. With Cockstock's recent exploits in mind, White warily scrutinized the visitors, whom he described as "painted and well armed."[15] He knew the Klamaths lived several hundred miles to the south and the Molallas over forty miles to the east; he feared they were "on an errand of mischief, being well informed of their marauding and desperate habits."[16] Nevertheless, White was on friendly terms with Caleb, who had already accepted his civil compact, and he allowed him to slaughter one of White's oxen in an attempt to curry favor with Caleb's Molalla and Klamath guests. White himself then joined the feast at Caleb's lodge.

Once the members of the gathering had their appetites sated, White seized the opportunity to present the same civil compact he had introduced to the Native groups of the Columbia Plateau and the Willamette Valley. Unbeknownst to him, Cockstock had infiltrated the meeting at some point during the evening, although White failed to recognize his erstwhile assassin. The Molallas and Klamaths listened patiently to White's proposal and agreed to discuss the matter further with their respective tribespeople at a council scheduled for March 15, 1844. At the conclusion of the meeting, the party, which now included Cockstock, rode away from Caleb's lodge to return home. When they arrived at a difficult stream and attempted to cross it, Cockstock allegedly gave a signal and rallied his five supporters and massacred the remaining Native men in retaliation for entertaining White's request.

By February 16, 1844, Saules's agitation regarding Cockstock's harassing behavior reached a breaking point. He drafted a letter to White, updating him on the current situation and demanding that he subdue Cockstock. The letter, which was later presented in White's 1844 report to the US Senate, is the only known document written by Saules:

SIR: I beg leave to inform you that there is an Indian about this place, of the name of "Cockstock," who is in the habit of making continual threats against the settlers in this neighborhood, and who had also murdered several Indians lately. He has conducted himself lately in so outrageous a manner, that Mr. Winslow Anderson has considered himself in personal danger, and on that account has left his place, and come to reside at the falls of the Wallamette; and were I in circumstances that I could possibly remove from my place, I would certainly remove also, but am so situated that it is not possible for me to do so. I beg, therefore, that you, sir, will take into consideration the propriety of ridding the country of a villain, against the depredations of whom none can be safe, as it is impossible to guard against the lurking attacks of the midnight murderer. I have therefore taken the liberty of informing you that I shall be in expectation of a decided answer from you on or before the 10th of March next; after that date, I shall consider myself justified in acting as I shall see fit, on any repetition of the threats made by the before-mentioned Indian or his party.

I am, &c., with respect, James D. Saules.[17]

Saules's letter is fascinating in several respects. First, it suggests Saules was not only literate but a facile writer. This is not surprising since literacy rates among northern blacks in 1850 ranged from 63 percent in Louisville, Kentucky, to 97 percent in Providence, Rhode Island.[18] And despite laws proscribing literacy, many southern free blacks and even a small percentage of enslaved people could read and write. Secondly, the letter demonstrated that Saules conceived of himself as part of the settler community in the Willamette Valley and wrote, at least partially, on their behalf. In addition, Saules also stated that, for whatever reason, he could not leave his farm in the Willamette Valley. This suggests he may have permanently settled as a farmer and abandoned his freight business. Or perhaps Saules's wife was physically incapable of making such a trip at the time. She may have been pregnant or nursing, as White later referred to Saules as having a family. If Saules and his wife had children by the winter of 1844, they would have been very young and perhaps unable to relocate. Finally, his letter demonstrates that Saules was a pragmatist who recognized and accepted the legal infrastructure created by the American settlers, and that he understood the efficacy of going through proper legal channels to fulfill his request for assistance. Saules was respectful toward White but never deferential. Saules essentially gave White an ultimatum to act or else he, Saules, would take the law into his own hands.

Saules's willingness to work with White demonstrates that the subagent had established at least some authority in the region despite having served for just slightly over a year.

White, who claimed in his report to have known Saules well, received his letter on February 20, along with corroborating testimony from Oregon City shopkeeper Philip Foster. The subagent sprung into action, likely dreading the consequences of Saules's acting alone. William H. Willson, an American settler and Methodist missionary, was present at White's residence when the news arrived. Years later, Willson recalled that Cockstock had been particularly vindictive toward Methodist missionaries who had admonished him for his behavior.[19] White was convinced that Cockstock might incite "all the horrors of savage warfare in our hitherto quiet neighborhood."[20] The subagent assembled a party of ten men to "secure the Indian without bloodshed."[21] This last point had nothing to do with mercy; White knew that Cockstock was affiliated with what he described as "formidable" tribes, and he worried his death might bring troubled waters to a boil. On February 27, White's posse located Cockstock and his five Molalla supporters, but bad weather thwarted them, and Cockstock's party easily fled.

As a last ditch effort, White offered a one hundred dollar reward—a considerable sum in 1844—for the successful capture of Cockstock. In the mid-1840s, the American settlers faced a chronic currency shortage, which heightened the reward's value. Most of the actual currency used in Oregon consisted of orders for merchandise redeemable at stores or wheat to be delivered to the order holder.[22] While White recognized that many settlers sought to kill Cockstock, his plan was to have him tried by the Nez Perces and Cayuses, whom he believed "would feel honored in inflicting a just sentence upon him."[23] This was a curious decision, since Cockstock was not a member of either group. Yet White was probably reluctant to leave legal proceedings to the Wasco headman Skiats, whom White had flogged only a few months earlier. White also contended that such a settlement would save the "colony" from an Indian war "so much to be dreaded in our present weak and defenceless condition."[24] White did not address the likelihood that Cockstock's allies might retaliate against the Nez Perces and Cayuses for flogging or hanging the accused man.

On March 4, 1844, Cockstock and his five Molalla supporters arrived in Oregon City on horseback in the early afternoon. Although Subagent White later presented his account of the subsequent confrontation to Secretary of

Oregon City, ca. 1846. Source: Henry J. Warre, *Sketches in North America and the Oregon Territory* (1848). Courtesy of the Oregon Historical Society.

War William Wilkins, it is unclear if he was actually present in Oregon City when Cockstock appeared. Many settlers were out of town that day attending a meeting of the provisional government about twenty miles upriver in Champoeg. White himself had actually called for the meeting; and while he did not preside, given his low standing among Anglo-American settlers, he most likely attended. White planned to petition the US Congress to extend its jurisdiction over the Oregon Country. To White's chagrin, a faction of French Canadian citizens dominated the meeting; they protested the establishment of American-style governance and instead advocated a more limited and local organization.[25] This debate was immediately set aside following the explosive events that occurred later that day.

Regardless of whether White was actually present in Oregon City during the fracas, the following description of the Cockstock Affair is culled from White's version of the events and occasionally augmented by details from Willson's 1857 retrospective account.[26] According to the subagent, Cockstock's party rode into town "horridly painted" and carrying firearms.[27] They first gathered at the home of the Reverend A. F. Waller, a Methodist missionary, and "halloed" for him to come out.[28] When Waller did not emerge, the band rode from house to house for several hours in an insulting and intimidating manner, evidently frightening the townspeople. Several hours later in the early evening, Cockstock and his men tied up their horses and paddled a boat across the Willamette River to a Kalapuyan village on the western bank. According to the village headman, Cockstock attempted to recruit local Natives to "join him and burn the town that night."[29] After the villagers refused, White claimed the band recrossed the river with an interpreter "for the purpose of calling the whites to an explanation for pursuing him [Cockstock] with hostile intentions."[30]

As Cockstock and his companions paddled toward Oregon City, a confused crowd of panicked townspeople gathered on the bank at the boat launch where the party attempted to land.[31] White reported that a few armed settlers arrived at a nearby sawmill, "some to take him alive and get the reward; others to shoot him at any risk to themselves, the wealthiest men in town promising to stand by them to the account of $1,000 each."[32] Among them were Willson, James W. Nesmith, and Sterling Rodgers. The armed settlers and Cockstock's men started firing rounds at each other, with each side claiming the other had fired first. According to Willson's version, when Cockstock stepped out of the boat and headed toward his horse, someone in the crowd shouted an insult at him. Cockstock allegedly responded by firing indiscriminately into the crowd. After an exchange of gunfire, George LeBreton, the official recorder for the provisional government, rushed unarmed at Cockstock and received three shots to his right arm. Cockstock then wrestled LeBreton to the ground and stabbed him with his knife. Saules's neighbor Winslow Anderson appeared and smashed Cockstock's skull with the barrel of his rifle, killing him instantly. The five Molallas avenged his death by firing guns and shooting poisoned arrows at the settlers, wounding both Willson and Rodgers in the process. Cockstock's companions then fled over the bluff and hid among the rocks on the east side of the town. The settlers followed them and managed to kill a horse and wound one of the Molallas, but the party remained at large. Local residents took LeBreton via canoe to Fort Vancouver to receive medical attention, but the journey took ten hours, and he soon died from blood poisoning. Rogers also died from his wounds, but Willson survived to regale future generations with his story.

Catholic priest Francois Norbert Blanchet was not in Oregon City on March 4, but his description of the Cockstock Affair—written soon after the event—was influential among some historians and deviated significantly from White's account.[33] Blanchet was a French Canadian Catholic priest who first arrived in the Oregon Country in 1839 with his fellow missionary, the Reverend Modeste Demers, at the request of the HBC. Blanchet was also involved in the formation of the provisional government but eventually split with the body due to its pronounced American character. The introduction of Catholic missionaries in Oregon inspired antipathy among many Methodist missionaries, who considered Blanchet a supercilious and elitist intruder.[34] Perhaps they were also resentful that the unmarried Catholic men made more headway in establishing positive relations with the region's indigenous population. Demers in particular worked closely with Native people and became fluent in the Chinook jargon.[35] Many of the American settlers were also staunchly anti-Catholic and intended to establish an egalitarian and decidedly Anglo-Protestant homeland in the Willamette Valley.

Blanchett described the Cockstock Affair as "an unfortunate and disgraceful affair, brought on by the indiscretion of two white men,"[36] presumably meaning White and LeBreton. He claimed Cockstock was innocent of massacring any Native people. Blanchet asserted that Cockstock only arrived in Oregon City to contest White's bounty and declare his innocence of all charges. He also contended that once Cockstock crossed the river to the Kalapuyan village, the townspeople conspired to apprehend him in order to claim White's reward. Blanchet wrote that John McLoughlin's store clerk admonished the greedy crowd by shouting, "That Indian is a good man, you should not molest him; if you do, you will repent!"[37] According to Blanchet, when Cockstock rowed back to Oregon City, LeBreton and the "Mulatto" [Anderson] demanded Cockstock surrender. When he refused, LeBreton ordered Anderson to shoot. Anderson wounded Cockstock, who allegedly only returned fire and shot LeBreton in self-defense. Cockstock then approached LeBreton and Anderson, both of whom tried to run away. When Cockstock caught up to LeBreton, he wrestled him to the ground. LeBreton then succeeded in firing a ball into his assailant's arm, and Anderson forced LeBreton's release by smashing Cockstock's skull with the butt end of his rifle. Upon witnessing their leader's death, Cockstock's companions shot arrows, hitting LeBreton, Rodgers, and Willson. Blanchet lamented the death of Rodgers, whom he described as a mere spectator, and concluded that most of the settlers were ignorant regarding what actually caused the event.[38]

Unlike Blanchet, Reverend Demers was present in Oregon City on March 4 and claimed he witnessed Cockstock's death. He wrote a letter to Blanchet a few days after the event that corroborated Blanchet's account and added a grisly detail: "But, O barbarity! The negro who said it was [Cockstock] who pierced his hat with a bullet, did pierce him after he was dead; and in the morning, his head had been found split and entirely separated above the forehead, the brains still clung to the axe which had been the instrument for such savage cruelty."[39] No other witness referred to this use of an axe, and it is unclear if the "negro" to whom Demers referred was Anderson or Saules, since the priest earlier referred to Anderson only as the "Mulatto."[40] Demers concluded that Cockstock's death was "true murder; based upon the extremely rash and unjustifiable action of poor LeBreton who will pay dearly for his apostasy and crime."[41] Regarding LeBroton's "apostasy," Demers was referring to LeBreton's abandonment of Catholicism.

It is impossible to determine the veracity of either account of the Cockstock affair. In his report to the secretary of war, White wanted to minimize his culpability in allowing events to escalate into an armed skirmish on the streets of an otherwise quiet frontier town. On the other hand, the French Canadian missionaries viewed the American overlanders and Methodist missionaries as rivals and had good reason to publicly denigrate them. Yet Blanchet's and Demers's perceptions of the event demonstrate how differently the French Canadian missionaries viewed the Native people of the region. They were also deeply skeptical regarding the intentions of American settlers, which Blanchett described as "another kind of savageness."[42] He especially objected to contemporary historians of the time like William H. Gray, who referred to the Cockstock Affair as an "attack." The priest insisted it was unlikely that a small band of Molallas would consider taking on the well-armed citizenry of an entire town. Years later, Blanchet reflected on the event and insisted that "all the Indian tribes were never so peaceable as they were then, having no reason to molest [settlers], as their fisheries, hunting-places and camas prairies had not yet been taken away from them."[43]

According to White's documentation, seventy armed Native people from The Dalles arrived in Oregon City following the events of March 4, demanding both an explanation and compensation for Cockstock's death. White remained resolute and refused to offer any gifts to the Wasco headman or other tribal leaders. According to White, "I told them we had lost two valuable innocent men, and they but one; and should our people learn that I had given them presents, without their giving me two blankets for one, they must expect nothing but the hottest displeasure from the whites."[44]

Notwithstanding his stern response, White was indeed concerned that the incident could lead to widespread conflict. He eventually brokered a settlement by presenting Cockstock's widow with two blankets, a dress, and a handkerchief, emulating the traditional Native practice of "covering the dead."[45] His handling of the situation suggested the influence of McLoughlin, who usually advocated for solving disputes according to Native customs. McLoughlin himself handled the actual transaction and later described the death of Cockstock as an unprovoked "assassination."[46] McLoughlin was an ideal figure to oversee the transaction: as a representative of the multiethnic fur trade, he had ample experience with similar negotiations. There is evidence that White was worried that such a settlement might not be enough to quell future violence. In his report, White mused, "I believe it morally impossible for us to remain at peace in Oregon, for any considerable time, without the protection of vigorous civil or military law."[47]

White's solution of offering gifts ultimately proved effective, but many American settlers were skeptical of his approach and believed it did nothing to prevent local Native people from rising up again. Alanson Beers, one of the provisional government's three executives, considered the score with the Wascos far from settled. He suggested that "the idea should be hooted out of countenance, that [American settlers] allowed Indians to be murdered, and paid for it with blankets."[48] Instead, he urged his fellow settlers to back White's gesture with military muscle. As a result, the provisional government responded to the Cockstock Affair in a manner far different than fur trade elites had reacted to previous instances of violent conflict with Native peoples. On March 9, 1844, five days after the Cockstock Affair, the executive committee held a public meeting in French Prairie in response to ongoing fears of a major Native revolt. After Subagent White presented his thoughts on the recent fray, the members voted to form the Oregon Rangers, a voluntary organization consisting of twenty-five mounted riflemen. This was the first military organization ever assembled in the Oregon Country.[49] The immediate purpose of the militia was to pursue Cockstock's accomplices and bring them to justice. Despite the Molallas remaining at large, relations between settlers and Natives remained peaceful, and the Oregon Rangers saw very little action in the subsequent months. According to historian Frances Fuller Victor, "The formation of the company was in fact a mere piece of braggadocio, intended quite as much to alarm the Hudson's Bay Company as to awe the natives."[50] This also suggests the extent to which the Cockstock Affair can be seen as a product of regional tensions between the recently arrived overlanders and the various previous inhabitants of the region.

William H. Gray, an original member of the Oregon Rangers, later wrote a history of Oregon partially confirming Victor's claim that the militia's purpose was to send a potent message to Great Britain and the officers of the HBC. Following the provisional government's bellicose response to the Cockstock Affair, Gray alleged that HBC factor James Douglas feared American settlers might attempt to overtake Fort Vancouver. HBC officers had also noted that local Native people had become more "hostile and dangerous" since American settlers arrived in large numbers. The British government was indeed concerned about Fort Vancouver's safety and ordered an eighteen-gun sloop, the HMS *Modeste,* to sail to Fort Vancouver as both protection and demonstration of Britain's naval supremacy. But Gray's claim attributing the arrival of *Modeste* to the formation of the Oregon Rangers is dubious since the ship arrived at the fort on July 14, 1844, suggesting the *Modeste's* voyage began long before the creation of the Oregon Rangers. Yet Gray correctly identified a larger issue: because the Oregon boundary question remained unsettled in the summer of 1844, the *Modeste's* appearance in the Pacific Northwest demonstrated how regional factionalism, struggles, and anxieties now intersected with international political tensions.

THE SAULES-PICKETT DISPUTE

In the two months following the Cockstock Affair, the mood of trepidation that gripped the nascent settler community in the Willamette Valley began to lift. On May 1, 1844, however, news of another potential Native uprising against an American settler shattered this fragile sense of calm. Earlier in the day, Justice of the Peace Robert Moore, a member of the 1839 Peoria Party, issued Sheriff Joseph L. Meek a warrant to apprehend the alleged ringleader and bring him to justice. Meek soon located the suspect, James D. Saules, and arrested him in connection with an alleged assault on a Virginian named Charles E. Pickett. Meek was a legendary mountain man and fur trapper from Virginia who had worked with William Sublette as part of the Rocky Mountain Fur Company in the 1820s and 1830s. He later befriended Presbyterian missionary Marcus Whitman and relocated to Oregon in 1840. The provisional government appointed Meek as its top law enforcement official in 1843.

On May 3, Meek arrived at the makeshift courtroom in Moore's residence with Saules, three witnesses, and a jury of six men. In his May 1 deposition, the "plaintiff," Charles E. Pickett claimed Saules had "threatened to incense the Indians against his property, to destroy the same; and that he . . . verily believes that unless measures are taken to prevent [Saules] . . . he will carry those threats into execution." Two of the three witnesses, William Hill and David Bird, corroborated Pickett's account and claimed, "Indians had come in a menacing manner; and that Saul [sic] said he would stand for the Indians' rights; and that [Saules] was armed and prepared to do so; and that the Indians would burn and destroy his house and property."[51] Moore determined that the charges against Saules were "of a higher character than the Oregon laws have cognizance of" and "that the United States sub Indian agent, Dr. Elijah White, is the proper officer to take cognizance of him."[52] Moore then instructed Sheriff Meek to deliver Saules to White.

Unlike the Cockstock Affair, which is covered extensively in several early Oregon history books, little is known about the circumstances surrounding the Saules-Pickett dispute. The only reference that exists beyond the scant legal documents is from Frances Fuller Victor: "Saules, the negro who had complained of Cockstock, was himself arrested for joining the Clackamas Indians in making threats against the life and property of Charles E. Pickett."[53] Why Saules allegedly made these threats and stood for the Natives' rights remains a mystery. Furthermore, none of the documentation identifies the specific "rights" Saules was willing to defend. Pickett's biographer, Lawrence Clark Powell, never mentions the case, although he discusses other events that took place in the spring of 1844 in considerable detail.

What is certain is that Saules did not receive a fair trial. The jury consisted entirely of Anglo-American immigrants, and two of the witnesses and half of the jury had traveled with Pickett as part of the Great Migration of 1843. Furthermore, one juror, future US senator James W. Nesmith, was Pickett's close friend.[54] Four jurors—Nesmith, William C. Dement, Philip Foster (who had earlier corroborated Saules's testimony against Cockstock) and Sydney W. Moss—were members of the Pioneer Lyceum and Literary Club, an organization led by Pickett.[55] Finally, it does not appear that Saules, whom the provisional government denied citizenship due to his race, received any legal representation or anything resembling a jury of his peers. The provisional government was not unusual in this regard, as no African American ever served on a jury in the United States until 1860.[56] Furthermore, Oregon's laws regarding jurisprudence recognized the primacy of the color line in protecting the rights of white citizens. The provisional government's organic laws, borrowed from Iowa, stipulated that "a negro, mulatto or Indian shall not be a witness in any court or in any case against a white person."[57] This precedent was firmly established in May 1832 in an opinion by US Supreme Court Justice Roger Taney. According to Taney, "The African race in the United States even when free, are every where a degraded class, and exercise no political influence. The privileges they are allowed to enjoy, are accorded to them as a matter of kindness and benevolence rather than of right. . . . They were never regarded as a constituent portion of the sovereignty of any state."[58] In this opinion, Taney was specifically referring to the ostensible rights of black sailors like Saules to freely travel to southern seaports. Taney was later the author of the notorious 1857 Dred Scott decision that denied citizenship and legal representation to black people living in the United States.

While many scholars have addressed Saules's arrest in relation to Oregon's first black exclusion law, no historian has ever considered the role of the complainant in the dispute, Charles E. Pickett. Pickett was a belligerent and eccentric southerner who arrived in Oregon at the age of twenty-four. But Pickett did not fit the profile of the typical 1843 overlander: he was the scion of a prominent and wealthy Virginia tidewater planter family, known as the Fighting Picketts. Unlike most of his fellow immigrants, Pickett had received a classical education, was adamantly pro-slavery, and harbored a notorious aversion to physical labor. He was also a self-professed philosopher and journalist with impressive political connections and counted future president James K. Polk as a personal friend. Prior to joining the Great Migration of 1843, he was part of a scheme to rob $1 million worth of merchandise and specie from two Mexican caravans engaged in trade in St. Louis. The plan failed when Governor Manuel Armijo of New Mexico learned of the plot and hired a small army of armed guards to protect the caravans.[59] During the three years he lived in Oregon, Pickett was active in the provisional government, secretary of the literary club, a member of the Oregon Rangers, and publisher of the improbably named *Flumgudgeon Gazette and Bumble Bee Budget*, the first newspaper west of the Rocky Mountains. In 1845 Oregon voters selected Pickett as Clackamas County judge, even though he later admitted he had never studied nor practiced law.[60]

Pickett earned as many enemies as friends during his stay in Oregon. By 1845 he was engaged in a bitter feud with Subagent White. The conflict stemmed from lyceum debates in which White revealed his intentions to become Oregon's governor. Pickett also believed that White conspired to block him from becoming the first editor of the *Oregon Spectator*.[61] Pickett not only pilloried White in the pages of his *Flumgudgeon Gazette,* he also sent President James K. Polk a packet of missives that derided White, including a transcript of the August 1845 legislative committee meeting in which the body refused to endorse White for any government position. Pickett's letters reached Washington, DC, before White could, and in 1847 President Polk relieved White of his duties and appointed Pickett as his replacement as Indian subagent.[62]

Pickett never served and instead relocated to pre-Gold Rush San Francisco, where he continued to court controversy. For the next several decades, Pickett was a prolific pamphleteer and critic of the California political scene, although he returned to Oregon in 1857 to agitate for slavery during the debate over the state constitution.[63] Perhaps the most notable incident in Pickett's contentious life occurred in 1874, when he served eight months in jail for physically dragging a California Supreme Court justice off his seat on the bench.[64]

Pickett was also an outspoken white supremacist, a fact that probably did not endear him to the nonwhite and mixed-race residents of the Willamette Valley. Even though many American overland settlers were openly racist, Pickett's views were considered extreme even in this context. For example, when President Polk appointed Pickett as Indian subagent, many Oregonians expressed astonishment. Some referred to a letter Pickett wrote to the *Oregon Spectator* in which he instructed those traveling to California to shoot Native people on sight: "After you get to the Siskiyou Mountains, use your pleasure in spilling blood . . . my only communication with these treacherous, cowardly, untamable rascals would be through my rifle." Pickett was also skeptical regarding the possibility for peaceful relations with Native people, claiming that "philanthropy must be set aside in cases of necessity, while self-preservation here dictates these savages being killed off as soon as possible."[65] Furthermore, Pickett was in favor of the expansion of slavery to the West Coast, and according to Powell, Pickett "looked upon the Indians as equivalent to the Negroes—a slave race."[66] Few settlers wrote as prolifically about race, and Pickett's pamphlets are a vivid example of the settler colonialist mentality. In 1857 he issued a jeremiad to the veterans of the Mexican War, warning of politicians with "false humanitarian notions" who sought to "raise the inferior orders or colored castes on a level with the white race."[67] In one passage, Pickett stressed the importance of white women's role in preserving racial differences in the nascent settler colonies of the multiethnic Far West and claimed advocates for racial equality would force "ye women of Caucasian lineage . . . to be enfolded as brides in an Ethiop's brawny embrace, and become the dams of a rising breed of tawny hybrids."[68]

Perhaps the most important clue regarding the events that immediately preceded the Saules-Pickett dispute pertains to Pickett's protracted feud with the Methodist establishment in the Willamette Valley. In early 1844, Methodist missionaries Reverend L. H. Judson and his wife invited Pickett to stay in their home and cared for Pickett after he fell ill. Pickett's manners failed to impress the Judsons, and they later sent him a bill for six dollars, decrying his "abusive and hoggish manner and ungentlemanly conduct." Infuriated, Pickett wrote the Judsons to remind them that "the house of a missionary . . . was a place where the stranger might have his wants supplied and the sick to be ministered unto without money." In a subsequent letter, Rev. Judson explained he denied Pickett free care because he was "a spunge and a loafer and above all a debaucher with Indian women."[69]

Surviving documents reveal that it was more than Pickett's poor manners and questionable morals that drew the ire of the Methodists. In his 1874 address to the California legislature, Pickett recalled his troubled stint in Oregon and his battle with the Methodists: "When first arriving in and becoming a citizen of Oregon . . . I found the existing rulers of the magnificent Willamette Valley to be certain American missionaries. These, in their pride, presumption, ignorance and greed, had—additional to their individual pre-emptions—set apart for 'church purposes' thirty-six sections of the choicest land of that valley."[70] Pickett claimed he immediately denounced the Methodist's "sacerdotal land monopoly" upon arrival in 1843 and encouraged his fellow American settlers to establish claims on Methodist land. According to Pickett, he had originally envisioned a temporary stay in Oregon and only acted in the interest of his fellow emigrants. In particular, he urged his compatriot and future Saules-Pickett juror James W. Nesmith to seize a portion of "holy land." Nesmith initially demurred and Pickett's explanation is telling: "But either fearful of the Church's anathemas, or of what came near being my fate—*assassination by Indians, at the instigation of those pious men*—he and others, though coinciding with me regarding their illegal and high-handed assumption in setting up title to such land, hesitated and deferred making off a pre-emption claim upon it" (emphasis added). Pickett eventually decided to remain in Oregon and single-handedly challenge Methodist landholdings. He marked off a square mile of Methodist land, erected a log cabin, and lived in it alone. Because the American tradition of preemption required cultivation and "improvements," he reluctantly engaged in the first prolonged manual labor of his stay in Oregon, growing grain, cabbages, and potatoes. Pickett later boasted, "This example was immediately followed by others and soon all the 'Holy Land' of Oregon was appropriated by settlers."[71]

Regarding potential motives behind the Saules-Pickett dispute, the most intriguing aspect of Pickett's testimony is his assertion that the Methodists encouraged local Natives to assassinate him. Unfortunately, he does not provide a date, making it difficult to determine if this was the same altercation in which Saules was allegedly involved. On the other hand, Pickett was a staunch supporter of Indian removal, and his behavior and temperament were such that it is conceivable he provoked Saules and his Native allies in an unrelated incident. But provided he was not delusional and imagined a conspiracy where there was none, Pickett's reference to his quarrel with the Methodists raises the question of whether Saules and the Natives acted on their own or if they allegedly assaulted Pickett at the behest of the Methodists. As previously mentioned, Saules's friend Winslow Anderson had a close association with the Methodists, and Saules later evinced a similar relationship with them. The Natives who allegedly joined Saules to threaten Pickett may have had similar connections with the missionaries; the Methodists, despite having mostly abandoned the conversion of local Natives to Christianity, still operated an Indian manual labor school and regularly employed Native and mixed-raced labor in their projects.[72]

Pickett's friend Nesmith later corroborated many of Pickett's charges against the Methodists, although he never mentioned the alleged assassination attempt. In 1876 Nesmith delivered an address to the Oregon Pioneer Association in which he recalled Pickett's exploits and confirmed the extent of the Methodists' land claims in the region. He also described how Pickett broke their monopoly on additional lands: "This claim of a principality outside of their regular donation claims caused about the first litigation in Oregon between the Mission and Chas. E. Pickett, who, in 1845, located upon vacant land near the mouth of the Clackamas, and the Mission brought suit to oust him, in which aided by all the lawyers in Oregon, they were unsuccessful."[73] When the Methodist Mission board sent the Reverend George Gary from New York to Oregon to curtail the activities of Methodists in Oregon and sell off their property, Nesmith resented the fact that Gary gave preference to

Methodist buyers.[74] It is noteworthy that Nesmith described Pickett's squatting experiment as occurring in 1845, a year later than the Saules-Pickett dispute. But it is possible that Nesmith misremembered the date, or that perhaps Pickett began jumping claims the previous year.

Rev. Gary's diary from his 1844 Oregon visit supports the theory that the overlanders attempted to squat on Methodist claims prior to 1845. The Methodist monopoly on land was entirely legal according to article four of the land claims section of the 1843 Organic Laws, which allowed for claims "of a religious character" not exceeding 3,840 acres.[75] On June 2, 1844, about one month after the Saules-Pickett dispute, Gary wrote, "The emigrants of 1843 brought with them a strong prejudice against the Mission as a powerful monopoly, especially in view of the number and location of sections of land to which it had already laid claim. And they came with the purpose of riding over and breaking down the Mission."[76] He also mentioned that Methodist missionary Rev. A. F. Waller was embroiled in a land claim controversy with John McLoughlin of the HBC regarding ownership of the nearly 640 acres that comprised Oregon City. Gary learned that many of the 1843 overlanders had broken into factions, with some supporting McLoughlin and others Waller. According to Gary, "In this state of affairs our claims in some places are being 'jumped,' as it is called. There can be little doubt, if any, but that the public feeling will sustain the jumpers, and it is probable that to dispute the point with them will tend to the injury and disadvantage of the Mission."[77] News of such land squabbles soon reached the East Coast and alarmed the Mission Board. Gary settled the dispute by selling Waller's claim back to McLoughlin for $5,400. Following the transaction, in which he had to reluctantly purchase land he once claimed, McLoughlin lamented with more than a trace of irony, "The first violation of the rights of another in this Country is committed by a Minister of the Gospel." He added that because of the protracted struggle, the Methodists had "lost all influence in the Country."[78]

The Saules-Pickett dispute occurred at a time in which several groups, Natives, overland settlers, missionaries, and the HBC, all vied for the same Willamette Valley land. When viewed in this context, it is not surprising that Saules might be compelled to "stand for the Indians' rights" against a white settler known for his hatred of Native people and willingness to encroach on other people's land. And regardless of whether Saules acted alone or in league with the Methodists, the dispute indicates a shift in Saules's allegiances. During the series of events that precipitated the Cockstock Affair, he showed a willingness to work through proper government channels to resolve his quarrel with Cockstock, even though he promised to take matters into his own hands if necessary. But if Saules actually threatened the life and property of a prominent white overland settler to defend the rights of local Native people (or Methodists), it demonstrates the fluidity of such allegiances and how Saules continued to navigate liminal space between colonizer and colonized.

Pickett's actions following the successful prosecution of Saules are telling. If Pickett led the charge to seize land from the Methodists in the Willamette Valley, he was also among the first settlers to engage in the time-honored American tradition of land speculation. By the time Pickett cultivated the land on which he squatted, he had already resolved to move to California and was residing at the City Hotel in Oregon City. Pickett subdivided the property and placed an advertisement for "town lots" in the February 5, 1846, edition of the *Oregon Spectator*. In the ad, Pickett boasted, "As the eligibility of this site for a town, has been attested by nearly all nautical men who have visited the river . . . it will be unnecessary to say any thing farther in its favor."[79] The advertisement suggests that neither Pickett nor his potential buyers fit the mold of the Jeffersonian yeoman of the agrarian myth.

Oregon had no newspaper at the time of the Saules-Pickett dispute, and Elijah White's report to Congress remains the only existing record of the incident. Therefore, it is difficult to gauge the impact it had on other Anglo-American settlers. Peter H. Burnett, one of the co-leaders of the 1843 Great Migration and a member of the provisional government's legislative committee, wrote a letter to his brother in Missouri on November 4, 1844. But he failed to mention either the Saules-Pickett dispute or the Cockstock Affair, two noteworthy events in which nonwhite residents allegedly assaulted settlers. Instead, Burnett devoted most of his letter to extolling the Willamette Valley's agricultural potential, as well as the regenerative effect of agrarian labor on the American immigrants: "I have never yet before seen a population so industrious, sober and honest as this. I know many young men who were the veriest vagabonds in the states, who are here respectable and doing exceedingly well."[80] While Burnett obviously intended the letter to promote and encourage American resettlement of Oregon, he did allude to how factional skirmishes over land claims justified the creation of a provisional government: "Difficulties were daily occurring between individuals in relation to their 'claims' . . . crimes were committed and the base and unprincipled and reckless and turbulent were hourly tramping upon the rights of the honest and peaceable."[81] But Burnett insisted that Meek, the newly hired sheriff who arrested Saules, had single-handedly established law and order in the community. In fact, he claimed he had witnessed only one serious incident of lawlessness, in which Missourian Joel Turnham attacked another settler.[82] Yet when the legislative committee met in June 1844, Burnett's actions suggested he was quite aware of Saules's and settlers' allegations against him.

OREGON'S FIRST BLACK EXCLUSION LAW

Saules's arrest and conviction ended his efforts to subsist and provide for his family as a yeoman farmer in the Willamette Valley. The provisional government had no jail or prison in the spring of 1844, and Subagent White held Saules in custody at his own residence. White contacted the captain of a local vessel to remove Saules from the area, but the captain refused. After several weeks, White urged Saules to leave the Willamette Valley and seek employment at the Methodist mission at Clatsop Plains on the south side of the Columbia River's mouth. Saules obeyed White's orders but was initially unable to find work with the mission. According to White, in a letter to the US secretary of war, Saules "remains in that vicinity with his Indian wife and family, conducting, as yet, in a quiet manner." It is unclear what happened to Saules's land claim near Willamette Falls or whether he was able to sell it.

In his letter, White drew a sweeping conclusion from the Saules-Pickett dispute: "[Saules] ought to be transported, together with every other Negro, being in our condition dangerous subjects. Until we have some further means of protection, their immigration ought to be prohibited. Can this be done?"[83] White offered no explanation for why Saules's alleged activities necessitated the wholesale deportation of all black residents of the Oregon Country, as well as a prohibition of future black settlement. His use of the term *subjects* to describe local black people is noteworthy in a law enforcement context since it implies they are all potential subjects of investigation. But White may have also employed the term in a colonial context, contrasting citizens capable of self-government with "subjects," or subordinated noncitizens. The urgency of his request is also striking, since there were probably fewer than fifteen blacks residing in the entire Oregon Country at the time Saules was arrested.[84] Furthermore, there are no surviving records indicating that any other black person was ever arrested or charged with any crime prior to Saules's arrest.

White's request to the secretary of war went unheeded since the US government had no jurisdiction over the region, but the provisional government took immediate action. On June 18, 1844, the executive committee recommended "that the laws of Iowa be taken into consideration concerning blacks and mulattoes, and that law be enacted for the punishment of offenders inciting the Indians against the whites."[85] This was a clear reference to the Saules-Pickett dispute, which had occurred less than two months earlier. On June 25, 1844, Peter H. Burnett, who had been recently elected to the legislative committee, introduced a bill proposing that "when any free negro or mulatto shall have come to Oregon, he or she . . . shall remove from and leave the country within the term of two years for males, and three for females."[86] The bill, which was actually more severe than Iowa's, prescribed corporal punishment for those who refused to leave. If a black person remained in Oregon beyond the stated terms, he or she would "receive upon his or her bare back not less than twenty nor more than thirty-nine stripes, to be inflicted by the constable of the country."[87] Such floggings would be repeated every six months until the guilty party left the region. On June 26, 1844, the legislative committee voted 6 to 2 to pass Oregon's first black exclusion law, later known as the Lash Law.

Many historians have explained Oregon's 1844 black exclusion law by drawing a connection between the Cockstock Affair and the Saules-Pickett dispute based on Saules's involvement in both. In 1888 Frances Fuller Victor wrote, "The trouble occasioned by Winslow and Saules aroused a strong prejudice against persons of African blood, which was exhibited in a communication sent by White to the secretary of war, inquiring if the emigration [sic] of negroes could not be prohibited, and in the subsequent legislation of the colonists."[88] While Victor, who did not live in Oregon until 1864, offered no evidence for this link, it has proven influential. Yet no witness who wrote about the incident ever blamed Saules for the Cockstock Affair, and Saules's written request for White to handle the situation was well within the bounds of settler society. Even so, most books or articles that mention Saules draw a similar connection between him and Winslow Anderson's role in the Cockstock Affair and Oregon's first black exclusion law.[89]

But were the Cockstock Affair and the Saules-Pickett dispute necessarily linked?

Both events involved Natives, blacks, and whites and occurred within weeks of each other, and Saules's alleged provocations in the latter occurred during a tense period in which white settlers felt vulnerable. Yet while it is logical to link the two, there is no historical evidence that one event was related to the other. As for Victor's claim that the two events "aroused a strong prejudice against persons of African blood," such prejudice obviously already existed, given the white supremacist views of most Anglo-American settlers and the provisional government's denial of black citizenship. The issue is further complicated by the fact that no members of the provisional government ever mentioned the Cockstock Affair or the Saules-Pickett dispute as a justification for the Lash Law. Settler and historian William H. Gray later attacked Burnett for drafting the initial black exclusion law, but Gray never mentioned either event. Nor did Burnett in his retrospective defense of the law in his memoirs. Finally, Subagent White, in his inquiry to the War Department regarding the possibility of expelling blacks from Oregon, never mentioned the Cockstock Affair as an inspiration. He simply established it as a given that Saules and other black people were "dangerous subjects."

Burnett justified the 1844 black exclusion law by framing it as a means to prevent slavery from taking root in the region. The act's first three sections reflect his position:

> SECTION 1. That slavery and involuntary servitude shall be forever prohibited in Oregon.
> SECTION 2. That in all cases where slaves have been, or shall hereafter be brought into Oregon, the owner of such slaves shall have the term of three years from the introduction of such slaves to remove them out of the country.
> SECTION 3. That if such owner of slaves shall neglect or refuse to remove such slaves from the country within the time specified in the preceding section, such slaves shall be free.[90]

Burnett later wrote of his desire to ban slavery in a letter to the *Jefferson Inquirer* in 1845: "We are in a new world, under most favorable circumstances, and we wish to avoid most of these great evils that have so much afflicted the United States and other countries."[91] Burnett, who hailed from the slave state of Missouri, contended that slavery was "injurious" to both whites and blacks and advocated instead for racial separation as a means to preserve the Jeffersonian ideal of an agrarian society of free white laborers.[92] In this sense, the law was in the tradition of the antislavery states of the Old Northwest, most of which also had similar black exclusion laws on their books.

Yet Burnett's claim that the law was an antislavery measure was mislead-
ing, since slavery was already banned according to the provisional government's 1843 Organic Code. Burnett's law, therefore, highlighted the fact
that in addition to being antislavery, many white settlers were also antiblack.
Most believed that if slavery were ever to end in the United States, emancipated slaves would be transformed overnight into a disruptive population
of free blacks. This hostility toward free black people among antislavery settlers is consistent with an observation Alexis de Tocqueville made in 1835
about race relations in the United States: "The prejudice of race appears to
be stronger in the states that have abolished slavery than in those where
it still exists; and nowhere is it so intolerant as in those states where servitude has never been known."[93] According to settler Jesse Applegate, who
was eventually instrumental in repealing Oregon's first black exclusion law
in 1845, "Many of those people hated slavery, but a much larger number of
them hated free negroes worse even than slaves."[94] Colonel Currey recalled a
northerner telling him he immigrated to Oregon to rid himself of "saucy free
negroes."[95] Burnett also came from a state, Missouri, in which black exclusion
was decoupled from the issue of slavery. For instance, when Missouri drafted
its pro-slavery state constitution in 1820, the framers included a provision
similar to Oregon's black exclusion law banning "free negroes and mulattoes
from coming to and settling in this State."[96]

In his 1880 memoir, Burnett defended his black exclusion law and
argued that, because the Organic Code of 1843 denied blacks voting rights
or the ability to hold office, he was actually doing potential black residents a
favor by banning their immigration. In essence, Burnett absolved himself by
shifting blame for the law to the original framers of Oregon's government:

> The principle is no doubt correct that when a State, for reasons
> satisfactory to itself, denies the right of suffrage and office to
> a certain class, it is sometimes the best humanity also to deny
> the privilege of residence. If the prejudices or the just reasons
> of a community are so great that they can not or will not trust a
> certain class with those privileges that are indispensable to the
> improvement and elevation of such class, it is most consistent, in
> some cases, to refuse that class a residence.[97]

Burnett warned, therefore, that disenfranchised black people would be a potentially dangerous burden on the rest of the population. He insisted that Oregon's white supremacist laws trapped black people "in a degraded and subordinate political and social position which continually reminds them of their inferiority ... they are left without adequate motive to waste their labor for that improvement which, when attained, brings them no reward."[98] He concluded that "surely every intelligent and independent man of color would have scorned the pitiful boon offered him of a residence under conditions so humiliating."[99] Despite Burnett's antislavery convictions, it evidentially never occurred to him to solve this issue by allowing black citizenship in Oregon. He did later admit that had he anticipated the monumental changes brought by the Union's victory in the Civil War, he never would have argued for black exclusion.

While the aftermath of the Saules-Pickett dispute forced the issue of black exclusion, the provisional government also warned of the dangers of black residents collaborating with Native people, urging that the "law be enacted for the punishment of offenders inciting the Indians against the whites." Beginning in the eighteenth century, many Americans had dreaded the potential alliance of these two marginalized groups. Such concerns may have been rooted in the realization that the astonishing economic growth of the United States was predicated on the appropriation and exploitation of Native and black peoples' land and labor and, therefore, some sort of retribution was imminent. Historians Peter Linebaugh and Marcus Rediker argue that such fears were heightened prior to the American Revolution due to formation of multiethnic resistance movements in eastern port cities: "At the peak of revolutionary possibility, the motley crew appeared as a synchronicity or an actual coordination among the 'risings of the people' of the port cities, the resistance of African American slaves, and Indian struggles on the frontier."[100] These alliances were particularly dangerous in eighteenth century colonial American society in which the notion of race was subsuming the idea of social class. Therefore, black-Native collaborations portended an explosive form of racial *and* class struggle. Similar forebodings persisted during the American Revolution, only this time among anti-British partisans. In a 1777 pamphlet, political theorist Thomas Paine lamented that the British crown had "tampered with Indians and Negroes to cut the throats of the freemen of America."[101]

In the slave societies of the Deep South, there was nothing abstract about slaveholders' anxieties regarding the potential of black-Native revolt and insurrection. In Louisiana in the 1720s, French tobacco planters attempted to import the plantation system by removing Natchez Indians from their land and installing five thousand enslaved black workers. However, Natchez fighters forged an alliance with enslaved blacks and staged a bloody revolt against the colonists that eventually led the French joint stock company *Compagnie des Indes* to surrender its charter in Louisiana.[102] During this same period in the plantations of South Carolina, Natives and enslaved blacks toiled together, and planters often lumped them together into one ethnic group. In the 1730s, many of these enslaved people escaped to Spanish Florida where Spanish authorities promised freedom. For several years, local Native people joined former slaves in raids on South Carolina plantations and attempted to prevent southern planters from importing the plantation system to Florida. Moreover, during the War of 1812, many free black, Native, and runaway enslaved people fought with the British against the United States. In particular, the British-equipped "Negro Fort" near Pensacola, Florida, was a major site of rebellion and boasted a garrison of runaway slaves, Seminoles, and Choctaws. Alarmed by a potential British-backed revolution in Florida in 1816, General Andrew Jackson destroyed the fort and killed hundreds of black and Native people in the process.[103]

For the generation of Anglo-Americans that traveled west via the Oregon Trail, however, the Second Seminole War (1935–1842) was the black-Native collaboration that made the strongest impact on their collective memory. The Second Seminole War—the most costly Indian war in US history up to that point—had ended mere months before the emigrants loaded up their wagons. The roots of the conflict went back much further, to the runaway enslaved people who found refuge among the Seminoles in Spanish-occupied Florida in the eighteenth and nineteenth centuries. When American slaveholders tried to recover their property, the Seminoles consistently refused all attempts to retrieve the slaves. In the First Seminole War (1814–1819), the US army—led by General Jackson—and Georgia's militia attempted to force the Seminoles to surrender the slaves, only to be humiliated by the combined resistance of Seminole and black fighters. In 1821 the United States acquired Florida and allowed the Seminoles to remain on reservations there. This arrangement proved temporary. When Jackson became president, he urged Congress to pass the 1930 Indian Removal

Act, which uprooted and relocated the Seminoles and other groups to the west of the Mississippi River. When the US army moved to enact this plan, the Seminoles and blacks again rose up against the might of the US Army. The Second Seminole War was a quagmire that lasted seven years, cost the US government $20 million—approximately $500 million in today's currency—and resulted in the deaths of approximately 1,500 American soldiers as well as 1,500 Seminoles and blacks.[104]

While no one in the provisional government specifically mentioned black-Native collaboration in the southeastern United States as a rationale for black exclusion, there is evidence it may have influenced the policy and led the legislative committee to attach added significance to the alleged actions of Saules and his accomplices against a white settler. Many of the men in the provisional government were educated and literate; they were almost certainly aware of what had happened in Florida only a few years prior. Missouri senator Thomas Hart Benton was a major influence on the movement to resettle Oregon; he served as chairman of the Senate Committee on Military Affairs for the duration of the Second Seminole War and was obsessed with bringing it to a satisfying end. More specifically, two early members of the Oregon Rangers, Captain Charles Bennett and Sergeant Thomas Holt, served as dragoons in the war.

Regardless of the lack of written testimony, most of the overland settlers of the 1840s were almost certainly aware of the 1835 Dade Massacre, which resulted in the rapid escalation of the Second Seminole War and dominated national news for two months in early 1836. Earlier in 1835, General D. L. Clinch had urged Congress to send more troops to Florida to enforce the removal of the Seminoles, and on December 23, 1835, Major Francis L. Dade and 110 US soldiers marched toward Fort King in Seminole territory. On December 28, several Seminoles and about forty black fighters led by Chief Micanopy ambushed the detachment and left only one survivor, Private Ransome Clark. Micanopy's forces, on the other hand, lost only three men. Clark's 1836 account of the clash outraged and alarmed many Americans, and some historians have compared the Dade Massacre to the Lakota-led routing of General George Custer's forces at Little Big Horn (Battle of Greasy Grass) in 1876.[105] In particular, Clark noted how "the Negroes," in fighting for their freedom, surpassed "their savage masters in hellish cruelty" by slitting the throats of wounded soldiers.[106]

The most explicit reference to the Second Seminole War in regard to black exclusion laws in Oregon came years later in 1857, when Oregon territorial Chief Justice George H. Williams specifically mentioned the Dade Massacre in his influential front-page *Oregon Statesman* editorial titled "The Free State Letter." In the piece, Williams made an economic rather than moral argument against allowing slavery in the soon-to-be state of Oregon. Yet he also dredged up old fears of enslaved black people joining forces with local Native groups:

> Eastward dwell numerous Indian tribes, to whose welcome embrace a slave might fly and be safe. . . . Some say that slave property will not be so unsafe here as I pretend, for negroes will not go to and consort with Indians, but otherwise is the evidence. General Jackson found fugitive slaves fighting with the Creoles in the war of 1812. Major Dade's command of 112 (except 4) was slaughtered in the Florida war by a party of Seminoles and 40 fugitive slaves, the negroes outstripping the Indians in ferocity and brutal treatment of the dead.[107]

When Williams invoked the Second Seminole War, he continued the long-standing tradition of Oregon policy makers conflating the issue of outlawing slavery with the banning of free black immigration in Oregon. Williams himself echoed earlier black exclusion policy when he asked, "Is it is not the true policy of Oregon to keep as clear as possible of negroes, and all the exciting questions of negro servitude?"[108]

There were also inherent similarities between the situations in Florida and Oregon as American expansionists saw both as part of the same larger project. For example, in late 1830s and early 1840s, Senator Benton argued forcefully for the colonization of both regions by Anglo-American settlers. In 1842, following the disastrous end of the Second Seminole War, Congress passed Benton's Armed Occupation Act, which offered settlers 160 acres of free land in Florida if they were willing to cultivate it and bear arms to protect it.[109] Benton proposed the bill at the same time he had urged the passage of his colleague Senator Lewis Linn's very similar 1841 Oregon Territorial Bill. General Thomas Jesup, the commander of US forces in the Second Seminole War, applauded Benton's idea of using settlers rather than soldiers to conquer indigenous peoples: "No force employed against [the Seminoles] . . . has ever been able to catch them. . . . Let them be crowded by settlers, and that which has invariably occurred throughout the whole history of our settlements will occur again, they will not only consent to remove, but will desire it as the greatest benefit the nation can confer upon them." Historian Paul W. Gates has argued that the later Oregon Donation Land Law can be linked to the success of Benton's Florida bill as both were intended to give "land to settlers in these territories where they might help to reduce the Indian menace."[110]

Perhaps the expulsion of Saules and his family from the Willamette Valley, as well as the passage of the first black exclusion law, can also be explained in terms of the logic of settler colonialism itself. When settler colonists arrive in a new region, they must contend with the previous inhabitants and determine who belongs in the community and who must be excluded. In the 1840s, the cultural and ethnic hybridity of the Oregon Country upset these categories and presented a challenge to the newly arrived American settlers. Saules, in particular, was a person who resisted the binary categories of "colonizer" and "colonized," as he moved between and among both communities. Lorenzo Veracini argues that settler colonialism creates a triangular "system of relationships comprising three different agencies: the settler colonizer, the indigenous colonized, and a variety of differently categorized exogenous others.[111] Settler colonizers attempt to manage these relationships by establishing which indigenous or exogenous inhabitants are righteous and therefore worthy of inclusion in the settler body politic, as well as which are degraded and must be excluded.[112] These categories are never fixed; they are contested, negotiated, and open to a modicum of enlargement. For example, the fur trade practice of intermarriage resulted in a generation of mixed-race children difficult to define as either indigenous or exogenous. Some early American settlers, such as Joseph Meek, also married Native women and fathered children with them. Some of these children—particularly the male offspring of prominent white American settlers like Meek himself—were later included in the settler body politic, even though Anglo-American settlers discouraged intermarriage and later made it illegal.

Despite the passage of the black exclusion law, Saules did not leave the Oregon Country. But he never lived in the Willamette Valley again. The fluid social and cultural space Saules once traversed had become severely challenged by the overlanders. This middle ground would continue to fade as thousands more Americans arrived in the region and further marginalized the previous inhabitants. At the same time in the next two years, tensions between the United States and Great Britain over which empire would ultimately claim the region increased to the point that many feared armed conflict. These imperial struggles would directly affect Saules, who again experienced displacement and humiliation. Even so, future changes within the composition of the provisional government allowed Saules to regain much of his cherished mobility and visibility. Unfortunately for Saules, his reclaimed freedoms would prove fleeting.

5

Saules in Exile, the Oregon Question, and the Return of Black Exclusion

As the American settler colonization of the Oregon Country continued in the mid-1840s, one might assume that the provisional government would hold fast to its segregative practices. Yet this was not exactly the case. James D. Saules and other nonwhites did not simply go away as many settlers had wished. The provisional government could pass laws but had difficulty enforcing them. This was due to both the vastness of the Oregon Country and the lack of an effective police force or jails to house criminals. Therefore, the heterogeneous culture of the lower Columbia River region continued to exist, in a somewhat muted form, for several more years. While the provisional government denied Saules citizenship and the right to participate in the provisional government, he was a significant presence in the region's economic and cultural life in the mid-to-late 1840s. The American settlers, however, continued to express fear and antipathy toward the ethnic complexity of the Oregon Country and the presence of black sailors in particular. Oregon also became embroiled in international imperial wrangling between Great Britain and the United States, the outcome of which accelerated the Americanization of the Pacific Northwest. Saules attempted to steer a course through these regional shifts and, at times, even resisted them. He also experienced how difficult it became to preserve his autonomy and freedom of movement once the region was officially incorporated into the United States.

By December 1844, some members of the provisional government expressed misgivings about the severity of the black exclusion law passed the previous June. On December 16, the executive committee recommended to the legislative committee "that the act passed by this assembly . . . relative to blacks and mulattoes, be so amended as to exclude corporal punishment, and require bonds for good behavior in its stead."[1] On December 18, 1844, Peter Burnett, who still led the legislative committee, responded to the request by proposing an amendment to the original law that removed the flogging provision. This was obviously only a partial measure, as Burnett retained all the exclusion provisions of the June law instead of introducing bonds for good behavior. Instead, his amendment proposed that if a black person refused to leave the Oregon Country, he or she would be arrested and brought before a justice of the peace. If found guilty, an officer would then auction off the guilty party as a laborer to the lowest bidder. Whoever agreed to hire the "free black or mulatto" for the shortest term of service would "enter into a bond . . . binding himself to remove said negro or mulatto out of the country within six months after such service shall expire."[2] In his autobiography, Burnett failed to mention the executive committee's recommendation and instead took credit for the removal of the flogging provision: "By the December session of 1844 I had found another and less objectionable remedy, and promptly adopted it."[3] He even went as far as to claim that he and the others on the legislative committee were not responsible for the original lash law, writing that "we ourselves corrected the error."[4]

In the summer of 1845, Saules and the other black people living in the region received even better news. On July 24, the original Organic Code of 1843 was replaced with a new set of laws that, among other changes, repealed the black exclusion law in its entirety. The revised provisional government of 1845 resulted from an influx of more moderate and politically experienced settlers who sought a more restrained and efficient government.[5] And unlike the first, this government would be less hostile toward McLoughlin and the HBC. Still, as in 1843, the new government recognized and endorsed the color line, proclaiming that only "free male descendants of a white man" were eligible for citizenship, meaning that Saules and Native people could not participate in the civil society. Male residents with Native mothers, on the other hand, could vote and hold office, reflecting the continued influence of the French-Indian families in the region.

Some historians have attributed this change to the election of Jesse Applegate to the legislative committee as well as the temporary absence of Burnett from the new provisional government.[6] Like Burnett, Applegate was one of the leaders of the Great Migration of 1843 and a fervent opponent of slavery. Unlike many of his fellow settlers who were Democrats, Applegate was a Whig, a party formed in opposition to the policies of President Andrew Jackson. While Applegate was somewhat skeptical regarding the possibility of white and black people living together harmoniously, he wrote of emancipated blacks in 1865 that "if we retain [the Negro] among us, for our good as well as his, we must take him like Onesimus, 'a brother and an equal.'"[7] In addition to repealing the black exclusion law, Applegate and others urged a new amendment banning slavery in the region. His stance on racial issues raised eyebrows among the Democratic faithful in Oregon in the 1840s, and Applegate's Whig political views, coupled with his friendly relationship with John McLoughlin and the HBC, led many settlers to refer to him as a sycophant of the British.[8]

The new provisional government also furthered the Americanization of the region through its new land office, which was used to record claims and sales. This move increased the legal backing for the commodification and dispossession of land once held in common by Native communities. The land office provided Anglo-American settlers with an advantage in land ownership by failing to protect the traditional lands of indigenous peoples. The official position of the provisional government toward Native land remained the same as US federal Indian policy circa 1843 and the Northwest Ordinance of 1780: the government promised not to seize Native lands without permission or remuneration.[9] Yet most settlers also ignored Native land claims, likely assuming that Indian removal and disease would clear the way for the inevitable white settlement of the Oregon Country.

SAULES AND THE OREGON BOUNDARY DISPUTE

At the time of the repeal of the black exclusion law, Saules resided in a cabin perched high atop Cape Disappointment at his original location overlooking Baker Bay. While the Willamette Valley was no longer a middle ground in which people of various ethnic backgrounds encountered and accommodated each other, the community that lived near the mouth of the Columbia seemed to retain more of the fluid, heterogeneous quality of Oregon prior to the Great Migration of 1843. Although Elijah White believed that Saules failed to gain employment with the Methodists at Clatsop Plains following his expulsion, Saules eventually found work at the mission, located near his residence on the south side of the mouth of the Columbia until the mission closed in 1846.[10] This is corroborated by the recollections of English settler John Minto, who remembered meeting a mission cook named "J.D. Sauls" in Clatsop County circa 1844.[11]

Saules's presence in Clatsop Plains is also confirmed by resident Silas B. Smith's vivid recollections of him performing fiddle tunes at various public gatherings in Clatsop County circa 1845–1846. Smith was the son of a Clatsop woman named Celiast (the daughter of Clatsop Chief Coboway) and Solomon H. Smith, a New Hampshire settler and schoolteacher who arrived in the region in 1832 with the overland expedition of Massachusetts business-man Nathaniel J. Wyeth.[12] Solomon Smith and Celiast worked at the mission and operated a ferry service across the Columbia as early as 1840. Their son, Silas, who later practiced law in New Hampshire, remembered Saules as a popular fixture at dances who "played the violin in true plantation manner, a vigorous wielding of the bow, loud beating on the floor with his heel, accom-panied with an animated action of the body."[13] According to Smith, local Columbia River bar pilots often promoted these dances, and Saules may have served alongside them to guide ships through the dangerous river entrance. Smith referred to the pilots as "mostly unmarried men" who were "leaders of the dancing gentry of the times."[14]

Saules was not only accepted at the Clatsop Plains mission, he was also allowed back in the Willamette Valley only a year after his exile. On June 10, 1845, Solomon H. Smith, Josiah Lamberson Parrish, and Calvin Tibbets hired Saules to deliver election returns for the June 3 provisional government election from Clatsop Plains to the office of Dr. John E. Long in Oregon City. Long served as the body's territorial recorder and ex officio clerk of commit-tee, and he hosted meetings at his home. Smith, Parrish, and Tibbets are listed as "judges" on the receipt. Parrish was a New Yorker who came to Oregon with Jason Lee aboard the *Lausanne* in 1839 and purchased the Methodist Mission at Clatsop Plains in 1844. He was also an early proponent of estab-lishing American-style governance in the region. Tibbets was a stonemason from Maine who had traveled to the region with Smith in 1832. Once Saules delivered the results, the judges instructed Long to draw funds from the provisional government and pay Saules $17.50, a considerable sum in 1845. To complete this task, Saules had to travel over one hundred miles via the Columbia and Willamette Rivers. A surviving receipt for this transaction complete with Saules's signature proves he was successful.[15]

Saules's 1845 journey to Oregon City is significant in several respects. First, it demonstrates that his social standing in Clatsop Plains was such that three prominent citizens trusted him to carry important information to the provisional government. Smith, Parrish, and Tibbets were all northeastern-ers who had lived in the region long before the Great Migration of 1843 and may have been less averse to free black men than the overland newcomers.

Sketch of Oregon City by Henry J. Warre, ca. 1846. Source: Henry J. Warre, *Sketches in North America and the Oregon Territory* (1970). Courtesy of the Oregon Historical Society.

Also, Saules delivered the election returns to the provisional government in the Willamette Valley—which, in turn, paid him—over one month before that same body repealed the initial black exclusion law, so the existence of the law did not dissuade him from entering the region and conducting business. Finally, unless Saules was traveling as a passenger, his journey suggests that he was again piloting a vessel up and down the Columbia and Willamette Rivers as early as the summer of 1845, providing crucial transportation and communication services to the settlers of the Oregon Country.

As Saules sailed from the mouth of the Columbia to Oregon City in 1845, he was unaware that British leaders were holding secret meetings in London to discuss the occupation of Cape Disappointment. The British government hoped to install artillery near his home in preparation for a potential war with the United States. Neither Great Britain nor the United States wanted to yield possession of the Oregon Country, but the large number of Anglo-American settlers flowing into the region startled the British government. The Anglo-American Convention of 1818, which established the joint occupation of the region, complicated matters by containing no means by which the two parties could resolve a territorial dispute through arbitration.[16] This meant that armed conflict was probable if a diplomatic solution failed. As a precautionary measure, Sir George Simpson, the Canadian governor of the HBC, recommended that Great Britain take possession of Cape Disappointment and "erect thereon a strong battery."[17] He claimed that ships entering the mouth of the Columbia "must pass so close under the Cape that shells might be dropped almost with certainty upon their decks from the battery."[18] Simpson was clearly willing to go to great lengths to ensure the survival of the HBC in Oregon.

On April 3, 1845, Simpson traveled to London to meet with British prime minister Sir Robert Peel and foreign secretary Lord Aberdeen to discuss how best to preserve the company's interests in the Oregon Country. Due to the growing number of Anglo-American settlers and the decline of fur-bearing animals south of the Columbia River, the British government planned to relinquish the area from the south bank of the Columbia to the Mexican California border (lat 42° N).[19] However, Simpson insisted that Great Britain retain the area north of the Columbia containing Fort Vancouver, Puget Sound, and the southern tip of Vancouver Island, site of the HBC's recently built Fort Victoria. Both Peel and Aberdeen dreaded the prospect of war but were confident in Great Britain's military supremacy over the United States. Two months earlier, Aberdeen had sent the HMS *America* on a mission to the Oregon Country to "let the Americans see clearly that Her Majesty's Government are alive to their proceedings and prepared, in case of necessity, to oppose them."[20] In addition to occupying Cape Disappointment, Simpson recommended that Aberdeen send four Royal Navy warships to the Oregon Country. Each ship would be stocked with a large number of marines augmented by a local army of two thousand Native and mixed-race soldiers. This scheme was too ambitious for Peel and Aberdeen, who decided instead to send two British spies to Fort Vancouver "to gain a general knowledge of the capabilities of the Oregon territory in a military point of view, in order that we may be enabled to act immediately and with effect in defense of our rights in that quarter."[21] The major objectives of this mission were to purchase Cape Disappointment, gather intelligence regarding American settlers, and investigate the practicability of sending British troops overland from Montreal to the Oregon Country.[22]

In November 1844, the election of President James K. Polk fueled the British government's fears of impending conflict with the United States. Polk, a southern Democrat and slaveholder, was an outspoken overland expansionist whose platform included the annexation of Texas, the purchase of California from Mexico, and the acquisition of the entire Oregon Country extending to the southern tip of Russian Alaska (lat 54°40' N). While many dismissed his demands as pre-election demagoguery, Polk's demand for Oregon far exceeded any previous position of the United States and later inspired the slogan "fifty-four forty or fight."[23] Although the British government understood Polk's saber rattling as an extreme bargaining position, Prime Minister Peel was distressed that Polk now considered setting the international boundary at the 49th parallel as a compromise. For the British, this meant they would lose Fort Vancouver, the Puget Sound, and Fort Victoria.

Many Anglo-American settlers in Oregon were delighted by Polk's expansionist rhetoric. One in particular was Charles E. Pickett, the man who had Saules arrested and removed from the Willamette Valley. Pickett later claimed he had a direct influence on Polk's position regarding the Oregon question. This is difficult to prove, but Pickett, a personal friend of Polk, did write to the president in the mid-1840s. He urged Polk to strike a deal with the British that would set the border at the 49th parallel and grant the United States sole possession of Vancouver Island.[24] This would open up even more land for settlement and speculation.

On August 12, 1845, the two spies sent by the British government, Lieutenants Henry J. Warre and Martin Vavasour, arrived at Fort Vancouver. Due to the sensitive nature of their visit, they were not allowed to divulge their true purpose to anyone, including the HBC's McLoughlin. They instead posed as a pair of young vacationers visiting the region "for the pleasure of field sports and scientific pursuits."[25] Warre and Vavasour had left Montreal on June 16 accompanied by their guide HBC chief factor Peter Skene Ogden and seven company servants. One month earlier, Ogden had received instructions from Simpson to purchase Cape Disappointment upon arrival from anyone living there, provided an American settler did not already own it. The journey, which required traveling horseback across the Rocky Mountains, proved so arduous that Warre and Vavasour concluded that sending British troops overland was not feasible. They were also convinced that Fort Victoria was "ill-adapted either as a place of refuge for shipping or as a position of defence."[26] Instead, they ascertained that Britain could best defend its interests by controlling the strategic waterways of the region, the Columbia River and Puget Sound.[27] And once they investigated the mouth of the Columbia, Warre and Vavasour concurred with Simpson's assessment that Cape Disappointment could function as the linchpin of a regional defense. To this end, Vavasour

Sketch of Baker Bay and Cape Disappointment by Henry J. Warre. Source: Henry J. Warre, *Sketches in North America and the Oregon Territory* (1970). Courtesy of the Oregon Historical Society.

submitted a request to his commanding officer to install three batteries of heavy guns on the cape.[28]

In early September 1845, Ogden himself traveled to Cape Disappointment to complete his instructions from Simpson to purchase the property. When he reached the desired location overlooking Baker Bay, he found Saules living there in his cabin. Because his mission was secret, Simpson had advised Ogden not to divulge the military purpose of the purchase and instead express a desire to establish an HBC trading post and pilot lookout on the Cape. Ogden requested that Saules sell him part of his large claim. Saules considered the offer and agreed to relinquish a large portion to Ogden for an undisclosed sum.[29] Although Ogden never mentioned Saules's race in any of his correspondence, Ogden's willingness to buy the property from him suggests he did not consider him an American. For his part, Saules may not have represented himself as such since the HBC strongly discouraged Americans from settling north of the Columbia.[30]

After finalizing the sale with Saules, Ogden traveled to Oregon City to file the purchase with the provisional government's land office. He arrived on September 11, and John E. Long, the territorial recorder, recorded his claim as follows:

To wit: taking in all the high lands East and West, from the
Easternmost point of Cape disappointment, down to the second
small Bay in Bakers Bay, bounded on the East by Bakers Bay, and
on the West by the Pacific Ocean and the mouth or entrance of the
Columbia river, containing about five hundred acres, the boundaries
and extent of said claim being defined and understood, between
said Ogden, and J.D. Sauls; said Sauls now claims the land adjoining
the aforesaid claim of P. Ogden. And the said claimant states that he
holds the same claim without occupancy.

It is unclear how much land Saules retained after the sale, but the remain-
der could not legally exceed 140 acres according to the land office terms.
Regardless of the amount he received, Saules probably felt satisfied with his
end of the deal. He still held an ample piece of land that would have included
his cabin and whatever remaining acres he cultivated for subsistence. Because
Ogden kept his strategic objectives secret, one can only imagine Saules's
bemusement while watching British military personnel enter his old claim.

But Saules never got the chance to witness any such developments. To
his consternation, Ogden soon discovered that two American settlers, Isaac
Newton Wheeler and William McDaniel, insisted they were the rightful
claimants of 1,280 acres of Cape Disappointment property, including Saules's
remaining portion. Both men were Anglo-American overlanders mentioned
in James W. Nesmith's diary of the Great Migration of 1843.[31] Long evidently
supported Wheeler and McDaniel and voided Ogden's claim.[32] It is impossible to determine the veracity of Wheeler and McDaniel's claim, or if they
had received an advance tip from Long or someone else regarding the HBC's
desire to purchase the land. Corruption and fraud had been pervasive at land
offices since the birth of an American land system in the late eighteenth century, and speculators often operated in tandem with corrupt land agents.[33]
Aware of the HBC's deep pockets, Wheeler and McDaniel offered to sell
their claim on Cape Disappointment to Ogden for the princely sum of $900.
Ogden refused, claiming he had "no authority vested in me to negotiate."[34] In
an October 1845 letter to Henry Warre, he revealed that he did not want to
appear "over-anxious to obtain it" since he was convinced he could purchase
the land for a much lower price.[35]

On November 7, 1845, Warre received Ogden's letter and responded with
an exasperated missive, reminding Ogden of Simpson's original instructions

to purchase Cape Disappointment using "whatever preliminary measures you may consider it desirable should be taken."[36] Ogden responded on November 16 and clarified that he did not believe he had the authority to purchase Cape Disappointment, since his instructions forbade him to purchase it "if already possessed or occupied on behalf of the United States Government or its citizens."[37] Warre countered by asking Ogden why he bought the property from Saules in the first place, who Warre reminded was also an American.[38] This suggests that Warre and Vavasour met Saules during their reconnoitering of Cape Disappointment. Warre also questioned the legitimacy of Wheeler and McDaniel's claim: "I consider it very probable that Wheeler or McDaniell may have claims in some other part of the Territory, or even that they may have 'jumped' Mr. Saules' claim."[39] On November 19, Ogden answered Warre's question, insisting that Saules had no right to sell the property and was "merely employed in the service of Wheeler and McDaniell as a guardian to their claim on Cape Disappointment."[40] Ogden also claimed that the two American settlers had erected a building on the land, "thereby rendering their right to it still more valid."[41] This response seemed to satisfy Warre, who concluded that neither he nor Ogden had the authority to purchase the land. On February 14, 1846, Ogden evidently changed his mind regarding his interpretation of Simpson's instructions and purchased Cape Disappointment from Wheeler and McDaniel for $1,000, plus $200 for surveyor's fees. He registered this claim on March 14.

What was Saules's strategy amidst the chaos of early Oregon land policy? One possibility is that Saules seized an opportunity to pocket Ogden's money for land he may not have actually owned. But it is difficult to accept that Saules would have jeopardized whatever social standing he had in the region for such a short-term gain. He would have also expected repercussions from not only Ogden but Wheeler and McDaniel as well, especially since the two settlers claimed they hired Saules to guard their property. Furthermore, if Saules had swindled Ogden, he probably would not have remained in his cabin at Cape Disappointment. But Saules did stay. Another possibility is that Saules believed he was acting on the American settlers' behalf and planned to share the proceeds with them. Lastly, there is the distinct possibility that Saules was ignorant of Wheeler and McDaniel's alleged claim, which was never officially surveyed and only filed with the land office once Ogden expressed his interest.

Despite Ogden's insistence that Saules never owned the property, there is evidence suggesting Warre was justified in suspecting that Wheeler and

Fort George, ca. 1846. Source: Henry J. Warre, *Sketches in North America and the Oregon Territory* (1848). Courtesy of the Oregon Historical Society.

McDaniel had jumped Saules's land claim. Early settler John E. Pickernell claimed that Saules was living on a cabin overlooking Baker Bay as early as 1842, at least one year before the Great Migration of 1843. At that time, land claims were established by simple preemptions and whatever improvements the landholder made. On the other hand, it is possible that Wheeler and McDaniel staked their claim—or purchased it from Saules—while Saules was living in the Willamette Valley, since Saules, having purchased Winslow Anderson's farm, was only legally permitted to hold one land claim at a time.[42] This rule was an attempt to uphold traditional republican values that favored small landholders over brazen speculators. Wheeler and McDonald may have actually hired Saules to protect their claim, but their timing in revealing their ownership is questionable. According to provisional government land claim records, Wheeler and McDaniel never registered their claim with the land office, although they apparently had two years to do so after erecting a building on the property. They officially filed their claim for Cape Disappointment on September 29, 1845, eighteen days after Ogden submitted his. Furthermore, Wheeler filed four more land claims in less than a year after selling Cape Disappointment, suggesting he was more speculator than Jeffersonian yeoman.

Saules was apparently not kept apprised of the situation and expressed bewilderment when informed that he was living on Ogden's claim. This supports the possibility he knew nothing about Wheeler and McDaniel's alleged claim. On May 9, 1846, Alexander Lattie, an HBC employee and noted bar pilot, received a dispatch from Fort Vancouver asking him to go to Cape Disappointment to "ascertain the mistake respecting the survey of Mr P S Ogdon's Claim."[43] The survey in question was likely the one Lattie witnessed Warre and Vavasour performing on March 1, 1846, although Lattie did not mention the nature of the "mistake."[44] According to Lattie's May 11, 1846, diary entry, when he arrived at Baker Bay he "found a person by the name of Saul a coloured man one quarter of a mile on Mr Ogdens Claim pointed out his error and made him Sensible of mistake he had committed himself."[45] Presumably, Saules's error was assuming he still held the remaining portion of property he did not sell to Ogden and not vacating immediately after Ogden's purchase. On May 30, 1846, Lattie spotted Newton Wheeler traveling near the mouth of the Columbia; it is possible Wheeler was also there to confer with Saules.[46] On June 5, 1846, Lattie reported that "Black Saul" had arrived in Fort George from Cape Disappointment "lamenting his misfortune in having to remoove off Mr Ogdens Claim after making improovements upon it." Regardless of the reason, the outcome was that almost exactly two years following his expulsion from the Willamette Valley, Saules was again displaced.

SAULES PILOTS THE SHARK

His encounter with Ogden, Warre, and Vavasour was not the last time Saules found himself in the midst of the imperialist struggle between the United States and Great Britain. On July 18' 1846, the USS *Shark*, an American naval schooner, arrived at the mouth of the Columbia. In April, Commodore John Drake Sloat had ordered the ship's captain, Lieutenant Neil Howison, to travel to the Oregon Country and "determine the disposition of the residents of those friendly to the United States compared to those friendly to Great Britain, and the extent, character, and tendency of emigration from the United States."[47] The navy also sent the *Shark* to Oregon to offset the presence of the HMS *Modeste*, the much larger British warship anchored at Fort Vancouver. Howison had earlier commanded a steamboat in Florida during the Second Seminole War and was later on the shortlist to serve on the US Ex. Ex. before Lieutenant Charles Wilkes's appointment. Sloat also instructed Howison to "cheer our citizens in that region by the presence of the American flag" and assure them that a favorable agreement with Great Britain was imminent.[48] However, before Howison could fulfill his duties, he had to first cross the Columbia bar. Howison initially planned to use the maps prepared by Wilkes of the US Ex. Ex. but soon realized that the sands of the bar had shifted dramatically since Wilkes had first surveyed the region in 1841. Howison's trepidation was increased when a crew member informed him that he had been aboard the USS *Peacock* exactly five years earlier to the day when it was wrecked at the bar.

The *Shark* carried no pilot with local experience, and Howison was determined to avoid the earlier mistake of *Peacock* commander Lieutenant Hudson. Therefore, he instructed his crew to fire their guns to summon a bar pilot. When none answered, Howison gingerly rounded Cape Disappointment. Once the ship approached Baker Bay, a boat came alongside the *Shark* containing William Gray, Asa Lovejoy, and the Reverend Henry Spalding. Gray was an Oregon politician, former Presbyterian missionary, and later author of a notoriously tendentious early history of Oregon. Lovejoy was the mayor of Oregon City and future co-founder of Portland. Spalding was a Presbyterian missionary who first traveled overland to the region with his wife, Eliza, where they joined Gray and fellow missionaries Marcus and Narcissa Whitman. This esteemed trio informed Howison that "no regular pilots were to be had for the river, but that there was a black man on shore who had been living many years at the cape, was a sailor, and said, if sent for he would come off and pilot us up to Astoria."[49] The man was Saules, who still apparently lived in the Cape Disappointment area despite his expulsion from Ogden's claim. It is also possible that Ogden eventually allowed Saules to remain at his previous residence since Ogden held the claim without occupancy. At any rate, it is noteworthy that Gray, Lovejoy, and Spalding knew how to contact Saules and engage his services, suggesting his location was no secret and he had earlier performed similar tasks.

According to Howison, once Saules was on board the *Shark*, he "spoke confidently of his knowledge of the channel" and "had been living here for the last six [years]."[50] Howison does not mention whether Saules informed him that he, too, was on board the *Peacock* when it suffered a total loss. Saules then "ordered the helm put up, head sheets aft, and yards brace" with an air of confidence that convinced Howison "that he was fully competent to conduct the vessel."[51] Howison then handed over command of the *Shark* to Saules. Unfortunately, after twenty minutes, Saules ran the ship ashore on Chinook shoal. The ship remained there for several hours, where it took a severe beating from the current without suffering any damage. Later that evening, the ship broke free from the shoal and Howison had it anchored in the channel until the following morning. In his fanciful piece about Saules for the *Overland Monthly*, Charles Melville Scammon suggested that Saules was then thrown overboard for his fecklessness, although Howison never mentions how Saules was treated immediately after the accident.[52] According to Howison, the three settlers, Gray, Lovejoy, and Spalding, had witnessed the entire incident and "feeling themselves somewhat responsible for the employment of this pretended pilot," went to Astoria to obtain the services of HBC bar pilot Alexander Lattie. Lattie sought the assistance of noted Chinookan pilot Old George (sometimes known as Chinook George), who had helped rescue the crew of the *Peacock* five years earlier. The duo successfully brought the *Shark* to Fort Vancouver.

Saules's failure to pilot the *Shark* to Astoria became one of the events for which he is best-known, and the mishap was even mentioned in Hubert Howe Bancroft's landmark *History of Oregon*. Had Saules been successful, he might have raised his stature as a pilot and his position in settler society. He would have vindicated the recommendation of three leading citizens and perhaps earned the respect of Howison and the *Shark's* crew members. Instead, the fiasco at the bar seemed to further his marginalization in Oregon. Like the Cockstock Affair and the Saules-Pickett dispute, the incident was preserved for posterity in a report presented to the US Congress that presented Saules in a poor light. The incident also attracted local attention, none of which reflected positively on Saules. On August 6, 1846, the *Oregon Spectator* reported, "The Shark was run aground upon Chenook shoal, through the unskillfulness of a negro man living at the Cape, who undertook to pilot her over to Astoria."[53] The *Spectator's* insistence on emphasizing Saules's race is noteworthy. The newspaper routinely featured minstrel show-type racial humor between news items, and the writer of the article may have seen Saules's mistake as a confirmation of racial stereotypes.

Howison's report also blamed Saules's incompetence as a bar pilot for the near disaster, and many historians writing about this episode have echoed this assessment.[54] What such historians often fail to mention is that three prominent and respected local residents recommended Saules. William Gray, in particular, lived in Oregon City at the time of the Cockstock Affair and the Saules-Pickett dispute and in 1845 moved to Clatsop Plains, where Saules was well-known. And Lattie, the pilot who took over for Saules, made no reference to Saules's presumed incompetence. Instead, he claimed the

Shark "took onboard Saul a coloured man as Pilot, who unluckly got the vessel on shore behind the west end of Chinook Spit."[55] At least one more sympathetic historian has suggested that Saules was likely more familiar with the shallow draft of the flat-bottomed scows more commonly found on the Columbia River, as opposed to the deeper keel of the *Shark*.[56] The *Shark* also had design quirks of which Saules was probably unaware. According to historian Gregory Shine, "Another cost of the extensive rig (masts, spars, and sails) and heavily laden foremast was the ship's inclination to lower its bow and dive under when pressed by the wind under full sail."[57] Therefore, while Saules was not as experienced a bar pilot as either Old George or Alexander Lattie, he was also facing one of the world's most difficult rivers to navigate in an unfamiliar vessel.[58]

Howison had ample reason to shift blame from himself in his report to Congress since his mission ultimately ended in disaster. After arriving in Fort Vancouver, Howison received a characteristically warm reception from the recently retired John McLoughlin as well as HBC chief factors James Douglas and Peter Skene Ogden. This was despite Howison's reassurance to American settlers that the United States would never accept any boundary settlement south of the 49th parallel. Howison and his crew members also experienced cordial relations with the crewmen of the *Modeste,* with whom they often drank and dined.[59] On August 23, 1846, the *Shark* departed from Fort Vancouver. Unfortunately for the crew members, they were again without a bar pilot since both Lattie and Chinook George were unavailable. On September 8, after two weeks of river travel, an impatient Howison attempted to cross the bar himself, having received strict orders to depart by September 1.[60] However, the *Shark* struck the bar and took heavy damage from the churning sea. Howison was able to get all twenty-four crew members safely to Clatsop Beach, but the *Shark* was completely demolished. Ironically, the shivering crew warmed themselves with a fire built from planks salvaged from the wreck of the *Peacock.*[61] Despite Howison's haste in crossing the bar without a pilot, the US Congress later absolved him of any wrongdoing.

It is not known what Saules thought of the wreck of the *Shark,* although he likely witnessed it from a prime vantage point on Cape Disappointment. Perhaps he felt some vindication after his previous humiliation aboard the vessel. He may have also experienced some traumatic memories of the wreck of the *Peacock.* But what did he make of the political struggle over his adopted homeland? He had inadvertently aided British interests through his deal with

Ogden and then openly tried to assist the US cause by piloting the *Shark*. In the case of the *Shark*, however, he was probably as motivated by his pilot's fee than any sense of patriotism. Both gambits ended poorly for him. But Saules had originally come to the lower Columbia as part of an imperialist mission that took on a distinct colonizing character once it reached the Pacific Northwest. And Saules himself, a de facto agent of empire who had not only worked for the US Navy but also established land claims, called on a US authority to settle his dispute with a Native man and aided Anglo-American settlers through his transport business. Yet the increasing Americanization of the region had dealt serious blows to Saules's ability to maintain a stable residence and an advantageous position in settler society.

LIFE ON THE COLUMBIA

By the latter half of the 1840s, Saules was earning his living aboard the *Callapooiah* (sometimes known as the *Calipooia* or *Callipooia*), a thirty-five-ton schooner based in Oregon that carried passengers and cargo throughout the region. Aaron Cook, a British settler with pro-American views, and three other settlers with no prior boat-building experience, constructed the *Callapooiah* in August 1844.[62] According to James W. Nesmith, who helped build it, the *Callapooiah* was a rustic craft that "did the principal part of carrying trade upon the lower Columbia and Willamette rivers."[63] The journey from Oregon City to Astoria took several days in the 1840s, and the vessel contained a cabin for women and children in the aft section and a fire pit for cooking near the front of the ship. At night, male passengers would cover themselves with blankets and sleep outside on the deck. The vessel was also often used to bring newly arrived settlers from the foot of the Columbia River rapids near the Cascade Mountains to Oregon City. In May 1846, Cook placed an advertisement in the *Oregon Spectator* announcing that the ship was for sale.[64] Brazil Grounds, a prominent figure in the early maritime history of the region, later commanded the schooner and may have purchased it at this time.[65] Grounds had recently arrived overland from Illinois and later built and commanded a steam scow he dubbed the *Black Republican*.[66] Yet it is also possible that Saules purchased the craft himself, as at least one source indicates that Saules had earned a decent living continuing to run his transportation between Astoria and Cathlamet.[67]

Saules's life remained anything but quiet, however, and an event even more mysterious and disturbing than the Saules-Pickett dispute occurred in

late 1846. As a result, Saules again found himself in the Willamette Valley facing serious charges. The December 24, 1846, edition of the *Oregon Spectator*
featured the following item: "A negro man named James D. Saul was brought
to [Oregon City] recently from the mouth of the river, charged with having caused the death of his wife, an Indian woman. He was examined before
Justice Hood, the result of which examination we have never been able to
ascertain, but the accused is at large and likely to remain so, we suppose."[68]

Justice Andrew Hood was a native of Ireland who traveled overland to
Oregon City in 1845.[69] Some historians have referred to this article as evidence that Saules murdered his Native wife, but the article does not actually
make this claim and implies something closer to manslaughter or negligence.
Little else is known about this case, including who brought Saules to Oregon
City or who pressed charges. It is also not known whether the case was
dropped due to lack of evidence or if the life of a Native woman was not considered important enough to pursue charges.

Despite the fact that Saules remained free, it is, of course, possible he
intentionally or unintentionally killed his wife. Saules was known as a heavy
drinker and may have harbored violent tendencies. He was most likely
involved in massacres against Native people in the South Pacific, and he was
arrested for allegedly threatening the life of Charles E. Pickett. Saules may
have also been the black deserter who threatened to kill Captain Edward C.
Barnard, his commanding officer aboard the whaling bark *Winslow*. Saules's
personal problems in subsequent years may have exacerbated marital difficulties. Some settlers later referenced Saules's strange and erratic behavior and
even questioned his sanity.

Judge Hood's lack of interest in pursuing the case against Saules also suggests that his unnamed wife's social position in the lower Columbia area was
also diminished by the arrival of Anglo-American settlers. At the height of
Oregon's fur trade, Native women played a key role as laborers and forged
social and economic ties between the fur trade and indigenous groups
through intermarriage. Chinookan women, both first wives and headwomen,
also had genuine power within their communities.[70] The settler invasion of
the mid-1840s began a process that pushed Native women to the margins of
settler society. Many Anglo-American settlers despised interracial marriages
as an affront to their desire to see white wives raising white families. At the
same time, many settlers conceived of Native women as little more than pros-
titutes. Historian Sylvia Van Kirk saw this same pattern occur throughout fur

trade communities in North America: "In the period of frontier settlement, unions between white men and native women became increasingly rare; they were frowned upon by the dominant white culture, while at the same time the sexual exploitation of native women was allowed to increase."[71]

Saules's wife's Native relatives also would have been unable to bring her killer to justice. The nature of the justice system in Oregon in the mid-nineteenth century continued to make it nearly impossible for Natives to seek redress from non-Natives. In July 1851, two white settlers were brought before Oregon chief justice Thomas Nelson for the assault and battery of a Clackamas woman. Yet when the prosecution offered a Native woman named Kezika as a witness, Nelson cited the provisional government's law that "a negro, mulatto or Indian shall not be a witness in any court or in any case against a white person."[72] Although Oregon had become a US territory by then, Nelson ruled that the old law still disqualified Kezika from serving as a witness. This raises the interesting question of whether a Native would be able to serve as a witness against a black person like Saules.

The 1897 diary of Silas B. Smith does not provide any additional information on the aforementioned case, but Smith recalled witnessing Saules receiving corporal punishment for an unnamed crime. According to Smith, "After a while, Saul got into bad ways and the settlers decided that he should be given a public flogging."[73] This may have been related to the death of Saules's wife, who may have had familial connections among the mixed-raced families of Clatsop Plains. Smith wrote that settlers tied Saules to a tree and whipped him with the end of a rawhide lariat. Smith, a young child at the time, provided a chilling account of the punishment: "From the first blow, he gave agonized shrieks and frantically tore and struggled at his fastenings and piteously begged them to desist. He continued his screams all through the whipping."[74] Smith claimed that because of Saules's public disgrace, "troubles affected his mind and he became partially insane."[75] Smith places the onset of Saules's mental problems to early 1848, although he does not offer a date for the public whipping. Despite the antiblack Lash Law of 1844, Smith insisted that such punishments were very rare in Clatsop County and that settlers only flogged one other man during this period. The other victim, also nonwhite, was a Coos Bay Native who allegedly stole a tool from an American settler and threatened him with a knife when the settler tried to retrieve it. Smith, whose mother was a Clatsop Native, contrasted the two whippings to demonstrate that, unlike Saules, the Native "displayed the traditional stoicism of his race" as a means of denying his enemies any evidence of weakness.[76]

Saules's problems in Oregon did not seem to affect his professional life, and by 1848 he apparently commanded the *Callapooiah* by himself. This might be because Grounds, the previous captain, moved to San Francisco that same year.[77] Samuel T. McKean was an early resident of Astoria who recalled meeting Saules during a voyage down the Columbia River. According to his diary, McKean was seven years old when he arrived with his family in Oregon from Illinois in 1847. The family settled in Linnton, a few miles west of Portland. In 1848 John McClure encouraged McKean's father to move to Astoria, where McClure had established a land claim. In September 1848, the family members and their belongings traveled aboard the *Callapooiah*, which McKean described as "a queer kind of craft . . . built like a scow and rigged as a schooner."[78] According to McKean, "She was commanded by a man of the African persuasion called 'Nigger Sol,' an odd character who felt the dignity of this position as captain of so fine a craft."[79] McKean added that Saules was "good natured, however, and we got along very well."[80] The voyage took eight days, as difficult river conditions often required Saules to either anchor the craft or tie it to the banks while the tide was flooding.[81] Saules's anchor was apparently unusual for the time and combined the crotch of a tree, an oblong stone, and the root of a sapling.[82] Charles Melville Scammon claimed that Saules later survived the sinking of the *Callapooiah* near Astoria, although he does not provide a date. This story is perhaps corroborated by the fact that, in 1975, an Astoria fisherman snagged a strange looking object in his gillnet that matched the description of Saules's anchor.[83]

McKean's recollections regarding Saules are brief but fascinating. This is the only instance in which a settler referred to him as "Nigger Sol," although McKean implied that this moniker was commonly used. In fact, it is only Anglo-American settlers that referred to Saules as "Saul" or "Sol." In any official writings, Saules referred to himself as "J.D. Saules" or "James Saules," although it is possible he suggested "Saul" as an informal nickname. It is unfortunate that McKean did not elaborate on why he found Saules "odd," but the reference recalls Smith's questions about Saules's sanity during this period. Regardless, Saules's solo command of the Callapooiah demonstrates that despite his previous difficulties with the law and authority figures, he was still permitted to serve his important function as a local river man. He also evidently retained warm and agreeable relations with the incoming Anglo-American settlers he aided.

AN AMERICANIZED OREGON AND THE 1849 BLACK EXCLUSION LAW

On June 16, 1846, Warre sent a letter to Ogden informing him that Simpson had approved the purchase of Cape Disappointment. Yet such machinations were for naught, as at the same time Ogden and Warre fretted over the particulars of the land deal, Great Britain and United States were negotiating over the location of the Oregon border. On June 18, 1846, two days after Ogden received Warre's final letter regarding the purchase, the US Congress ratified the Oregon Treaty, establishing the international border at the 49th parallel while granting Great Britain sole possession of Vancouver Island. This agreement meant that Great Britain lost both Puget Sound and access to the lower Columbia. However, the British government's desire to preserve its Oregon holdings was tempered by severe domestic problems. These included a failed potato crop in Ireland, a below-average grain harvest in England, and unrest over the repeal of Britain's Corn Laws. The United States, on the other hand, pulled back from its bellicose insistence on 54°40'N, since the government was preoccupied by tensions with Mexico that erupted into full-scale war in May 1846.[84] All of this occurred unbeknownst to anyone living in the Pacific Northwest, as news of the treaty did not reach Oregon until late October 1846.

By 1847 Saules seemed to have regained much of his mobility and visibility in the region, but this proved temporary. Developments during the year challenged the notion that Oregon could continue to exist as a heterogeneous middle ground in which mutual interests superseded military force. As in other middle grounds in North America, Great Britain's presence in the region allowed the Native people to exploit imperial rivalries to their advantage. Yet when the HBC left the Oregon Country following the settlement of the boundary question, local Natives lost considerable leverage and a financial partner. And as was often the case with settler colonialism, it was not the US government that initiated this shift but rather the inhabitants of the region themselves. Richard White describes this peculiar brand of American imperialism as "a world system in which minor agents, allies, and even subjects at the periphery often guide the course of empires."[85] This was particularly true when regional tensions exploded into violence several hundred miles upriver from Cape Disappointment on the Columbia Plateau.

On November 29, 1847, a small group of Cayuse and Umatilla men killed Marcus and Narcissa Whitman, as well as twelve other settlers, at the Whitmans' house at the Waiilatpu Mission. Relations between the Whitmans and Cayuses had become strained due to Whitman's continued assistance to Oregon Train immigrants. A faction of Cayuses also believed Marcus Whitman, a physician, had intentionally infected Cayuses with deadly diseases following a measles outbreak. The killings sent shockwaves throughout the region and sparked a series of wars with the Native groups of the Columbia Plateau. These conflicts often followed a pattern of Native attacks met with severe retribution from American settlers and the military. These attacks were largely a reaction to the various pressures American settlement placed on Native communities, such as the extinguishment of Native title to land, the enclosure of hunting and gathering grounds, and the imposition of exogenous laws and values. In May 1848, Sheriff Joseph Meek, the man who once brought Saules before a county judge for allegedly inciting Native people to violence, traveled to Washington, DC, to bring news of the Waiilatpu tragedy and convince President Polk that the residents of the Oregon Country needed the protection of the US military. On August 1848, Polk signed the Oregon Territorial Act, which established Oregon as the first territorial government west of the Rocky Mountains. By the following year, the US Army had established bases at the two sites previously occupied by the HBC, Fort Vancouver and Fort Nisqually.

The aftermath of the Whitman Massacre ended much of Oregon's political isolation from the United States. It also inspired a renewed outcry among Oregonians against allowing black people to reside in the territory. Like the provisional government before it, the territorial government promoted the vision of Oregon as an ethnically homogenous region dominated by Anglo-Protestant farm families. Many residents continued to see the presence of nonwhites as a threat to their growing community and would again utilize the state apparatus to attempt to regulate the racial composition of the region. Applying military force on recalcitrant indigenous populations was one way to accomplish this. Another was the resurrection of black exclusion legislation. While the Oregon Territory retained its ban on slavery, several politicians wanted to ensure that free black people would not immigrate to the new territory. On September 26, 1849, the territorial House of Representatives voted 12 to 4 to pass a bill "to prevent Negroes and Mulattoes from coming to, or residing in Oregon."[86] The bill narrowly passed the Territorial Council by a vote of 5 to 4. The new law prohibited free black or mulatto people from immigrating to Oregon, although it allowed black or mulatto settlers already living in the territory, like Saules, to remain. Unlike the earlier black exclusion law, the 1849 version did not specify punishment for those who refused to leave and instead left the matter to the discretion of individual judges.

The circumstance regarding the specific origins of the law remain unclear, although Samuel Thurston, Oregon's territorial delegate to the US House of Representatives, defended it before Congress in 1850. According to the *Oregon Spectator*, when Ohio Whig congressman Joshua Reed Giddings voiced his objections to the bill, Thurston countered by insisting "the people of Oregon were not pro-slavery men, nor were they pro-negro men; there were but few negroes in the territory and [we] hoped there never would be more."[87] Thurston contended that "the people themselves excluded [blacks]" and he "trusted that Congress would not introduce them in violation of their wishes."[88] While it was somewhat disingenuous for Thurston to claim the "the people" had approved the law, since it was not decided by popular vote, he was correct about the small number of black people living in Oregon. According to the 1850 census, Oregon contained 13,294 people, but census takers counted only 54 they considered "Negroes."[89]

While he was never mentioned by name, it is likely that Saules partly influenced the language of the 1849 black exclusion bill. For example, the preamble dredged up old fears about black-Native collaboration: "Whereas, situated as the people of Oregon are, in the midst of an Indian population, it would be highly dangerous to allow free negroes and mulattoes to reside in the Territory, or to intermix with the Indians, instilling into their minds feelings of hostility against the white race."[90] This could be an indirect reference to the Second Seminole War of the previous decade or even the long-running anxieties heightened by the Whitman Massacre two years earlier. However, that particular event did not involve any black people. On the other hand, the specific wording is far more suggestive of the Saules-Pickett dispute of 1844. Saules was a black man with marital and familial ties to the local indigenous population. Saules had also once allegedly joined forces with Native people to defend their rights against a white settler. Furthermore, no other incident involving this sort of racial alliance ever took place in the region.

The preamble also implies that, due to Anglo-American encroachment, Native people had ample reasons for hostility. Some Oregonians feared rebellious black men could take advantage of this hostility and provide Native people with valuable intelligence regarding the ways of white men. And if one applies the racialist logic and binary thinking of many Anglo-American set-tlers, blacks and Native people had a natural affinity for one another due to their lowly positions on the racial hierarchy. Furthermore, the use of the term "intermix" connotes interracial sexual activity, which was one of the hallmarks of the middle ground. This also suggests that a prohibition on interracial rela-tions would be necessary to preserve order in the new settler colonial society. Even Jesse Applegate, a settler who believed in the fair treatment of ethnic minorities, wrote of free blacks in 1865, "But it is not among the rights he is entitled to that his sons shall marry our daughters, or that our sons shall marry his; a power higher than man's has forbidden such connection."[91] According to historian Gray Whaley, Oregon legislators believed "the supposedly infe-rior, savage races would naturally combine and form a sort of Super-Rogue and deny American citizens ('whites') the security of their birthright."[92]

Yet even in the nineteenth century, many found this logic dubious. In 1886 historian Frances Fuller Victor wrote that fears of black-Native collabo-ration "could not be advanced as a sufficient explanation . . . to keep negroes out of the territory, because all the southern and western frontier states had possessed a large population of blacks, both slave and free, at the time they had fought the savages, without finding the negroes a dangerous element of their population."[93] Victor, however, fails to consider the Second Seminole War or other instances in which Native and black people rebelled against Anglo-American hegemony.

Even more remarkable is that the bulk of the exclusion law addresses the behavior of black sailors arriving on ships, especially potential deserters, of which Saules was likely the most visible in Oregon during this period. And since black sailors continued to comprise a sizeable portion of most sea crews, territorial legislators seemingly viewed them as a particular threat. Section two of the law allowed masters and owners of ships to bring blacks to Oregon but also made them responsible for the actions of their black crew members and "liable to any person aggrieved by such negro or mulatto."[94] Despite fears of what black sailors like Saules might do if left unattended, this provision reveals that legislators recognized that maritime commerce was necessary to the economic health of the region. Therefore, legislators remained pragmatic about the need for commercial ships to come to Oregon. Section three stipu-lated that blacks and mulatto sailors must not leave the immediate vicinity of their vessels unless accompanied by their vessel's master, while section four required that the master must remove all black or mulatto crew members from the territory within forty days.[95] These measures were obviously intended to prevent black sailors from deserting their ships and establishing residency in Oregon, something Saules had done in 1841. Finally, section five stated that if the master or owner of a ship failed to abide by the previous sections, a territorial court would have them indicted, imprisoned, and fined.[96] This was a bold move, as legislators were willing to risk the possibility that some ships might bypass Oregon altogether due to the severity of the law.

Laws confining black sailors to their ships were nothing new in the United States, demonstrated by the aforementioned Negro Seaman Acts enacted by various southern states. However, the southern statutes were intended to prevent free black men from having contact with enslaved laborers working in seaports and either helping them to freedom or introducing abolitionist ideas. In this regard, some southern legislators likened restricting the movement of black sailors to quarantining a "moral contagion."[97] Yet in a free territory like Oregon, black sailors would have found few slaves to incite. Instead, the contagion Oregon politicians repeatedly invoked pertained to black sailors fomenting unrest among local Native people. It remains unclear whether any of the politicians who invoked this notion actually believed it themselves or if it was mere demagoguery designed to arouse the deep-seated fears of their constituents. Nonetheless, the strategy was apparently successful, as the specter of black-Native collaboration remained the key justification of black exclusion in antebellum Oregon.

Oregon's receptiveness to black exclusion was somewhat unique in the Far West. For example, in 1849, the same year Oregon passed its territorial black law, California rejected a similar black exclusion law. That year, at the height of the Gold Rush, California voters elected Peter Burnett, the architect of Oregon's original Lash Law, as the state's first governor. Burnett immediately urged the California legislature to ban black immigration, warning that the lure of gold "would bring swarms of [black people] to our shores."[98] Burnett's word choice is interesting in light of the Oregon law's emphasis on black sailors, as he assumes black people would arrive on ships as opposed to overland. Burnett contended that the arrival of black settlers would only add to an already "heterogeneous mass of human beings, of every language and of every hue."[99] California's legislature, dominated by Whigs, rejected Burnett's proposal, denouncing it as "unduly influenced by prejudice and behampered by fear and favor."[100] R. G. Gilbert, the Whig editor of the *Alta*, a California newspaper, believed free black men should have the opportunity to improve their economic position in the state, but he also doubted that enough blacks would migrate to California to significantly alter the racial composition of the state.[101] Yet black people would not experience anything resembling legal equality in the new state, and California's first state constitution forbade black people from voting or serving in the militia.[102] Some Californian legislators may have had less than noble reasons for rejecting black exclusion, since despite California's status as a free state, many slaveholders brought their enslaved workers with them to the goldfields. A black exclusion law like the one Burnett proposed would have denied California slaveholders their workforce.[103]

THE 1850 DONATION LAND ACT

Although the 1849 black exclusion law boldly declared Oregon a white man's territory, Saules remained in the region. Because he was already living in the vicinity of the territory when it passed, he was not legally subject to exclusion. Nevertheless, the passage of the law sent a clear signal to black residents that they were unwelcome. Yet at the same time as black exclusion became territorial law, Oregon politicians and elites were encouraging the passage of a federal act that was arguably more instrumental in establishing a racial status quo in Oregon by promoting the Anglo-American resettlement through the distribution of free land to potential white settlers.

The 1850 Donation Land Act was largely written by Oregon territorial delegate Samuel R. Thurston as a response to the original Oregon Territorial Act, which did nothing to honor land claims recorded by the provisional government's land office. To add to this insult, the US government had initially granted 640 acres to each missionary station in the new territory.[104] The Donation Land Act, which President Millard Fillmore signed into law on September 27, 1850, not only validated the legal title of land claimed by early overlanders, it also granted 320 acres of free land to white male American citizens (or mixed-race Native men with white fathers), provided they lived on it and improved it through cultivation. If the male settler was married, his wife was granted an additional 320 acres, thus encouraging families to settle in the male-dominated region.[105] Passage of the five-year act resulted in eight thousand Anglo-American claimants receiving three million acres of land from 1850 to 1855, as well as a population increase of 300 percent.[106] This also meant that the number of white settlers now exceeded the entire Native population of the region, thoroughly upsetting the delicate balance that had characterized the region for much of the nineteenth century.

The Donation Land Act was also a decisive victory over the last vestiges of the middle ground forged by indigenous peoples and the fur trade. The act was intended to usurp land claims made prior to the formation of the provisional government, particularly those of non-Americans associated with the fur trade. Thurston, in advocating for the act in Congress, insisted on the phrase "American citizen" in the law itself, a designation he contrasted with "every servant of the Hudson's Bay Company."[107] For example, section eleven stipulated that the territorial legislature would receive the majority of John McLoughlin's Oregon City land claim. According to Thurston during a congressional debate on May 28, 1850, "[The HBC] has been warring against our government these forty years."[108] This recalls the earlier unfounded belief among some American settlers that the HBC was arming local Native people to undermine their nascent community. Thurston also singled out one culprit in particular: "Dr. McLoughlin has been their chief fugleman, first to cheat our government out of the whole country, and next to prevent its settlement."[109]

The Donation Land Act was an emphatic endorsement of the color line in Oregon, and the law essentially functioned as an affirmative action program for Anglo-American settlers. Saules, like most nonwhite residents of Oregon, was unable to take advantage of this free land bonanza, and the Donation Land Act was, in many ways, a more effective racial exclusion act than either the 1844 or 1849 black exclusion laws. Although previous governments had denied citizenship to nonwhites, earlier land laws had never specified whiteness as a prerequisite for land ownership.

The Donation Land Act's racial exclusion element had an enormous impact on regional power dynamics and the racial composition of Oregon. In the nineteenth-century American West, wealth and power was measured by land ownership. A settler could use free land claims to grow crops and graze livestock for subsistence or the marketplace. In a capitalist economy, land was also a commodity that one could subdivide and sell for profit. Yet only males with white fathers and their wives qualified for free land according to the law. In drawing up the initial draft of the bill, Thurston was therefore conflating whiteness with legitimate American citizenship. This notion had its origins in the 1790 Naturalization Act, which limited American citizenship to whites. The act's exclusionary provisions therefore racialized Oregon land claims as both American *and* white spaces. Those forbidden from owning land in

Oregon included blacks, indigenous people without white fathers, Chinese, and Pacific Islanders. Thurston's justification for excluding Pacific Islanders was partially due to their prominent role as Oregon fur industry workers and ties to the HBC. Yet his stance also revealed that he, like so many racialists of the nineteenth century, held a binary view of race based more on skin tone than specific ethnicity. On May 28, 1850, when defending the racial exclusion clause before the US House of Representatives, Thurston referred to "Canakers" or Pacific Islanders as "a race of men as black as your negroes of the South, and a race, too, that we do not desire to settle in Oregon."[110]

The Donation Land Act was significant in that it allowed some women, namely the wives of claimants, to own large parcels of land in their own name. This was one means to address Oregon's imbalanced sex ratio: in the 1850 census, white women were only 37.8 percent of the 13,294 people counted.[111] By granting land claims to the wives, and eventually widows, of white male settlers, the US federal government found an effective means to encourage the racial and ethnic homogenization of the region, thus increasing the marginalization of nonwhite residents. In 1850 thousands of women living in Oregon could not qualify for land, as they were married to either Native, Pacific Islander, Chinese, black, British, or French Canadian men. The exclusionary aspects of the Donation Land Act further marginalized these women by elevating the position of white women in the region. These white women would presumably also give birth to the next generation of white residents. Margaret D. Jacobs argues that the mobilization of white women is a necessary component of settler colonialism because it encourages settlement by white families, balances sex ratios, reproduces colonial gender systems, and makes "the home" a "means of establishing dominance in the new settlement."[112] The increasing number of white women in the Pacific Northwest also allowed promoters of racial exclusion to exploit fears that nonwhites in the region would pose a sexual threat to the white wives and daughters of settlers.[113]

As in the cases of the first two black exclusion laws, Saules may have influenced the rhetoric used to defend the bill in Congress. When faced with a possible amendment to remove various exclusionary aspects from the bill, Thurston continued to raise the familiar threat of black-Indian collaboration. During the May 28, 1850, congressional session, Thurston softened his stance toward the British and French Canadians living in Oregon; he consented to include them in the land law if they were willing to become American citizens. At the same time, Thurston reaffirmed his rigid stance against nonwhites: "I am not for giving land to Sandwich Islanders or negroes." He then cited the danger of interracial sexual relationships, claiming that "the Canakers and negroes, if allowed to come there, will commingle with our Indians, a mixed race will ensue, and the result will be wars and bloodshed in Oregon."[114] During a congressional debate two days later, Thurston stressed the supposed affinity between black people and Natives, claiming that that the few black residents in Oregon "preferred to rove with Indians, encouraging them to acts of hostility against the whites instead of settling down and laboring like the settlers."[115]

The proposed bill did make an exception by allowing land grants for "American half breeds." This was probably due to the influence of the French-Indian families of French Prairie and the fact that many prominent American male settlers had Native wives and wanted their progeny to receive land.[116] As for full-blood Native people, Thurston successfully lobbied Congress to authorize the president to appoint commissioners who would negotiate treaties with Native groups "for the extinguishment of their claims to lands lying west of the Cascade Mountains."[117] This was the first stage in a process that later resulted in the removal of several Native groups from their ancestral lands.

The Donation Land Act was an also an example of settler colonists driving US policy rather than the reverse. In other words, Oregon politicians like Thurston were instigating Jacksonian Democracy from the fringes of empire. Despite the expansionist rhetoric of President Polk and Missouri senator Thomas Hart Benton, in the 1840s Manifest Destiny remained a contentious topic among US politicians, especially when combined with the question of whether slavery would extend to the Far West. Yet many Oregonians believed the federal government had tacitly promised settlers free land in the West, even though Senator Lewis Linn's Oregon Territorial Bill, a precursor to the Donation Land Act, failed to pass the US House of Representatives in 1843. In 1849, when the Oregon legislature appointed Thurston as its delegate to Congress, his first and most important assignment was to draft a new land bill and take it to Washington, DC. In a remarkable case of the periphery guiding the empire, the resulting Donation Land Act was virtually identical to Thurston's proposed bill.[118] This process began decades earlier and was far from unidirectional—it involved Oregon politicians and their constituents placing pressure on the federal government to help enact their own particular vision of a culturally and ethnically homogenous West.

On September 27, 1850, Saules's vacated plot of land on Cape Disappointment became a donation land claim. The claimant was none other than Elijah White, the former Indian agent who had contributed to regional tensions by imposing foreign laws on Native groups. White had also convinced Saules to leave the Willamette Valley and later urged the provisional government to remove all black people from the region. White, who had moved back to Ithaca, New York, in 1845, returned to Oregon in 1849 to refashion Cape Disappointment into Pacific City, a future metropolis he hoped would eclipse both Oregon City and San Francisco in importance.[119] In 1850 White and his business partner, James D. Holman, subdivided the property, erected a sawmill there, and transported a luxury hotel in pieces by ship from New York via San Francisco. White's reputation in Oregon, however, was tarnished, and in 1851, the *Oregon Spectator* warned readers against doing business with him. Yet White still managed to convince Henry and Jane Fiester to move from Aurora, Oregon, to Pacific City; he gave them two city lots for free, citing his desire to have an all-white family begin populating the town.[120] Reports vary on how many Anglo-Americans White convinced to resettle in Pacific City, ranging from seventy-five to five hundred people.[121] On February 26, 1852, White's ambitions were nevertheless dashed when President Fillmore, citing the fourteenth section of the Donation Land Act, ordered that Pacific City be turned over to the federal government and converted it into a military reservation later known as Fort Canby.[122] While White was compensated for the land, this demonstrated how bringing the federal government into the region for protection could have unforeseen consequences.

The Donation Land Act was also the culmination of a colonial project that began when Saules, Lieutenant Charles Wilkes, and the rest of the US Ex. Ex. arrived on the lower Columbia in the summer of 1841. As he surveyed the region, Wilkes was confident that it would one day belong solely to the United States. He employed the era's most advanced surveying and cartographic techniques to create accurate yet abstract representations of physical space that could be then presented to politicians in Washington, DC. For those who sought to absorb the Pacific Northwest into United States, these images seemed to reinforce and legitimate their imperial desires. Geographer Daniel Clayton argues that the appropriation of territory by the nation-state is often "underpinned by imperial intentions that were at once public and scientific."[123] The Donation Land Act also used surveys and cartography to apply a gloss of scientific objectivity to the colonial project of seizing and privatizing land once held in common. Unlike the more primitive techniques of the provisional land office, the Donation Land Act brought a surveyor general to the area in 1851. He implemented a formal survey that converted what the federal government called the "unsurveyed public domain" into square-shaped private land plots easily identified and referenced on official maps.[124] According to historian Katherine G. Morrissey, "Representing land as state-regulated property, accessible for private individual ownership, a commodity to be bought and sold on the market, the maps connected their users to national, economic, legal, and political systems."[125] The process of surveying and mapmaking integral to the Donation Land Act therefore reified land itself as political space fit only for those whose race qualified them for citizenship.

THE DEATH OF SAULES?

Oregon's racist policies pushed nonwhites to the margins of settler society. Perhaps it is only a coincidence, but Saules virtually disappears from the historical record following the passage of the 1850 Donation Land Act. This is in stark contrast with the previous nine years, in which Saules regularly appeared in government reports, settler diaries, and newspaper articles. It is possible that Oregon's dramatic population growth in the late 1840s and early 1850s made Saules's presence less noticeable in the region. On the other hand, if the aforementioned racist legislation is any indication of how white Oregonians treated nonwhites, Saules probably did not feel welcome anywhere near the Willamette Valley. Saules was further pushed to the sidelines of settler society due to his legal inability to take advantage of the federal government's redistribution of free land, which would have at least provided him with some property, a means of subsistence, and a stake in the economic future of the region.

There is some evidence that Saules may have lived north of the Columbia River in the vicinity of Cathlamet. In 1851 Saules's name was on the ledgers of the Cathlamet general store. Two years later, the store still listed him as an outstanding debtor.[126] Throughout the nineteenth century, many black people in the region preferred to remain on the north side of the Columbia River in what later became Washington Territory. For example, in 1845 a prosperous Missourian of black and Irish descent named George Bush arrived in the Willamette Valley with his German American wife, Isabella. When he learned of the provisional government's black exclusion law, he settled near Fort Vancouver, which was beyond the government's jurisdiction. He later

relocated to Puget Sound and—with the aid of several white allies—successfully petitioned the US Congress to obtain a donation land claim in 1854.
George Washington was another black settler who opted for the north side
of the Columbia. Washington arrived in Oregon City in 1850 with his adop-
tive white parents, Anna and James Cochrane. In 1852 he obtained a donation land claim in his parents' names at the future town site of Centralia,
Washington, which he founded.

Definitive information regarding Saules's death has never surfaced, but
some sources suggest he died in the early 1850s. Charles Melville Scammon's
1875 profile of Saules for the *Overland Monthly* suggests that he drowned
somewhere on the Columbia River between the mouth of the Willamette
River and the town of Astoria and was buried near the shore of Cathlamet
Bay.[127] Silas B. Smith believed that Saules died sometime after 1848, although
he did not know the cause or location.[128] Historian Elizabeth McLagan specu-
lated that Saules died in a boat accident in December 1851. Her evidence is an
article in the December 30, 1851, edition of the *Oregon Spectator*:

> We learn that three negro men have been engaged for some time past
> in selling liquor to Indians, a short distance from Milton, Washington
> county, and that the citizens of that place were so much annoyed
> by their continued drunkenness and debauchery, that several of the
> citizens started in a boat to take the negroes into custody. This they
> succeeded in doing, and when taking them before the Magistrate, by
> some means the boat was capsized, and one of the negroes drowned.
> For want of sufficient evidence to commit them, the other two were
> discharged. Upon the examination it was stated by these negroes that
> they were in the employ of a resident of [Oregon City], and that the
> liquor they were engaged in selling was his property.[129]

It is certainly possible that the drowned man was Saules, although it is
somewhat surprising the article did not state his name, given his local notoriety. But the location of the event does suggest Saules's involvement. While
the town of Milton no longer exists, it was located on the south side of the
Columbia River near the town of St. Helens—less than fifty miles upriver
from Cathlamet. It is also noteworthy that settlers accused the three black
men of selling liquor to Natives, an illegal activity in Oregon Territory. Saules
had a long-standing relationship with local Native communities and, given the

economic opportunities available to a marginalized black man living Oregon in the 1850s, selling liquor may have been among the few viable means of employment he found.

For Anglo-American setters, the idea of three black men furnishing alcohol to Native communities would have again triggered fears of black residents inciting Natives to violence. In June 1844, the provisional government not only passed the first black exclusion law; it also passed a ban on the sale, manufacture, and importation of liquor. The bill particularly targeted fur traders and ocean vessels sailing into the Oregon Country for allegedly profiting from selling intoxicating spirits to local Native communities. In 1845 George Abernathy used the specter of Indian violence to justify a liquor ban in Oregon: "We are in an Indian country. . . . If [liquor] should be introduced among the Wallawallas, and other tribes in the upper country, who can foretell the consequences; there we have families exposed out, off from the protection of the settlements, and perhaps, at the first drunken frolic of the Indians in that region, they may be cut off from the face of the earth."[130] On October 14, 1847, the *Oregon Spectator* accused Saules's old friend Winslow Anderson, described as the "mulatto from the [Methodist] Institute," of entering a Native community while drunk and sharing his alcohol with Native residents. The *Spectator* identified this act as a security risk to the growing settler community: "Citizens of Oregon City! How can you pass such conduct without notice? A few such drunken rats may cause much damage to be done."[131] By 1847 the law was amended to include imprisonment of up to two years for providing intoxicating spirits to Indians.[132]

There is evidence, however, that suggests Saules died in a more valiant way than the one McLagen hypothesized. Mildred Colbert, a Pacific County historian active in the mid-twentieth century, was a collector of pioneer lore. She claimed Saules was the first settler at Jim Crow Point in Wahkiakum County. According to Colbert, Saules was still alive in 1860s and made his living by gillnetting, a fishing technique common on the lower Columbia. She also believed Saules drowned in a storm.[133] This is plausible, as Saules would have been in his fifties or sixties at that time. In 1997 Rodney K. Williams published a history of the Whealdons, an Anglo-American family who settled in the area later known as Ilwaco, in Washington state, in the late 1850s. Williams compiled several primary source items apparently written by Whealdon family members themselves. The following item, titled "Negro Jim, Gentleman" was included as part of an early area history:

When Ilwaco was very young, there drifted to the village a Negro, "Jim" by name. A kinder soul never lived. That characteristic, coupled with his good nature and temperate, industrious habits, soon endeared him to the settlers and their children.

Once, while out in a boat with a young white man and his wife at the mouth of Wallicut [the Wallicut River empties into Baker's Bay], a sudden storm sweeping in from sea capsized their little craft. The three clung to the bottom of the boat, Jim cheering and encouraging the young couple all the while. Finally someone on the shore did discover their plight and came after them. However, the rescue boat could only take two of the unfortunate ones. Jim, though numb form the cold water and realizing that the end was near, without hesitation solved the question by insisting that the man and wife be taken first and that he was all right until another trip. Before they had reached shore, poor Jim had disappeared beneath the water. The entire community assembled to pay a tribute of respect when the body was buried in the old Whealdon Cemetery near the present city reservoir.[134]

This account of a hero's death is consistent with Colbert's claims that Saules drowned in a storm. Ilwaco was also a major center of gillnetting in the nineteenth century, and Saules probably fished there if he lived into the 1860s.[135] Unfortunately, the unknown author did not provide a date, making it difficult to verify. The only vague clue is that the black man came to town when Ilwaco was "very young." The community that became Ilwaco—located less than three miles from Saules former residence on Cape Disappointment—was platted on James D. Holman's 1852 donation land claim, located east of the former site of Pacific City. Isaac Whealdon and his family arrived in 1859, and by 1868 he was postmaster of a community called Unity, which became Ilwaco in 1870.[136] Saules would have been sixty-five years old that year. Still, the fact that the drowned black mariner's named was Jim, a diminutive of James, is compelling. Furthermore, although Saules himself was never included in any census, if he was still alive in the 1860s, he was probably one of the only black men living in the lower Columbia region on either side of the river. US Census records suggest there were very few black people living north of the Columbia River in Washington Territory in the 1860s, and the census recorded no black men living in either Pacific or Wahkiakum Counties.[137]

The murkiness of these accounts and the lack of any specific mention of Saules's death in the local media or government records is indicative of how marginalized he and the other nonwhite residents of Oregon had become by the early 1850s. His absence from the 1850 and 1860 US Censuses further reinforces this impression. Many of the American settlers who began arriving in the early 1840s blamed the nation's problems on nonwhites and hoped to establish an ethnically homogeneous community in Oregon. After some furtive steps in this direction, settlers soon realized how problematic and contentious racial exclusion could be. Yet through the 1848 Territorial Act, the 1849 black exclusion law, and the 1850 Donation Land Act, the territorial legislature and federal government further enshrined the color line in Oregon. The threat of efficient state violence, in the form of more organized forms of law enforcement and the US armed forces, supported such laws. Finally, the initial trickle of westward expansion became a torrential storm in the 1850s, and Oregon's white population increased from approximately 1,000 in 1844 to 52,465 by 1860.[138] As the nation became embroiled in sectional tensions that eventually erupted in the Civil War, Oregonians continued to reaffirm the principle of racial exclusion. However, blacks, Natives, Chinese, and Pacific Islanders continued to live in the region despite the presence of laws excluding them, and like Saules, had to resort to creative means to navigate and resist the daunting forces of white supremacy.

Conclusion

The last specific mention of Saules in the historical record places him in Astoria on July 4, 1849. In 1869 Charles Melville Scammon penned an article for the *Overland Monthly* titled "In and around Astoria." In it, Scammon quoted an attendee of the 1849 Fourth of July celebration who remarked, "Old nigger Saul, one of the *Peacock's* crew, was the fiddler. When we began to dance, the floor was a little wavy; but it was all on a level afore morning, though!"[1] Scammon was never one to avoid poetic license, but this is an apt final image of the protean Saules: earning money by performing for white American settlers celebrating the anniversary of their nation's founding. It also demonstrates that Saules was still attempting to maintain his place in a colonized space. As Scammon's interlocutor implies, this was a spirited affair since it was the first Fourth of July after Oregon had become a US Territory the previous August. The location was also appropriate, as it was held in the Shark House, built as winter quarters for officers and crew of the USS *Shark* after their ship—once briefly helmed by Saules himself—was wrecked at the Columbia bar. Three years earlier, the US government had sent the *Shark* to the lower Columbia to warn residents that the future of the region belonged to Anglo-American settlers.

One wonders what Saules himself thought about the Fourth of July affair, a holiday commemorating the signing of the Declaration of Independence, a document that declared "all men are created equal." In his famous 1852 Fourth of July address, the black abolitionist and social reformer Frederick Douglass remarked, "I am not included within the pale of this glorious anniversary! Your high independence only reveals the immeasurable distance between us. . . . The rich inheritance of justice, liberty, prosperity and independence, bequeathed by your fathers, is shared by you, not by me."[2] The US Constitution, which contained scant legal protections for free black people living in the United States, also allowed individual states and territories to disenfranchise or exclude them. Oregon, for instance, was one of many so-called "free" territories to restrict citizenship to white adult men. And if Saules had been a runaway slave, the Constitution also contained a fugitive slave clause that required the return of escaped slaves. The arrival of American settlers had provided some employment opportunities for him, both as riverman and musician. But these immigrants also sought to transform the previously multiethnic region into a white man's country with a rigid color line. As a black man attempting to navigate a social hierarchy increasingly predicated on race, Saules attracted attention, much of it unwanted. This resulted in legal troubles, dispossession, dislocation, and harrowing physical punishment. Anglo-American settlers also used his presence and activities to garner support for several racist laws in the region. At approximately the same time Saules was performing at the Shark House, Oregon politicians were busy conceiving two of these: the 1849 black exclusion law and the 1850 Donation Land Act.

Despite Oregon's fervent opposition to black immigration, the territory only convicted and removed one man, Jacob Vanderpool, under the 1849 territorial black exclusion law. Vanderpool, like Saules, was a black sailor who had traveled widely.[3] Vanderpool came to Oregon to become a businessman, yet his former occupation is a reminder that the law was specifically intended to regulate the behavior of black seamen. In 1850 Vanderpool, who was denied a generous donation land claim due to his race, opened a saloon and boarding house in Oregon City. In 1851 his growing business interests apparently attracted the attention of Theophilus Magruder. Magruder was a former land claim recorder for the provisional government and proprietor of the Main Street House, an Oregon City hotel that likely competed with Vanderpool's establishment. Magruder had Vanderpool arrested and jailed for violating the 1849 exclusion law. On August 25, 1851, a territorial court ordered Vanderpool to leave the territory within thirty days. In a brief article on the case, the *Oregon Spectator* applauded the court's decision and mentioned Saules's old friend Winslow Anderson as a deserving candidate for exclusion: "A notorious villain, who calls himself Winslow, has cursed this community with his presence for a number of years. All manner of crimes have been laid to his charge—we shall rejoice at his removal."[4] However, the article fails to mention that Anderson, like Saules, was exempt from the law since he already resided in the territory when the law was passed. It is unknown what became of Vanderpool following his expulsion, but the 1870 US Census recorded a fifty-year-old black man named Jacob Vanderpool and his wife Mary—both natives of New York—residing in San Francisco, where he worked as a hardware packer.[5]

While generous land claims lured thousands of white Americans to Oregon in the 1850s, the racialist attitudes of these new Oregonians resembled those of their predecessors. In 1857, as Oregon headed toward statehood, white male voters in the territory approved adding a black exclusion clause to the state constitution by a margin of 8,640 to 1,081.[6] This clause banned any further immigration of black people once the US government approved statehood and also compounded the exclusionary aspects of the Donation Land Law by forbidding blacks from owning real estate.[7] Oregon elites during this period pushed for such proscriptions with antiblack rhetoric reminiscent of the language once used against Saules, referencing both black sailors and black-Native collaboration. Oregon's new state constitution's exclusionary aspects also clearly placed nonwhite people in the category of colonized rather than colonizers.

Only one delegate to the constitutional convention, William Watkins, a New Yorker by birth, spoke out in opposition to this clause. According to Watkins, "The free negro has claims upon us which we can neither ignore nor destroy; he was born upon our soil, he speaks our language, he has been taught our religion, and his destiny and ours are eternally linked."[8] Yet Watkins was no abolitionist. His primary reasons for objecting to the law were commercial. Watkins believed that Oregon's future was in overseas commerce rather than agriculture. He contended that the benefits of maritime commerce outweighed the risk that black sailors like Saules would come to the region and remain there permanently. And because so many free blacks served aboard vessels, Watkins reasoned that the clause would discourage captains from bringing their ships to Oregon's ports since they would have no means to protect their black crew members.[9] Sympathetic to the plight of black sailors, he offered this hypothetical situation:

Suppose, sir, as we are a commercial people, that some negro, unlearned and unlettered in your constitutional provision, who honestly earns his living by serving as cook or waiter on one of your many vessels, lands at the emporium of commerce. His property may be taken, his life endangered, his limbs broken by some fiend in human shape; but your laws, framed to protect the weak, the innocent, the helpless, and to administer justice, could give him no redress.[10]

Watkins's emphasis on commerce highlights the growing economic importance of the city of Portland, where merchants and financiers prospered through the transport of raw materials to national and international markets. Watkins was hardly free of racist vitriol; at the same time he defended the rights of black sailors, he argued forcefully in favor of excluding Chinese people from living in Oregon.[11]

In 1857 Oregon voters also voted to ban slavery by a large margin, although many territorial residents were ambivalent regarding the actual rights of enslaved people living in the territory. Most opponents of slavery in Oregon were more concerned with the potential economic effects of slavery rather than its human costs. For instance, in his "Free State Letter," Oregon judge George H. Williams invoked "free soil" ideology to attack the notion of bringing slavery to Oregon, claiming the institution would impair the ability of white workingmen to compete in a free labor system. Perhaps more importantly, Williams offered no condemnation of southern slavery and instead argued that Oregon's climate was unsuitable for the production of cotton, rice, and sugar.[12] Furthermore, Oregonians often ignored or tolerated the small but significant number of enslaved blacks brought to the region via the Oregon Trail in the 1840s and 1850s. For instance, Robin Holmes, a former slave, fought a protracted legal battle to free his two children from their owner, Oregon politician Nathaniel Ford.[13] While in 1853 Holmes was ultimately successful, his difficulty in freeing his children suggested that the residents of antebellum Oregon respected the property rights of slave owners more than the rights of black people to their own liberty and labor.

At the same time as white Oregon elites and settlers collaborated to ban black immigration, their collective desire to commodify and claim Native land resulted in the familiar Jacksonian pattern of war, treaty, and removal—although not always in that order. Following the Whitman Massacre and resulting Cayuse War (1847–1855), Anglo-American settlers formed volunteer militias to fight Natives and defend their land claims. In the meantime, Indian commissioners negotiated with ostensible tribal leaders to remove Natives to reservations, open land to settlers, and guarantee settler safety. For instance, in 1855 US troops defeated the Cayuses and forced them and other Columbia Plateau Native groups to relocate to the Umatilla Indian

Reservation. When settlers discovered gold deposits in southern Oregon's Rogue River Valley—once home to a fur trade middle ground similar to the lower Columbia—in the early 1850s, Anglo-American miners and farmers, many of them Donation Land Act claimants, collaborated to expel the remaining Rogue Natives from the area. When Rogue fighters resisted the obvious land grab, US troops joined forces with the volunteer militia to spark the Rogue River Wars (1855–1856) and the eventual removal of Rogue Natives to the Siletz and Grand Ronde reservations. Oregon superintendent of Indian affairs Joel Palmer, backed by a US presidential executive order, ordered the removal of many of Oregon's remaining Native groups without treaty stipulations. Like Saules in the early 1840s, some Natives had attempted to join the Anglo-American settlers and subsist as yeoman farmers. By the late 1850s, however, the threat of white militias had forced most Native farmers to seek the protection and safety of reservations.[14]

Mixed-race Oregon residents did not fare much better in the 1850s, and they too were subjected to the settler colonialist logic of exclusion and removal. In 1855 the territorial legislature passed a law denying citizenship to mixed raced men, including those with white fathers able to claim under the Donation Land Act. Framers of Oregon's state constitution reaffirmed this ban two years later.[15] Moreover, Oregon's embrace of Indian removal left the French-Indian families of Willamette Valley in a quandary. While some remained in French Prairie, many French-Indian families elected to join their maternal relatives at various Indian reservations in western and eastern Oregon, Washington, Idaho, and Montana. This severed the continuity of their original community; those families who relocated to reservations developed stronger connections to Native culture and traditions, while those who remained in the Willamette Valley were increasingly drawn into Anglo-American society.[16]

With Saules and Oregon's color line at the center of this narrative, a different kind of Oregon Trail story emerges. Considering Oregon's historically small black population—and unlikely future prospects for significant black immigration—the members of Oregon's body politic pursued racial exclusion with a zeal that some modern observers find strange. Yet an examination of Saules's life within the context of antebellum American imperialism and settler colonialism provides an opportunity to historicize white supremacy and gain some understanding of why settlers deemed Saules and others black residents dangerous subjects. Saules lived in Oregon at a time when

Anglo-Americans conquered the region. These were people who had difficulty imagining that racial difference would not lead to violent social divisions. For the majority of them, the creation of their ideal settler community
required the marginalization and often the removal of people they marked
as nonwhite. Their racialist views compelled them to see black people not as
fellow colonizers but as a threat to colonization itself. Therefore, the color line
in Oregon marked a distinction between the colonizers and the colonized.

At the same time, Saules's struggles and successes shed light on how the
Americanization of Oregon affected ordinary people of color living in the
region, particularly those who found themselves pushed to the periphery of
Anglo-American settler society. Saules's life also calls attention to the various
strategies and tactics he employed to resist marginalization. Saules initially
came to the Pacific Northwest as an agent of empire and aspiring colonist. But
Saules was a colonist on the terms of the multiethnic fur trade with its permeable color line. The economic colonialists of the fur trade operated under
a logic of exploitation of the colonized (meaning indigenous communities)
rather than a logic of removal. This was a world Saules fully understood and
to which he could adapt. When the Anglo-American setters arrived, Saules
attempted to join them until it became apparent that his skin color would
make him a permanent outsider. But even after his exile from the Willamette
Valley, Saules continued to employ various means to participate in, profit
from, and at times even resist the new settler social order. The forces of colonization and racial exclusion were overwhelming, however, and Saules ultimately failed to maintain his position among the colonizers.

In recent years, Oregon's early black exclusion laws have received attention as the state experiences another wave of relocation-based population
growth. Most Oregonians, when they learn about the state's past, are rightfully embarrassed, and some are moved to reflect on the laws' lingering impact
on contemporary racial demographics. Yet the laws banning black immigration were indifferently enforced and subject to challenges. And regardless of
their significant symbolic power, a small number of black people defied the
laws and continued to move to Oregon to make better lives for themselves.
With the ratification of the Fourteenth and Fifteenth Amendments to the US
Constitution, black exclusion became illegal and black men could theoretically vote in elections and participate in the legal system, although Oregon
did not strike the law from its state constitution until 1926.

But it was not the black exclusion laws of 1844, 1849, and 1857 alone, or even the denial of black citizenship, that made Oregon a white man's country. Instead, it was ultimately land policy—epitomized by the 1850 Donation Land Act—that had the longest and deepest impact. Historian and educator Darrell Millner called the Donation Land Act "by far the most devastating anti-black law passed during this era."[17] As historian William Robbins has observed, "Until the onset of the railroad era in the 1870s, the Donation Land Law had a greater influence in shaping the course of Oregon history than any other event or legislative enactment." In the nineteenth century, the notion of extending property rights—and in particular land rights—to nonelite citizens was crucial to Jeffersonian and Jacksonian democracy, the market economy, and the settler colonialist project itself. But the preservation of landed independence for Anglo-American settlers also required the legal protection of a state apparatus, something Oregon settlers were quick to develop. Yet even before the overland immigrants arrived in the Pacific Northwest, Oregon boosters and soon-to-be settlers devised and refined a system, eventually coupled with Indian removal, through which they could expropriate and redistribute land with a complete disregard for the previous inhabitants they displaced or dispossessed. But such an ambitious system required more legal and military muscle than the provisional government could muster. Therefore, Oregon politicians and elites urged the US government to enshrine and enforce it. The US government, in turn, had a vested interest in the establishment of an Anglo-American community in the region, even though the law violated federal policy by allowing for the extinguishment of Indian title without purchase or treaty.

As early settler land policy gave way to the Donation Land Act and Indian removal, the redistribution of land became explicitly race-based and the land claims themselves racialized as white spaces. While Saules once thought he could join the nascent Anglo-American settler community in Oregon, this legal manifestation of the color line made his goal even more unlikely. The distribution of free land to settlers was born of a populist impulse, but the egalitarianism of Jacksonian democracy was inseparable from its attendant white supremacy. Indeed, for a community that conceived of human difference, social divisions, and inequality in racial terms, only a racially homogenous society could be truly free and democratic. This study contains several examples of displacement, most involving members of the previous multiethnic social order such as Native people; Methodist missionaries; HBC employees; and, of course, Saules himself. Yet those members of the middle ground whom Anglo-American settlers recognized as white could rejoin settler society as long as they accepted American hegemony. This was never a possibility for blacks or the Native people living in the region in the nineteenth century, as any further enlargement of the idea of whiteness remained closed to them.[18] American settlers used legal means to draw a color line that helped dismantle any last remnants of the middle ground and ensured that Oregon's white citizens would control the distribution of land and, by extension, the distribution of wealth and power.

The land-centered, race-based settler colonialist project was remarkably successful in the Pacific Northwest, and Oregon remained essentially a white man's country for several generations. In addition to black people, many racial and ethnic groups, such as Chinese, Japanese, and Mexicans, also faced exclusion and dislocation in Oregon, and Native groups have been engaged in a long struggle for self-determination, economic justice, civil rights, and tribal recognition. In the nineteenth and twentieth centuries, many Oregon residents embraced nativism as a bulwark against unwanted immigration, and in the 1920s, the Ku Klux Klan gained considerable power as a mainstream political organization. Only the exigencies of the war effort in the 1940s and a demand for labor forced Oregonians to relax their exclusionary posture somewhat.

Despite the illegality of black exclusion laws following the end of the Civil War, Oregon remained a place where many black people did not feel welcome. The black people who did live in Portland were marginalized and often experienced residential isolation. As a potent symbol of this fact, Oregon did not officially ratify the Fifteenth Amendment, which granted voting rights to adult black males, until 1959. Oregon's black population remained small—less than two thousand people—until the United States entered World War II, and an enormous need for workers to staff Oregon's shipyards brought over fifteen thousand black people to the lower Columbia. Yet these black laborers and their families encountered a racial atmosphere in Oregon that rivaled the Jim Crow South. Because of this, many black people left Oregon following the war, and those who remained struggled to find adequate housing, schools, and economic opportunities. And once again, land policy emerged as a means of black exclusion. In the city of Portland, banks and real estate companies engaged in a process known as redlining, creating real estate covenants that

excluded nonwhite home buyers from all but the least desirable neighborhoods. Because of these practices, by 1960, 66 percent of Oregon's 18,133
black residents were confined to the Portland Albina District, a two-and-a-
half square mile area with substandard housing, resource-starved schools,
poor environmental protections, and discriminatory policing.[19]

In the 1960s, long before the new western historians began writing about
westward expansion in terms of American conquest and colonization, many
black residents in Portland's Albina District interpreted racial segregation
and isolation of the color line in colonial terms. Following the 1967 Albina
Riot, Frank Fair, a young black activist, drew a colonial analogy to explain
his generation's militancy: "They come to realize that if Albina is going to be
categorized as a colony, something separate and foreign from the city, they'll
have to deal with their problems on those terms."[20] Fair was referring to the
growing tendency of black militants to view their struggles as part of a global
postwar decolonization movement aligned with liberation efforts in Africa,
the Caribbean, and the Middle East. Anticolonial theorist Frantz Fanon, in
particular, was a major influence on the Black Power movement in Portland
and elsewhere. In their study on discriminatory policing in Portland, Leanne
C. Serbulo and Karen J. Gibson wrote how black residents in inner-city neighborhoods throughout the United States saw their communities as colonized
spaces "dependent on outsiders for political and economic resources and
subject to the authority of white-dominated institutions such as the school
district, police, and welfare bureaucracy."[21] The colonial model led black activists in Portland and elsewhere to reject liberal assimilation and integration in
favor of advocacy of the redistribution of economic and political power, self-
sufficiency, and self-determination. This thread in the black freedom movement later gave rise to Portland groups like the Black United Front, which
used direct action to affect social change, especially in regard to education and
police brutality.[22]

Even with massive waves of gentrification in early twenty-first-century
Portland, postwar patterns of racial segregation in Portland remain clearly
visible, and many critics of gentrification argue that major financial invest-
ments in traditionally black neighborhoods—well intentioned as they may
be—have actually resulted in the displacement of nonwhite residents and
a resegregation of the city. Despite the fact that most modern Oregonians
disavow the notion of race as a biological determinant of behavior, Oregon
remains one of the whitest states in an American West increasingly defined

by racial diversity. The color line remains, particularly in regard to education, housing, law enforcement, mass incarceration, political representation, and distribution of wealth.

But like Saules in 1841, many people of various ethnic backgrounds have continued to come and live in Oregon despite these challenges. They have come for many different reasons and, like Saules, have often had to find creative ways to navigate and confront racial prejudice in the region and assert their Fourth of July rights to life, liberty, and the pursuit of happiness. Despite the impact of gentrification, Oregon's black population is actually growing. Many black Portlanders have challenged conventional wisdom and media coverage about the "whitening" of Portland to insist that the local black community is instead evolving and flourishing.[23] In addition, Native people in Oregon have defied the expectations of early Anglo-American settlers and missionaries. According to the 2010 US Census, Oregon is home to 109,223 people who identify as American Indian or Alaskan Native. Moreover, Oregon residents who identify outside the category of American whiteness have also been a part of a crucial process of mutual cultural transmission that has continually challenged Oregon's reputation for racial homogeneity, suggesting that Oregon's middle ground has never gone away in its entirety. They have also forced Oregonians to confront its history of colonialism, white supremacy, economic injustice, and other dangerous subjects.

Notes

INTRODUCTION

1 "Sen. Pramila Jayapal—Washington State Senate Democrats—Jayapal Initiates First-Ever State Review of Racist Geographic Names." http://sdc.wastateleg. org/jayapal/2016/03/31/jayapal-initiates-first-ever-state-review-of-racist-geographic-names/ (accessed August 29, 2016).

2 Pramila Jayapal, "Guest Editorial: We Must Do More to Change Racist Geographic Place Names in Our National Parks," *The Stranger*. http://www. thestranger.com/blogs/slog/2015/11/12/23140108/guest-editorial-we-must-do-more-to-change-racist-geographic-place-names-in-our-national-parks (accessed August 31, 2016).

3 For scholarly studies on the development of Jim Crow stereotypes in nineteenth-century minstrelsy, see Stephen Johnson, ed., *Burnt Cork: Traditions and Legacies of Blackface Minstrelsy* (Amherst: University of Massachusetts Press, 2012); Eric Lott, *Love and Theft: Blackface Minstrelsy and the American Working Class: Blackface Minstrelsy and the American Working Class* (New York: Oxford University Press, 1993).

4 In his 1987 book *Reach of Tide, Ring of History*, Sam McKinney claimed Jim Crow Point was named for James D. Saules. This was probably based on Mildred Colbert's claim in historian Lucile McDonald's 1966 book *Coast Country*. Mildred Colbert, a collector of pioneer lore, told McDonald that Saules was the first settler on Jim Crow Point. Sam McKinney, *Reach of Tide, Ring of History: A Columbia River Voyage* (Portland: Oregon Historical Society Press, 1987); Lucile Saunders McDonald, *Coast Country: A History of Southwest Washington*, (Portland, OR: Binfords & Mort, 1966).

5 "Jim Saules, Not Jim Crow," http://www.chinookobserver.com/co/local-news/20160419/jim-saules-not-jim-crow (accessed November 17, 2016).

6 According to Natalie St. John of the *Chinook Observer*, the theory that Jim Crow Point was named for an abundance of crows is based on an early 1900s letter written by Nellie Megler, the wife of Brookfield founder Joseph G. Megler. Andrew Emlen, a local bird watcher, disputes this notion. St. John, "Jim Saules, Not Jim Crow."

7 "Commissioners Support Change of Jim Crow Names," *The Wahkiakum County Eagle*, http://www.waheagle.com/story/2016/05/12/news/

commissioners-support-change-of-jim-crow-names/11411.html (accessed September 2, 2016).

8 St. John, "Jim Saules, Not Jim Crow."

9 "Brookfield Names Will Replace Jim Crow," *The Daily Astorian*, http://www. dailyastorian.com/Local_News/20160602/brookfield-names-will-replace-jim-crow (accessed August 29, 2016).

10 Charles Melville Scammon, "Pioneer Nig Saul," in *The Overland Monthly*, ed. Bret Harte (A. Roman & Company, 1875), 273.

11 Lucile McDonald, "Cape Disappointment's First Settler," *Seattle Times*, November 22, 1964, Sunday edition, Sunday magazine, 4.

12 Hubert Howe Bancroft and Frances Fuller Victor, *History of Oregon*, vol. 1 (History Company, 1886), 284.

13 John Hope Franklin and Alfred A. Moss, *From Slavery to Freedom: A History of African-Americans*, 7th ed. (New York: Knopf, 1994), 146–152.

14 Although dated in some respects, Eugene H. Berwanger's 1967 work on this subject remains a useful text. Eugene H. Berwanger, *The Frontier against Slavery: Western Anti-Negro Prejudice and the Slavery Extension Controversy* (University of Illinois Press, 2002).

15 Peter Hardeman Burnett, *Recollections and Opinions of an Old Pioneer* (New York: D. Appleton, 1880), 150.

16 Ibid., 219.

17 Ibid.

18 Elizabeth McLagan and Oregon Black History Project, *A Peculiar Paradise: A History of Blacks in Oregon, 1778–1940* (Georgian Press, 1980), 29.

19 Postcolonial theory is obviously instructive here, particularly Homi K. Bhaba's discussion of concepts like colonial ambivalence, mimicry, and third spaces. Frantz Fanon had earlier developed the concepts of racial imitation and appropriation in a colonial context. Homi K. Bhabha, *The Location of Culture* (New York: Psychology Press, 1994); Frantz Fanon, *Black Skin, White Masks*, trans. Richard Philcox, rev. ed. (Berkeley, CA.: Grove Press, 2008).

20 Roxanne Dunbar-Ortiz, *An Indigenous Peoples' History of the United States* (Beacon Press, 2015), 2. For an example of recent scholarship on settler colonialism, see the following: James Belich, *Replenishing the Earth: The Settler Revolution and the Rise of the Angloworld* (Oxford University Press, 2011); Walter L. Hixson, *American Settler Colonialism: A History* (New York: Palgrave Macmillan, 2013); Margaret D. Jacobs, *White Mother to a Dark Race: Settler Colonialism, Maternalism, and the Removal of Indigenous Children in the American West and Australia, 1880–1940* (University of Nebraska Press, 2011); Lorenzo Veracini, *Settler Colonialism: A Theoretical Overview* (Palgrave Macmillan, 2010); L. Veracini, *The Settler Colonial Present* (New York: Palgrave Macmillan, 2015); Patrick Wolfe, "Settler Colonialism and the Elimination of the Native," *Journal of Genocide Research* 8, no. 4 (2006): 387–409; Patrick Wolfe, *Traces of History: Elementary Structures of Race* (London: Verso Books, 2016).2015

21 James Belich, *Replenishing the Earth: The Settler Revolution and the Rise of the Anglo World* (Oxford: Oxford University Press, 2011), 149.

22 Ibid., 181.

23 Michael Omi and Howard Winant, *Racial Formation in the United States: From the 1960s to the 1990s* (New York: Routledge, 1994), 55.

24 Colette Guillaumin, *Racism, Sexism, Power and Ideology* (New York: Routledge, 2002), 61.

25 Wolfe, "Settler Colonialism," 387.

26 Patrick Wolfe, "Race and Racialisation: Some Thoughts," *Postcolonial Studies* 5, no. 1 (2002): 59.

27 Ibid., 58.

28 Richard White, *The Middle Ground: Indians, Empires, and Republics in the Great Lakes Region, 1650–1815* (Cambridge: Cambridge University Press, 2011), x.

29 White originally used the term to describe the common world shared for over 150 years by French-speaking fur industry workers and Algonquians in the region around the Great Lakes. The notion that the Oregon Country was a cultural "middle ground" during the fur trade period (1820s-1840s) is somewhat controversial among historians. Regarding the Oregon Country, Gray H. Whaley insists that "nothing as elaborate or coherent as a syncretic middle-ground culture developed." Yet Whaley also admits that "colonials and Natives did have to meet each other 'halfway' with their diplomacy." Nathan Douthit, on the other hand, argues that the Oregon Country *was* a middle ground, even though it "lacked the depth of cultural exchanges described by White." I agree with Douthit's assessment that even though Oregon's middle-ground status was comparatively brief and had limited reach, it "involved trade, sexual relations, diplomatic negotiations, and legal issues similar to those that existed on the seventeenth- and eighteenth-century colonial frontier described by White." See Gray H. Whaley, *Oregon and the Collapse of Illahee: U.S. Empire and the Transformation of an Indigenous World, 1792–1859* (Chapel Hill: University of North Carolina Press, 2010), 57. Nathan Douthit, *Uncertain Encounters: Indians and Whites at Peace and War in Southern Oregon, 1820s–1860s* (Corvallis: Oregon State University Press, 2002), 2.

CHAPTER ONE

1 Charles Wilkes, *Narrative of the United States Exploring Expedition: During the Years 1838, 1839, 1840, 1841, 1842* (Philadelphia: C. Sherman & Sons, 1858), lii.

2 W. Jeffrey Bolster, *Black Jacks: African American Seamen in the Age of Sail* (Cambridge, MA: Harvard University Press, 1997), 5

3 George Simpson, "Secret Mission of Warre and Vavasour," *Washington Historical Quarterly* 3, no. 2 (April 1, 1912): 141.

4 Silas H. Smith, "Celebrations in Clatsop County," *Cumtux: Clatsop County Historical Society Quarterly* 24, no. 1 (Winter 2004): 40.

5 Bolster, *Black Jacks*, 165.

6 "James Saules, Crew List Index," n.d., Microfilm, reel #168; drawer -029, New Bedford (MA) Free Public Library Special Collections.

7 Ira Berlin, *Generations of Captivity: A History of African-American Slaves* (Cambridge, MA: Belknap Press of Harvard University Press, 2003), 104–105, 136–137.

8 "Saules—1810 United States Federal Census—Ancestry.com," http://search. ancestry.com/cgi-bin/sse.dll?db=1810usfedcenancestry&gss=sfs28_ms_db& new=1&rank=1&msT=1&gsln=Saules&gsln_x=0&MSAV=1&uidh=ehg (accessed February 16, 2016).

9 Ira Berlin, *Slaves Without Masters: The Free Negro in the Antebellum South* (New York: Pantheon Books, 1974), 136.

10 "Sauls—1870 United States Federal Census—Ancestry.com," http://search. ancestry.com/cgi-bin/sse.dll?db=1870usfedcen&gss=sfs28_ms_db&new=1 &rank=1&msT=1&gsln=sauls&gsln_x=1&_83004002=black&MSAV=0&ui dh=ehg (accessed February 16, 2016).

11 John Hope Franklin, *The Free Negro in North Carolina, 1790–1860* (New York: W. W. Norton, 1971), 7.

12 For instance, Astoria historian Russell Dark claimed Saules had been called a "runaway slave." See Russell Dark, "Information Sought on Black Navigator," *The Oregonian*, February 23, 1973.

13 Franklin, *The Free Negro in North Carolina*, 43.

14 John Hope Franklin and Alfred A. Moss, *From Slavery to Freedom: A History of African-Americans*, 7th ed. (New York: Knopf, 1994), 151–153.

15 James Oliver Horton and Lois E. Horton, *In Hope of Liberty: Culture, Community and Protest among Northern Free Blacks, 1700-1860* (Oxford: Oxford University Press, 1998), 107, 168.

16 Ibid., 165.

17 Solomon Northup, *Twelve Years a Slave* (Lexington, KY: SoHo Books, 2011).

18 Berlin, *Slaves Without Masters*, 309.

19 Although it is outside of the scope of this book, much the same can be said for how enslaved people carved out meaningful lives and created a lasting culture. Many historians have addressed the agency of enslaved people in antebellum America. For a small sample, see Eugene D. Genovese, *Roll, Jordan, Roll: The World the Slaves Made* (New York: Knopf Doubleday Publishing Group, 2011); Herbert Gutman, *The Black Family in Slavery and Freedom: 1750-1925* (New York: Pantheon Books, 1976); John W. Blassingame, *The Slave Community: Plantation Life in the Antebellum South* (Oxford: Oxford University Press, 1979); and Walter Johnson, *River of Dark Dreams: Slavery and Empire in the Cotton Kingdom* (Cambridge, MA: Harvard University Press, 2013).

20 Neil M. Howison, "Report of Lieutenant Neil M. Howison on Oregon, 1846: A Reprint," *Quarterly of the Oregon Historical Society* 14, no. 1 (March 1, 1913): 5.

21 Robert Austin Warner, *New Haven Negroes: A Social History* (New York: Arno Press, 1969), v.

22 Franklin and Moss, *From Slavery to Freedom*, 81.

23 Warner, *New Haven Negroes*, 15.

24 Ibid., 21.

25 Elizabeth J. Normen, *African American Connecticut Explored* (Middletown, CT: Wesleyan University Press, 2014), 57.

26 Eric Jay Dolin, *Leviathan: The History of Whaling in America* (New York: W. W. Norton, 2008), 206.

27 Edward C. Barnard, *Naked and a Prisoner: Captain Edward C. Barnard's Narrative of Shipwreck in Palau, 1832–1833* (Sharon, MA.: Kendall Whaling Museum, 1980).

28 Martha S. Putney, *Black Sailors: Afro-American Merchant Seamen and Whalemen Prior to the Civil War*, Contributions in Afro-American and African Studies, no. 103 (New York: Greenwood Press, 1987), 52.

29 Mary Malloy, *African American in the Maritime Trades: A Guide to Resources in New England* (Sharon, MA: Kendall Whaling Museum, 1991), 1.

30 Nathaniel Philbrick, *Sea of Glory: America's Voyage of Discovery: The U.S. Exploring Expedition, 1838–1842* (New York: Penguin, 2004), xxiv.

31 For examples of contemporary studies of the role of race in *Moby-Dick*, see Fred V. Bernard, "The Question of Race in Moby-Dick," *Massachusetts Review* 43, no. 3 (2002): 384–404; Valerie M. Babb, *Whiteness Visible: The Meaning of Whiteness in American Literature* (New York: NYU Press, 1998); Elizabeth Schultz, "Visualizing Race: Images of Moby-Dick," *Leviathan* 3, no. 1 (May 29, 2013): 31–60.

32 Herman Melville, *Moby Dick* (Toronto: Bantam Books, 1981), 186–193.

33 Ibid., 308–315.

34 Bolster, *Black Jacks*, 161–162.

35 Dolin, *Leviathan*, 273.

36 Alexander Starbuck, *History of the American Whale Fishery* (Castle, 1989), 298–299.

37 Henry J. Dally, E. F. Murray, and Hubert Howe Bancroft, *Narrative of His Life, and Events in Cal. since 1843. Henry J. Dally.* (Manuscript, Bancroft Collection, University of California, Berkeley, 1878) 5–9.

38 Bolster, *Black Jacks*, 162.

39 Berlin, *Generations of Captivity*, 107.

40 Ibid.

41 Bolster, *Black Jacks*, 70.

42 Wilkes, *Narrative of the United States Exploring Expedition*, xxxiii–lvi.

43 Philbrick, *Sea of Glory*, 293.

44 Bolster, *Black Jacks*, 158.

45 Ibid., 4.

46 Ibid., 161.

47 Ibid., 176.

48 Martha S. Putney, *Black Sailors: Afro-American Merchant Seamen and Whalemen Prior to the Civil War* (New York: Greenwood Press, 1987), 2.

49 Ibid., 120.

50 Bolster, *Black Jacks*, 235.

51 Ibid., 77.

52 Ibid., 168–169.

53 Richard Henry Dana, *Two Years Before the Mast: A Personal Narrative* (New York: Houghton Mifflin Company, 1911), 9; William Hussey Macy, *There She Blows! Or The Log Of The Arethusa* (Boston: Lee & Shepard, 1877), 39.

54 George Musalas Colvocoresses, *Four Years in the Government Exploring Expedition: Commanded by Captain Charles Wilkes, to the Island of Madeira, Cape Verd Island, Brazil.* (New York: J. M. Fairchild, 1855), 56.

55 William Ragan Stanton, *The Great United States Exploring Expedition of 1838–1842* (Berkeley: University of California Press, 1975), 112.

56 Charles Erskine, *Twenty Years Before the Mast: With the More Thrilling Scenes and Incidents While Circumnavigating the Globe Under the Command of the Late Admiral Charles Wilkes, 1838–1842,* (Chicago: Lakeside, 2006.), 79.

57 Bolster, *Black Jacks,* 168.

58 Scammon, "Pioneer Nig Saul," 275.

59 Barbara Tomblin, *Bluejackets and Contrabands: African Americans and the Union Navy* (University Press of Kentucky, 2009), 17.

60 Bolster, *Black Jacks,* 31.

61 Smith, "Celebrations in Clatsop County," 40.

62 Stanton, *The Great United States Exploring Expedition,* 162.

63 Erskine, *Twenty Years Before the Mast,* 190.

64 Dena J. Epstein, *Sinful Tunes and Spirituals: Black Folk Music to the Civil War* (Champaign: University of Illinois Press, 2003), 113–114.

65 Northup, *Twelve Years a Slave,* 216.

66 Epstein, *Sinful Tunes and Spirituals,* 114.

67 Bolster, *Black Jacks,* 34.

68 Baptist, *The Half Has Never Been Told,* 166.

69 Bolster, *Black Jacks,* 217.

70 Ibid.

71 Paul Gilroy, *The Black Atlantic: Modernity and Double Consciousness* (Cambridge, MA: Harvard University Press, 1993), 4.

72 Bolster, *Black Jacks,* 35.

73 Ibid., 42.

74 Smith, "Celebrations in Clatsop County," 40.

75 Scammon, "Pioneer Nig Saul," 273.

76 Ibid.

77 Jean Brownell, "Negroes in Oregon Before the Civil War" (unpublished manuscript, Oregon Historical Society, Portland), 30.

78 Gilroy, *The Black Atlantic,* ix.

79 Beatriz Gallotti Mamigonian and Karen Racine, eds., *The Human Tradition in the Black Atlantic, 1500–2000* (Lanham, MD: Rowman & Littlefield, 2009), 2–3.

80 Bolster, *Black Jacks,* 192–193.

81 Ibid., 2.

82 Elijah White, *Ten Years in Oregon: Travels and Adventures of Dr. E. White and Lady, West of the Rocky Mountains* (Ithaca, NY: Andrus, Gauntlett, & Co), 111–112.

83 Bolster, *Black Jacks,* 194.

84 Michael Schoeppner, "Peculiar Quarantines: The Seamen Acts and Regulatory Authority in the Antebellum South," *Law and History Review* 31, no. 3 (August 2013): 565.

85 Ibid., 560.

CHAPTER TWO

1 Wilkes, *Narrative of the United States Exploring Expedition*, xxv.

2 Stanton, *The Great United States Exploring Expedition*, 16.

3 Ibid., 200.

4 Wilkes, *Narrative of the United States Exploring Expedition*, xxviii.

5 Ibid.

6 Stanton, *The Great United States Exploring Expedition*, 4–5.

7 Earl Spencer Pomeroy, *The Pacific Slope: A History of California, Oregon, Washington, Idaho, Utah, and Nevada* (Reno: University of Nevada Press, 1965), 58.

8 Ibid.

9 "An Address Delivered By Daniel Webster," *Granite Monthly: A New Hampshire Magazine* 5, 1881, 9.

10 Stanton, *The Great United States Exploring Expedition*, 33.

11 Ibid., 25.

12 Ibid.

13 For an extended discussion on racial ideology in the early US Republic, see Reginald Horsman, *Race and Manifest Destiny: The Origins of American Racial Anglo-Saxonism* (Cambridge, MA: Harvard University Press, 1981), 98–115.

14 Stanton, *The Great United States Exploring Expedition*, 29.

15 Ibid.

16 Ray Allen Billington and Martin Ridge, *Westward Expansion: A History of the American Frontier* (Albuquerque: University of New Mexico Press, 2001), 208.

17 Jeremiah N. Reynolds, *Address on the Subject of a Surveying and Exploring Expedition to the Pacific Ocean and South Seas: Delivered in the Hall of Representatives on the Evening of April 3, 1836* (New York: Harper & Brothers, 1836), 297.

18 Henry Nash Smith, *Virgin Land: The American West as Symbol and Myth*, 2nd ed. (Cambridge, MA: Harvard University Press, 2007), 23.

19 Ibid., 27.

20 Constance Bordwell, "Delay and Wreck of the Peacock: An Episode in the Wilkes Expedition," *Oregon Historical Quarterly* 92, no. 2 (July 1, 1991): 120.

21 D. Graham Burnett, "Hydrographic Discipline among the Navigators: Charting an 'Empire of Commerce and Science' in the Nineteenth-Century Pacific," in *The Imperial Map: Cartography and the Mastery of Empire*, ed. James R. Akerman (University of Chicago Press, 2009), 201.

22 Ibid., 202.

23 Ibid., 216.

24 Benedict Anderson, *Imagined Communities: Reflections on the Origin and Spread of Nationalism* (London: Verso, 2006), 173.

25 James R. Akerman, *The Imperial Map: Cartography and the Mastery of Empire* (Chicago: University of Chicago Press, 2009), 185.

26 Michel Foucault, *Power/Knowledge* (New York: Pantheon Books, 1980), 63–77.

27 Erskine, *Twenty Years Before the Mast*, 116.

28 Ibid., 117.

29 Philbrick, *Sea of Glory*, 196.

30 William Reynolds, *The Private Journal of William Reynolds: United States Exploring Expedition, 1838–1842* (New York: Penguin, 2004).

31 Stanton, *The Great United States Exploring Expedition*, 200.

32 Philbrick, *Sea of Glory*, 211.

33 Stanton, *The Great United States Exploring Expedition*, 211.

34 Philbrick, *Sea of Glory*, 229.

35 Stanton, *The Great United States Exploring Expedition*, 237–239.

36 Ibid., 244.

37 Reynolds, *The Private Journal of William Reynolds*, 237.

38 Herman Joseph Viola and Carolyn Margolis, *Magnificent Voyagers: The U.S. Exploring Expedition, 1838-1842* (Washington, DC: Smithsonian, 1985), 221.

39 Anne F. Hyde, *Empires, Nations, and Families: A History of the North American West, 1800–1860* (Lincoln: University of Nebraska Press, 2011), 122.

40 James P Ronda, *Astoria & Empire* (Lincoln: University of Nebraska Press, 1990), 115.

41 Charles Wilkes, *Narrative of the United States Exploring Expedition: During the Years 1838, 1839, 1840, 1841, 1842, Volume Four* (Lea and Blanchard, 1845), 293.

42 Ibid., 305.

43 Ibid., 417.

44 Richard White, *The Roots of Dependency: Subsistence, Environment, and Social Change among the Choctaws, Pawnees, and Navajos* (Lincoln: University of Nebraska Press, 1988), xv.

45 Stanton, *The Great United States Exploring Expedition*, 255.

46 Wilkes, *Narrative of the United States Exploring Expedition, Volume Four*, 332.

47 Melinda Marie Jetté, *At the Hearth of the Crossed Races: A French-Indian Community in Nineteenth-Century Oregon, 1812–1859* (Corvallis: Oregon State University Press, 2015), 54.

48 Adele Perry, "Reproducing Colonialism in British Columbia, 1849–1871," in *Bodies in Contact: Rethinking Colonial Encounters in World History*, ed. Tony Ballantyne and Antoinette Burton (Durham, NC: Duke University Press, 2005), 149.

49 Jetté, *At the Hearth of the Crossed Races*, 140.

50 Ibid., 51.

51 Ibid., 175–178.

52 Melinda Marie Jetté has provided a fascinating and likely definitive account of French Prairie before and after the rise of American settler colonialism in the Willamette Valley. She convincingly dismantles the long-standing historical trope that the French-Indian community challenged Anglo-American settlers out of fealty to John McLoughlin and the Hudson's Bay Company. See Jetté, *At the Hearth of the Crossed Races*.

53 For more information on the Flathead Delegation, see Albert Furtwangler, *Bringing Indians to the Book* (Seattle: University of Washington Press, 2005).

54 Ibid., 64.

55 For a further discussion of the outbreak, which contemporary observers often described as "intermittent fever" or "fever and ague," see Robert Boyd, *The Coming of the Spirit of Pestilence: Introduced Infectious Diseases and Population Decline among Northwest Indians, 1774–1874* (Seattle: University of Washington Press, 1999).

56 Jetté, *At the Hearth of the Crossed Races*, 139.

57 Ibid., 74–75.

58 Cornelius J. Brosnan, *Jason Lee, Prophet of the New Oregon* (Rutland, VT: Academy Books, 1985), 78.

59 Jetté, *At the Hearth of the Crossed Races*, 131.

60 Oregon Pioneer Association Reunion, *Transactions of the Eighth Annual Reunion of the Oregon Pioneer Association* (Salem, OR: E. M. Waite, 1881), 21.

61 Edmond S. Meany, "Diary of Wilkes in the Northwest," *Washington Historical Quarterly* 16, no. 1 (January 1, 1925): 51.

62 Wilkes, *Narrative of the United States Exploring Expedition*, vol. 4, 1845, 352.

63 Ibid.

64 John D. Unruh, *The Plains Across: The Overland Emigrants and the Trans-Mississippi West, 1840–60* (University of Illinois Press, 1993), 119.

65 Wilkes, *Narrative of the United States Exploring Expedition*, vol. 4, 1845, 358.

66 Bordwell, "Delay and Wreck of the Peacock," 145.

67 Wilkes, *Narrative of the United States Exploring Expedition*, vol. 4, 1845, 347.

68 Meany, "Diary of Wilkes in the Northwest," 46.

69 Wilkes, *Narrative of the United States Exploring Expedition*, vol.4, 1845, 353.

70 William L. Hudson, *Journal of William L. Hudson, Comdg. U.S. Ship Peacock, on the Vessels Attached to the South Sea*, vol. 2, 357–360, Microfilm Cabinet, drawer 1C—Q115.U46H83 1950, American Museum of Natural History Archives, New York, NY; Philbrick, *Sea of Glory*, 272.

71 Stanton, *The Great United States Exploring Expedition*, 253.

72 Ibid.

73 Ibid.

74 Charles Wilkes, *Voyage Round the World: Embracing the Principal Events of the Narrative of the United States Exploring Expedition* (G. P. Putnam, 1851), 574.

75 Wilkes, *Narrative of the United States Exploring Expedition*, vol. 5, 1845, 151.

76 Philbrick, *Sea of Glory*, 304.

77 Ibid., 341.

78 Warren Johnson joined the US Ex. Ex. during its 1841 stop in Oahu, so he had not sailed long before he deserted. According to the 1842 census, Warren Johnson seemed to prosper in the Oregon Country; he had an Indian servant and possessed considerable grain, livestock, and three horses. See "Elijah White's 1842 Oregon Census," MSS 1, Oregon Historical Society Microfilm, Portland.

79 Russell Dark, *Bar Sinister: The Story of the Columbia River Bar Pilots* (unpublished manuscript), 6, Clatsop County Historical Society, Astoria, OR.

80 Wilkes, *Narrative of the United States Exploring Expedition*, vol. 1, xxxiii–lvi.

81 Bolster, *Black Jacks*, 29.

82 Ibid., 213.

83 Schoeppner, "Peculiar Quarantines," 754.

84 Quintard Taylor, *In Search of the Racial Frontier: African Americans in the American West, 1528–1990* (W. W. Norton, 1999), 48.

85 Hudson, *Journal of William L. Hudson,* vol. 2, 380.

86 Gordon B. Dodds, *Oregon: A History* (New York: W. W. Norton, 1977), 68.

87 Bordwell, "Delay and Wreck of the Peacock," 178.

88 Scammon, "Pioneer Nig Saul," 273.

89 Ibid.

90 McDonald, "Cape Disappointment's First Settler," 4.

91 Herbert Hunt and Floyd C. Kaylor, *Washington, West of the Cascades: Historical and Descriptive; the Explorers, the Indians, the Pioneers, the Modern* (Chicago: S. J. Clarke, 1917), 436.

92 William Bittle Wells and Lute Pease, *Pacific Monthly,* vol. 6 (Pacific Monthly Pub. Co., 1900).

93 Daniel Lee and Joseph H. Frost, *10 Years in Oregon* (New York: J. Collard, 1844), 224.

94 Bruce McIntyre Watson, "Lives Lived West of the Divide: A Biographical Dictionary of Fur Traders Working West of the Rockies, 1793–1858," 989, http://www.lulu.com/shop/bruce-mcintyre-watson/lives-lived-west-of-the-divide-a-biographical-dictionary-of-fur-traders-working-west-of-the-rockies-1793-1858/ebook/product-20951764.html;jsessionid=A6B2B4ABA 128846DBE5D81F1E3BBD496 (accessed September 29, 2013).

95 E. W. Wright, *Lewis & Dryden's Marine History of the Pacific Northwest: An Illustrated Review of the Growth and Development of the Maritime Industry, from the Advent of the Earliest Navigators to the Present Time, with Sketches and Portraits of a Number of Well Known Marine Men* (Lewis & Dryden, 1895), 21.

96 Thomas Nelson Strong, *Cathlamet on the Columbia: Recollections of the Indian People and Short Stories of Early Pioneer Days in the Valley of the Lower Columbia River* (The Holly Press, 1906), 10.

97 Wright, *Lewis & Dryden's Marine History,* 21.

98 See the work of Gray H. Whaley for an in-depth discussion of the evolution of exogamous marriage, slavery, and prostitution in the lower Columbia region following the arrival of Euro-American explorers and the fur trade. Gray Whaley, "'Complete Liberty'? Gender, Sexuality, Race, and Social Change on the Lower Columbia River, 1805–1838," *Ethnohistory* 54, no. 4 (September 21, 2007): 669–695.

CHAPTER THREE

1 William G. Robbins, *Landscapes of Promise: The Oregon Story, 1800–1940* (Seattle: University of Washington Press, 1999), 72.

2 Robert Boyd and Robert Thomas Boyd, *People of The Dalles: The Indians of Wascopam Mission* (Lincoln: University of Nebraska Press, 2004), 235.

3 William Henry Gray, *A History of Oregon, 1792–1849: Drawn from Personal Observation and Authentic Information* (Portland, OR: Harris & Holman, 1870), 191.

4 White, *Ten Years in Oregon,* 232.

 5 "U.S., Atlantic Ports Seamen's Protection Certificates, 1792–1869," M2003, Roll 1, National Archives and Records Administration, Washington, DC.

 6 Hubert Howe Bancroft and Frances Fuller Victor, *History of Oregon*, vol. 1 (The History Company, 1886), 77.

 7 John Forsyth and William A. Slacum, "Slacum's Report on Oregon, 1836–7," *Quarterly of the Oregon Historical Society* 13, no. 2 (1912): 212.

 8 Boyd and Boyd, *People of The Dalles*, 309.

 9 A.B., "Rather beneath the Calling of a Worthy Act!," *Oregon Spectator*, October 14, 1847.

10 Berlin, *Slaves without Masters*, 66.

11 Ibid., 67.

12 Furtwangler, *Bringing Indians to the Book*, 27–28.

13 Mitchell Snay, *Gospel of Disunion: Religion and Separatism in the Antebellum South* (UNC Press Books, 2014), 128–129.

14 In American and black history, the term *Great Migration* is more commonly used to describe the mass movement of African Americans from the South to northern industrial cities during the early to mid-twentieth century. For an example of the term used in the context of the Oregon Trail, see Robbins, *Landscapes of Promise*, 72.

15 William G. Robbins, *Oregon: This Storied Land* (Portland: Oregon Historical Society Press, 2005), 44.

16 Charles Wilkes, "Report on the Territory of Oregon," *Quarterly of the Oregon Historical Society* 12, no. 3 (September 1, 1911): 291.

17 Ibid.

18 Quintard Taylor, "Slaves and Free Men: Blacks in the Oregon Country, 1840–1860," *Oregon Historical Quarterly* 83, no. 2 (July 1, 1982): 153–154.

19 John Mack Faragher, *Women and Men on the Overland Trail* (New Haven, CT: Yale University Press, 2001), 31.

20 David Alan Johnson, *Founding the Far West: California, Oregon, and Nevada, 1840–1890* (Berkeley: University of California Press, 1992), 8.

21 Robbins, *Oregon*, 43.

22 Fred S. Rolater, "The American Indian and the Origin of the Second American Party System," *Wisconsin Magazine of History* 76, no. 3 (1993): 180–203.

23 Ted Morgan, *Shovel of Stars: The Making of the American West 1800 to the Present* (New York: Simon and Schuster, 1996), 145.

24 Dorothy O. Johansen, *Empire of the Columbia: A History of the Pacific Northwest*, 2nd ed. (New York: Harper Collins, 1967), 255.

25 Oregon Pioneer Association, *Transactions of the Fifteenth Annual Reunion of the Oregon Pioneer Association*, (Portland, OR: Press of Geo. H. Himes,1887), 35.

26 Lee and Frost, *10 Years in Oregon*, 104–105.

27 Samuel T. McKean, "Memoirs of Samuel T. McKean," *Cumtux: Clatsop County Historical Society Quarterly* 13, no. 1 (Winter 1992): 3.

28 Ibid., 3–4.

29 Ibid., 6.

30 Johansen, *Empire of the Columbia*, 232.

31 Tom Chaffin, *Pathfinder: John Charles Frémont and the Course of American Empire* (London: Macmillan, 2004), 147.

32 Peter Hardeman Burnett, *Recollections and Opinions of an Old Pioneer* (New York: D. Appleton, 1880), 150.

33 Lorenzo Veracini, "Introducing," *Settler Colonial Studies* 1, no. 1 (2011): 3.

34 Lorenzo Veracini contends that settler colonists legitimate their sovereignty claims by positing their own de facto indigeneity. See Lorenzo Veracini, *Settler Colonialism: A Theoretical Overview* (Basingstoke, UK: Palgrave Macmillan, 2010), 18.

35 John O'Sullivan, "Annexation," *United States Magazine and Democratic Review* 17, no. 1 (August 1845): 5–10.

36 Thomas Jefferson, *Notes on the State of Virginia* (1785; Richmond, VA: J. W. Randolph, 1853), 55.

37 Horsman, *Race and Manifest Destiny*, 102.

38 Ibid., 10.

39 Ibid., 43–61.

40 Senator Benton, 29th Cong., 1st Sess, *Congressional Globe* (May 28, 1846), 917.

41 Ibid., 917–918.

42 Horsman, *Race and Manifest Destiny*, 205.

43 French Canadians and perhaps some mixed race people, however, were able to participate in the government. The ideas of whiteness and nonwhiteness are historical; they are never fixed and always subject to limited expansions and enlargements. Such enlargements were most often predicated on the embrace of white supremacy. See Nell Irvin Painter, *The History of White People* (New York: W. W. Norton, 2011); David R. Roediger, *The Wages of Whiteness: Race and the Making of the American Working Class* (New York: Verso, 1999).1999

44 Robert J. Loewenberg, "Creating a Provisional Government in Oregon: A Revision," *Pacific Northwest Quarterly* 68, no. 1 (January 1, 1977): 18.

45 Carlos Arnaldo Schwantes, *The Pacific Northwest: An Interpretive History*, rev. ed. (Lincoln: University of Nebraska Press, 2000), 114.

46 Melinda Marie Jetté has pointed out that the French Canadians were in favor of creating a provisional government. They simply wanted a government more amenable to their community interests than the one the Americans proposed. Jetté, *At the Hearth of the Crossed Races*, 169–173.

47 Ibid., 114.

48 Senator Lewis Linn's failed Oregon Bill had originally prescribed that Oregon adapt Iowa's laws, including the Northwest Ordinance. Ibid.

49 Robbins, *Landscapes of Promise*, 82.

50 Shannon Applegate, *Talking on Paper: An Anthology of Oregon Letters and Diaries* (Corvallis: Oregon State University Press, 1994), 19.

51 Ibid.

52 Johnson, *Founding the Far West*, 42.

53 Robbins, *Oregon*, 46.

54 Gray H. Whaley, *Oregon and the Collapse of Illahee: U.S. Empire and the Transformation of an Indigenous World, 1792–1859* (Chapel Hill: University of North Carolina Press, 2010), 161.

55 Ibid.

56 Dorothy Nafus Morrison, *Outpost: John McLoughlin & the Far Northwest* (Portland: Oregon Historical Society Press, 1999), 174–175.

57 Jetté, *At the Hearth of the Crossed Races*, 130.

58 At some point during the journey, many travelers became disenchanted with White, and the party split into two factions: one led by White and the other by Hastings. See David Lavender, *Westward Vision: The Story of the Oregon Trail* (Lincoln: University of Nebraska Press, 1985), 353–356.

59 Theodore Stern, *Chiefs and Change in the Oregon Country: Indian Relations at Fort Nez Percés, 1818–1855*, vol. 2 (Corvallis: Oregon State University Press, 1996), 131.

60 Johansen, *Empire of the Columbia*, 237.

61 As for the Presbyterians at the Columbia Plateau, Elijah White delivered a message from the American Board of Commissioners of Foreign Missions (ABCFM) to a bewildered Marcus Whitman, informing him that he must abandon his mission site at Waiilatpu, relocate to Chimakain, and make major personnel changes.

62 Stern, *Chiefs and Change in the Oregon Country*, 131.

63 Bancroft and Victor, *History of Oregon*, vol. 1, 274.

64 Historian Theodore Stern also suspected White's laws were inspired by his experience with Native people stealing goods and horses during his journey to Oregon in 1842. Stern, *Chiefs and Change in the Oregon Country*, 132.

65 Ibid., 133.

66 Alvin M. Josephy Jr., *The Nez Perce Indians and the Opening of the Northwest* (Boston: Mariner Books, 1997), 229.

67 "Laws of the Nez Perces." in *A History of Oregon, 1792–1849: Drawn from Personal Observation and Authentic Information*, by William Henry Gray (Portland, OR: Harris & Holman, 1870), 228.

68 Stern, *Chiefs and Change in the Oregon Country*, 136.

69 Ibid., 135.

70 Josephy, *The Nez Perce Indians*, 235.

71 Stern, *Chiefs and Change in the Oregon Country*, 139.

72 Bancroft and Victor, *History of Oregon*, vol. 1, 276–280.

73 Stern, *Chiefs and Change in the Oregon Country*, 160.

74 Ibid., 138.

CHAPTER FOUR

1 Josephy, *The Nez Perce Indians*, 239.

2 Bancroft and Victor, *History of Oregon*, vol. 1, 264.

3 *The Missouri Republican*, December 14, 1843.

4 Ibid.

5 Antebellum Americans' fears of the British backing Native and black fighters were rooted in collective memories of the forging of such alliances in the American Revolution and the War of 1812. See White, *The Middle Ground*; Daniel Walker Howe, *What Hath God Wrought: The Transformation of America, 1815–1848* (Oxford University Press, 2009), 74; and Gerald Horne, *Negro Comrades of the Crown: African Americans and the British Empire Fight the U.S. Before Emancipation* (New York: NYU Press, 2013).

6 "Documents," *Oregon Historical Quarterly* 4, no. 4 (December 1903): 405.

7 In his diary, Gustavus Hines refers to the horse theft victim as Winslow Anderson, although this does not line up with the details of Subagent White's version of the story. It is possible that Hines was mistaken or that he had misheard the story from his Clackamas informants. Historian Theodore Stern believed that the victim was Saules, and I follow his lead for the sake of narrative consistency and continuity. If Cockstock did steal that particular horse from Anderson and not Saules, this fact does not alter the chain of events that followed. See Stern, *Chiefs and Change in the Oregon Country*, 140.

8 Gustavus Hines, *Oregon, Its History, Condition and Prospects Containing a Description of the Geography, Climate and Productions, with Personal Adventures among the Indians during a Residence of the Author on the Plains Bordering the Pacific While Connected with the Oregon Mission* (New York: G. H. Derby, 1851), 144.

9 Ibid., 145.

10 *Boston* was a term many Native people used to refer to American settlers. Ibid.

11 "Elijah White's 1842 Oregon Census."

12 Hines, *Oregon*, 146.

13 Ibid.

14 Gray, *A History of Oregon, 1792–1849*, 252; Stern, *Chiefs and Change in the Oregon Country*, 151–152.

15 Gray, *A History of Oregon, 1792–1849*, 253.

16 Ibid.

17 US Congress, Senate, *Report of the Commissioner of Indian Affairs*, 28th Cong., 2d Sess., 1844, vol. 1, S.Doc. 1, serial 449, 502.

18 William Jeynes, *American Educational History: School, Society, and the Common Good* (Thousand Oaks, CA: SAGE Publications, 2007), 82.

19 Sallie Applegate Long, "Reminiscence of Early Days," in *The Oregon Native Son*, vol. 2 (Portland: Native Son Publishing, 1900), 394.

20 United States Office of Indian Affairs, *Annual Report of the Commissioner of Indian Affairs*, (Washington, DC: C. Alexander, Printer, 1844), 202.

21 Ibid., 200.

22 Morrison, *Outpost*, 432; Burnett, *Recollections and Opinions of an Old Pioneer*, 184.

23 United States Office of Indian Affairs, *Annual Report of the Commissioner of Indian Affairs*, 201.

24 Ibid.

25 Unfortunately, no minutes survived from this meeting, so it is unclear who actually attended. J. Neilson Barry, "The Champoeg Meeting of March 4, 1844," *Oregon Historical Quarterly* 38, no. 4 (December 1, 1937): 425–432.

26 It is worth noting that White's version was written shortly after the incident occurred, while William H. Willson's account was transcribed decades later by Willson's Yoncalla neighbor, Sallie Applegate Long.

27 United States Office of Indian Affairs, *Annual Report of the Commissioner of Indian Affairs*, 201.

28 Long, "Reminiscence of Early Days," 394.

29 United States Office of Indian Affairs, *Annual Report of the Commissioner of Indian Affairs*, 201.

30 Ibid.

31 In his history of Oregon, William H. Gray claimed that unnamed sources told him LeBreton had taken Cockstock into custody under armed guard and that the melee only occurred after Cockstock escaped. See Gray, *A History of Oregon, 1792–1849*, 371.

32 United States Office of Indian Affairs, *Annual Report of the Commissioner of Indian Affairs*, 201.

33 For Blanchet's version, see Francis Norbert Blanchet, *Historical Sketches of the Catholic Church in Oregon, During the Past Forty Years* (Portland, OR, 1878), 145–148.

34 Jetté, *At the Hearth of the Crossed Races*, 120–121.

35 Blanchet, *Historical Sketches of the Catholic Church in Oregon*, 145.

36 Ibid., 141.

37 Ibid., 146.

38 Ibid.

39 Ibid., 147.

40 Ibid.

41 Ibid.

42 Ibid., 148.

43 Ibid.

44 United States Office of Indian Affairs, *Annual Report of the Commissioner of Indian Affairs*, 204.

45 Robert H. Ruby and John A. Brown, *Indians of the Pacific Northwest: A History* (Norman: University of Oklahoma Press, 1988), 51.

46 Bancroft and Victor, *History of Oregon*, vol. 1, 283–284.

47 United States Office of Indian Affairs, *Annual Report of the Commissioner of Indian Affairs*, 204.

48 Bancroft and Victor, *History of Oregon*, vol. 1, 1888, 282.

49 Gray, *A History of Oregon, 1792–1849*, 241–248; Thomas C. McClintock, "James Saules, Peter Burnett, and the Oregon Black Exclusion Law of June 1844," *Pacific Northwest Quarterly* 86, no. 3 (July 1, 1995): 126–128.

50 Bancroft and Victor, *History of Oregon*, vol. 1, 285.

51 United States Office of Indian Affairs, *Annual Report of the Commissioner of Indian Affairs*, 1846, 182.

52 Ibid.

53 Bancroft and Victor, *History of Oregon*, vol. 1, 284.

54 Lawrence Clark Powell, *Philosopher Pickett: The Life and Writings of Charles Edward Pickett, Esq., of Virginia, Who Came Overland to the Pacific Coast in*

1842–43 and for Forty Years Waged War with Pen and Pamphlet against All Manner of Public Abuses in Oregon and California; Including Also Unpublished Letters Written by Him from Yerba Buena at the Time of the Conquest of California by the United States in 1846–47 (Berkeley: University of California Press,, 1942), 10, 18.

55 Various, *Quarterly of the Oregon Historical Society,* vol. 4, *March, 1903-December, 1903,* ed. Frederic George Young (2012), 390, http://www.gutenberg.org/ebooks/41493 (accessed April 10, 2017).

56 Michelle Alexander, *The New Jim Crow: Mass Incarceration in the Age of Colorblindness* (New York: The New Press, 2010), 117.

57 United States Office of Indian Affairs, *Annual Report of the Commissioner of Indian Affairs to the Secretary of the Interior for the Fiscal Year Ended . . .* (Washington, DC: US Government Printing Office, n.d.), 474.

58 Howe, *What Hath God Wrought,* 442.

59 Powell, *Philosopher Pickett,* 5.

60 Ibid., 28.

61 Ibid., 12.

62 Ibid., 13–14.

63 Ibid., 70.

64 Ibid., 92–96.

65 Ibid., 34.

66 Ibid., 39.

67 Charles Edward Pickett, *Address To The Veterans Of The Mexican War: Embodying A Historical Contrast Of The Two Great Political Parties Of The United States On Vital Issues* (San Francisco: Public Domain, 1880), 21.

68 Ibid.

69 Powell, *Philosopher Pickett,* 9.

70 Charles Edward Pickett, *Address of Charles E. Pickett to the California Legislature: Upon the Government Fee in the Public Domain—Intercommunication and Land Monopolies and Correlative Topics.* (Sacramento, CA.: Public Domain, 1874), 4.

71 Powell, *Philosopher Pickett,* 11–12.

72 Native adults and children were part of the Methodist missionaries' workforce and are accounted for in the missionaries' ledgers. See Whaley, *Oregon and the Collapse of Illahee,* 119.

73 Oregon Pioneer Association Reunion, *Transactions of the Eighth Annual Reunion of the Oregon Pioneer Association,* 21

74 Ibid.

75 La Fayette Grover, *The Oregon Archives: Including the Journals, Governors' Messages and Public Papers of Oregon, from the Earliest Attempt on the Part of the People to Form a Government, Down To, and Inclusive of the Session of the Territorial Legislature* (Salem, OR: Asahel. Bush, public printer, 1853).

76 Charles Henry Carey, "Diary of Rev. George Gary," *Quarterly of the Oregon Historical Society* 24, no. 1 (1923): 81.

77 Ibid.

78 Morrison, *Outpost,* 396.

79 C. E. Pickett, "Town Lots for Sale," *Oregon Spectator*, February 5, 1846, 3.

80 Peter H. Burnett, "Letter from Peter H. Burnett, Esq.," *Quarterly of the Oregon Historical Society* 24, no. 1 (1923): 105.

81 Ibid., 106.

82 Ibid., 106–7.

83 Gray, *A History of Oregon, 1792–1849*, 396.

84 McClintock, "James Saules, Peter Burnett, and the Oregon Black Exclusion Law of June 1844," 125.

85 Bancroft and Victor, *History of Oregon*, vol. 1, 429–430n8.

86 Burnett, *Recollections and Opinions of an Old Pioneer*, 213.

87 Ibid., 213–214.

88 Bancroft and Victor, *History of Oregon*, vol. 1, 284.

89 Works that have followed Frances Fuller Victor's lead in linking the Cockstock Affair with black exclusion include Taylor, "Slaves and Free Men"; McClintock, "James Saules, Peter Burnett, and the Oregon Black Exclusion Law of June 1844"; R. Gregory Nokes, *Breaking Chains: Slavery on Trial in the Oregon Territory* (Corvallis: Oregon State University Press, 2013); and Jetté, *At the Hearth of the Crossed Races*.

90 Burnett, *Recollections and Opinions of an Old Pioneer*, 213.

91 Elizabeth McLagan and Oregon Black History Project, *A Peculiar Paradise: A History of Blacks in Oregon, 1778–1940* (Athens, GA: Georgian Press, 1980), 29.

92 Burnett, *Recollections and Opinions of an Old Pioneer*, 221–222.

93 Alexis de Tocqueville, *Democracy in America*, vol. 1, *The Henry Reeve Text* (New York: Knopf, 1945), 327.

94 McLagan and Oregon Black History Project, *A Peculiar Paradise*, 29.

95 Oregon Pioneer Association Portland and Oregon Pioneer Association Reunion, *Transactions of the Annual Reunion of the Oregon Pioneer Association*, 1887, 35.

96 Article 4, Section 2, Clause 3: Missouri Constitution of 1820, ART. 3, SECS. 26–28, http://press-pubs.uchicago.edu/founders/documents/a4_2_3s12.html (accessed March 28, 2016).

97 Burnett, *Recollections and Opinions of an Old Pioneer*, 220.

98 Ibid.

99 Ibid., 221.

100 Peter Linebaugh and Marcus Rediker, *The Many-Headed Hydra: Sailors, Slaves, Commoners, and the Hidden History of the Revolutionary Atlantic* (New York: Verso, 2000), 213–214.

101 Thomas Paine, "American Crisis III," in *Collected Writings*, ed. Eric Foner, 137 (New York: Library of America, 1995).

102 Ira Berlin, *Generations of Captivity: A History of African-American Slaves* (Cambridge, MA: Belknap Press of Harvard University Press, 2003), 42.

103 Horne, *Negro Comrades of the Crown*, 82–83.

104 Kenneth W. Porter, ed., *The Black Seminoles: History of a Freedom-Seeking People* (Gainesville: University Press of Florida, 1996); John Missall and Mary

Lou Missall, *The Seminole Wars: America's Longest Indian Conflict* (Gainesville: University Press of Florida, 2004).

105 Horne, *Negro Comrades of the Crown*, 113.

106 *Sketch of the Seminole War, and Sketches during a Campaign. By a Lieutenant of the Left Wing* (Charleston, SC: Dan J. Dowling, 1836), 38.

107 George H. Williams, "The 'Free-State Letter' of Judge George H. Williams. Slavery in Oregon," *Quarterly of the Oregon Historical Society* 9, no. 3 (September 1, 1908): 263.

108 Ibid.

109 James W. Covington, "The Armed Occupation Act of 1842," *Florida Historical Quarterly* 40, no. 1 (July 1, 1961): 41–52.

110 Paul W. Gates, *History of Public Land Law Development* (Washington, DC: US Government Printing Office, 1968), 390.

111 Lorenzo Veracini, "The Settler-Colonial Situation," *Native Studies Review* 19, no. 1 (July 2010): 101.

112 Ibid., 104.

CHAPTER FIVE

1 Gray, *A History of Oregon, 1792–1849*, 382.

2 Peter Hardeman Burnett, *Recollections and Opinions of an Old Pioneer* (New York: D. Appleton, 1880), 215.

3 Ibid., 218.

4 Ibid.

5 Dorothy O. Johansen, *Empire of the Columbia: A History of the Pacific Northwest*, 2nd ed. (New York: Harper Collins, 1967), 244–245.

6 R. Gregory Nokes, *Breaking Chains: Slavery on Trial in the Oregon Territory* (Corvallis, OR: Oregon State University Press, 2013), 49.

7 Joseph Schafer, "Jesse Applegate: Pioneer, Statesman and Philosopher," *Washington Historical Quarterly* 1, no. 4 (January 4, 2010): 232.

8 Johansen, *Empire of the Columbia: A History of the Pacific Northwest*, 244.

9 Whaley, *Oregon and the Collapse of Illahee*, 161.

10 Elizabeth McLagan and Oregon Black History Project, *A Peculiar Paradise: A History of Blacks in Oregon, 1778–1940* (Athens, GA: Georgian Press, 1980), 11.

11 Jean Brownell, "Negroes in Oregon Before the Civil War" 1962, 30, MSS 1468, Oregon Historical Society, Portland.

12 Boyd, *Chinookan Peoples of the Lower Columbia*, 2013, 333.

13 Silas H. Smith, "Celebrations in Clatsop County," *Cumtux: Clatsop County Historical Society Quarterly* 24, no. 1 (Winter 2004): 40.

14 Ibid., 39.

15 "Receipt for $17.50 for Forwarding Election Returns to Office of J.E. Long," June 10, 1845, Territorial and Provisional Government Papers, 109 (Microfilm), Oregon Historical Society, Portland.

16 Barry M. Gough, "The Royal Navy and Oregon Crisis, 1844–1846," *BC Studies: The British Columbian Quarterly*, no. 9 (1971): 15.

17 George Simpson et al., "Secret Mission of Warre and Vavasour," *Washington Historical Quarterly* 3, no. 2 (April 1, 1912): 32.

18 Ibid.

19 Gough, "The Royal Navy and Oregon Crisis, 1844–1846," 19.

20 Joseph Schafer, "Documents Relative to Warre and Vavasour's Military Reconnaissance in Oregon, 1845–6," *Quarterly of the Oregon Historical Society* 10, no. 1 (March 1, 1909): 5.

21 Ibid., 16.

22 Gough, "The Royal Navy and Oregon Crisis, 1844–1846," 21.

23 Johansen, *Empire of the Columbia*, 265.

24 Powell, *Philosopher Pickett*, 16–17.

25 Schafer, "Documents Relative to Warre and Vavasour's Military Reconnaissance in Oregon, 1845–6," 9.

26 Gough, "The Royal Navy and Oregon Crisis, 1844–1846," 22.

27 Simpson et al., "Secret Mission of Warre and Vavasour," 34.

28 Gough, "The Royal Navy and Oregon Crisis, 1844–1846," 8.

29 Many historians have claimed that Ogden paid Saules two hundred dollars for the property. While this may be true, the sum is not included in Ogden's correspondence with Warre and Vavasour. Historian T. C. Elliott probably made the first reference to this amount in 1910, although he also misidentifies Saules as "James Sanler." See T. C. Elliott, "Peter Skene Ogden, Fur Trader," *Quarterly of the Oregon Historical Society* 11, no. 3 (September 1, 1910): 9.

30 Neil M. Howison, "Report of Lieutenant Neil M. Howison on Oregon, 1846: A Reprint," *Quarterly of the Oregon Historical Society* 14, no. 1 (March 1, 1913): 20.

31 James W. Nesmith, "Diary of the Emigration of 1843," *Quarterly of the Oregon Historical Society* 7, no. 4 (December 1, 1906): 329–359.

32 Simpson et al., "Secret Mission of Warre and Vavasour," 140.

33 See Malcolm J. Rorhbough's work for a history of American land policy from the early Republic to the Jacksonian Age. Malcolm J. Rohrbough, *The Land Office Business: The Settlement and Administration of American Public Lands, 1789–1837* (New York: Oxford University Press, 1968). See also Daniel Walker Howe, *What Hath God Wrought: The Transformation of America, 1815–1848* (New York: Oxford University Press, 2009), 127–128; and Patricia Nelson Limerick, *The Legacy of Conquest: The Unbroken Past of the American West* (New York: W. W. Norton, 1987), 55–65.

34 Simpson et al., "Secret Mission of Warre and Vavasour," 140.

35 Ibid.

36 Ibid.

37 Ibid., 141.

38 Ibid.

39 Ibid., 141–142.

40 Ibid., 142.

41 Ibid.

42 William G. Robbins, *Landscapes of Promise: The Oregon Story, 1800–1940* (Seattle: University of Washington Press, 1999), 82.

43 "Alexander Lattie's Fort George Journal, 1846," *Oregon Historical Quarterly* 64, no. 3 (September 1, 1963): 225.

44 Ibid., 210–211.

45 Ibid., 227.

46 Ibid., 239.

47 Gregory Paynter Shine, "'A Gallant Little Schooner': The U.S. Schooner Shark and the Oregon Country, 1846," *Oregon Historical Quarterly* 109, no. 4 (December 1, 2008): 546, doi:10.2307/20615903.

48 Ibid., 547.

49 Howison, "Report of Lieutenant Neil M. Howison on Oregon, 1846," 5.

50 Ibid.

51 Ibid.

52 Charles Melville Scammon, "Pioneer Nig Saul," in *The Overland Monthly*, ed. Bret Harte (A. Roman & Company, 1875), 275.

53 "The U.S. Schooner Shark," *Oregon Spectator*, August 6, 1846, 2.

54 In his 2008 article on the USS *Shark*, Gregory Paynter Shine referred to Saules as a "self-proclaimed bar-pilot" who "hoodwinked Howison into engaging his services." See "A Gallant Little Schooner," 21.

55 "Alexander Lattie's Fort George Journal, 1846," 49.

56 Roger T. Tetlow, "Black Saul Details," *Daily Astorian*, March 12, 1975.

57 Shine, "A Gallant Little Schooner," 538.

58 Chinook George, a prominent bar pilot and interpreter, also helped rescue the crew members of the USS *Peacock*. He is sometimes referred to as Indian George, One-eyed George, and George Ramsay. See J. Neilson Barry, "Astorians Who Became Permanent Settlers," *Washington Historical Quarterly* 24, no. 3 (July 1, 1933): 300.

59 Shine, "A Gallant Little Schooner," 549–550.

60 Ibid., 555.

61 Ibid., 557.

62 Oregon Pioneer Association, *Transactions of the Eighth Annual Reunion of the Oregon Pioneer Association*, 1876, 12.

63 Ibid., 14.

64 *Oregon Spectator*, May 28, 1846.

65 E. W. Wright, *Lewis & Dryden's Marine History of the Pacific Northwest: An Illustrated Review of the Growth and Development of the Maritime Industry, from the Advent of the Earliest Navigators to the Present Time, with Sketches and Portraits of a Number of Well Known Marine Men* (Portland: Lewis & Dryden, 1895), 21.

66 Ibid., n4. Southern and northern Democrats first used the term *Black Republican* in the mid-1850s to insinuate that black political interests controlled the new Republican Party. It is not known whether Grounds used the term derisively or not.

67 Ibid., 21.

68 *Oregon Spectator*, December 24, 1846.

69 Ichabod Sargent Bartlett, *History of Wyoming* (Chicago: S. J. Clarke Publishing, 1918), 348.

70 Gray Whaley, "'Complete Liberty'? Gender, Sexuality, Race, and Social Change on the Lower Columbia River, 1805–1838," *Ethnohistory* 54, no. 4 (September 21, 2007): 678.

71 Sylvia Van Kirk, *Many Tender Ties: Women in Fur-Trade Society, 1670–1870* (Watson and Dwyer, 1996), 240.

72 *Statutes of a General Nature Passed by the Legislative Assembly of the Territory of Oregon: At the Second Session, Begun and Held at Oregon City, December 2, 1850.* (Asahel Bush, Territorial Printer, 1851), 206.

73 Smith, "Celebrations in Clatsop County," 40.

74 Ibid.

75 Ibid.

76 Ibid., 40–41.

77 Wright, *Lewis & Dryden's Marine History of the Pacific Northwest*, 21n4.

78 Samuel T. McKean, "Memoirs of Samuel T. McKean," *Cumtux: Clatsop County Historical Society Quarterly* 13, no. 1 (Winter 1992): 6.

79 Ibid., 6–7.

80 Ibid., 7.

81 Ibid. While McKean's claim that his trip took eight days seems like a misprint, Columbia River travel was arduous during the mid-nineteenth century. For instance, the first journey of the *Callapooiah* took four days to travel from Oregon City to Astoria in August 1845. See Reunion, *Transactions of the Annual Reunion of the Oregon Pioneer Association*, 12.

82 Scammon, "Pioneer Nig Saul," 274.

83 Tetlow, "Black Saul Details."

84 Dorothy Nafus Morrison, *Outpost: John McLoughlin & the Far Northwest* (Portland: Oregon Historical Society Press, 1999), 440.

85 Richard White, *The Middle Ground: Indians, Empires, and Republics in the Great Lakes Region, 1650—1815* (Cambridge: Cambridge University Press, 2011), xi.

86 *Statutes of a General Nature Passed by the Legislative Assembly of the Territory of Oregon*, 182.

87 "Oregon," *Oregon Spectator*, August 22, 1850, 1.

88 Ibid.

89 McLagan and Project, *A Peculiar Paradise*, 185.

90 *Statutes of a General Nature Passed by the Legislative Assembly of the Territory of Oregon*, 182.

91 Schafer, "Jesse Applegate," 232.

92 Gray H. Whaley, "Oregon, Illahee, and the Empire Republic: A Case Study of American Colonialism, 1843–1858," *Western Historical Quarterly* 36, no. 2 (July 1, 2005): 176.

93 Bancroft and Victor, *History of Oregon*, vol. 1, 157.

94 *Statutes of a General Nature Passed by the Legislative Assembly of the Territory of Oregon* 181.

95 Ibid.

96 Ibid., 182.

97 Michael Schoeppner, "Peculiar Quarantines: The Seamen Acts and Regulatory Authority in the Antebellum South," *Law and History Review* 31, no. 3 (August 2013): 559–586.

98 Eugene H. Berwanger, *The Frontier against Slavery: Western Anti-Negro Prejudice and the Slavery Extension Controversy* (Champaign: University of Illinois Press, 2002), 70–71.

99 Ibid., 71.

100 Ibid.

101 Ibid.

102 Ibid., 65.

103 Stacey L. Smith, "Remaking Slavery in a Free State: Masters and Slaves in Gold Rush California," *Pacific Historical Review* 80, no. 1 (February 1, 2011): 28–63.

104 Bancroft and Victor, *History of Oregon*, vol. 2, 261.

105 This number was halved for married couples arriving after 1850, who received 320 acres in total. See William G. Robbins, *Oregon: This Storied Land* (Portland: Oregon Historical Society Press, 2005), 49.

106 Schwantes, *The Pacific Northwest*, 121.

107 *Statutes of a General Nature Passed by the Legislative Assembly of the Territory of Oregon*, 52.

108 Bancroft and Victor, *History of Oregon*, vol. 2, 120.

109 Ibid.

110 Whaley, *Oregon and the Collapse of Illahee*, 176.

111 "Center for the Study of the Pacific Northwest," https://www.washington.edu/uwired/outreach/cspn/Website/Classroom%20Materials/Pacific%20Northwest%20History/Lessons/Lesson%209/Census%20Data.html (accessed February 17, 2014).

112 Margaret D. Jacobs, *White Mother to a Dark Race: Settler Colonialism, Maternalism, and the Removal of Indigenous Children in the American West and Australia, 1880–1940* (Lincoln: University of Nebraska Press, 2011), 22.

113 Ibid.

114 Whaley, *Oregon and the Collapse of Illahee*, 176.

115 *Oregon Spectator*, August 22, 1850, 1.

116 Bancroft and Victor, *History of Oregon*, vol. 1, 120.

117 William Wharton Lester, *Decisions of the Interior Department in Public Land Cases: And Land Laws Passed by the Congress of the United States: Together with the Regulations of the General Land Office* (Philadelphia: H. P. & R. H. Small, 1860), 156.

118 Robbins, *Landscapes of Promise*, 83.

119 Mildred Colbert, "Naming and Early Settlement of Ilwaco, Washington," *Oregon Historical Quarterly* 47, no. 2 (June 1, 1946): 182.

120 Lucile Saunders McDonald, *Coast Country: A History of Southwest Washington* (Portland, OR: Binfords & Mort, 1966), 52.

121 Ibid., 53.

122 US Congress, House, *Index to the Reports of Committees of the House of Representatives for the First and Second of the Forty-Fifth Congress 1877-1878*, 45th Cong., 2d Sess., 1878, 176.

123 D. Clayton, "The Creation of Imperial Space in the Pacific Northwest," *Journal of Historical Geography* 26, no. 3 (July 1, 2000): 341.

124 Whaley, *Oregon and the Collapse of Illahee*, 162, 187.

125 Katherine G. Morrissey, *Mental Territories: Mapping the Inland Empire* (Ithaca, NY: Cornell University Press, 1997), 29.

126 Lucile McDonald, "Cape Disappointment's First Settler," *Seattle Times*, November 22, 1964, Sunday edition, Sunday magazine, 5.

127 Scammon, "Pioneer Nig Saul," 275–276.

128 Smith, "Celebrations in Clatsop County," 40.

129 "Drowned," *Oregon Spectator*, December 30, 1851, 2.

130 Gray, *A History of Oregon, 1792–1849*, 452.

131 A.B., "Rather beneath the Calling of a Worthy Act!," *Oregon Spectator*, October 14, 1847.

132 Bancroft, *History of Oregon*, vol. 2, 207.

133 McDonald, *Coast Country*, 35–36.

134 "A Partial History of the Whealdon Family in America," *The Sou'Wester* 32 (Fall 1997): 15.

135 Colbert, "Naming and Early Settlement of Ilwaco, Washington," 181.

136 McDonald, *Coast Country*, 54, 81–84.

137 According to the 1860 US Census, black people represented only 0.24 percent of Oregon's population and 0.26 percent of Washington Territories' population. "1860 Census: First Census to Count Washington Territory as Discrete Entity; Population Nearly 75 Percent Male; Native Americans; Counted for First Time, but Badly," HistoryLink.org," http://historylink.org/File/9463; McLagan and Project, *A Peculiar Paradise*, 185 (accessed October 25, 2016).

138 McLagan and Project, *A Peculiar Paradise*, 185.

CONCLUSION

1 Charles Melville Scammon, "In and Around Astoria," *Overland Monthly and Out West Magazine* 3, December 1869, 497.

2 James A. Colaiaco, *Frederick Douglass and the Fourth of July* (Macmillan, 2015), 52.

3 According to court documents, Vanderpool had been in Philadelphia and China prior to arriving in Oregon. See "Theophilus Magruder v. Jacob Vanderpool Case Documents," August 1851, Leaf 7, B 122, Special Collections and University Archives, University of Oregon Libraries, Eugene, OR.

4 *Oregon Spectator*, September 2, 1851.

5 "1870 U.S. Federal Census: 1870; San Francisco Ward 6," n.d., M593_81; Page: 106B; Image: 217, Family History Library Film: 545580, Salt Lake City, UT.

6 R. Gregory Nokes, *Breaking Chains: Slavery on Trial in the Oregon Territory* (Corvallis: Oregon State University Press, 2013), 142.

7 Ibid.

8 Oregon Constitutional Convention and Oregon Historical Society, *The Oregon Constitution and Proceedings and Debates of the Constitutional Convention of 1857* (Salem, OR: State Printing Dept., 1926), 385.

9 Ibid.

10 Ibid.

11 Nokes, *Breaking Chains*, 137.

12 George H. Williams, "The 'Free-State Letter' of Judge George H. Williams: Slavery in Oregon," *Quarterly of the Oregon Historical Society* 9, no. 3 (September 1, 1908): 266.

13 In 2013 historian Gregory Nokes published the definitive account of slavery in Oregon and *Holmes v. Ford*. See Nokes, *Breaking Chains*.

14 For an extended discussion of Indian removal in Oregon in the 1850s, see Whaley, *Oregon and the Collapse of Illahee*, 227–239.

15 Melinda Marie Jetté, *At the Hearth of the Crossed Races: A French-Indian Community in Nineteenth-Century Oregon, 1812–1859* (Corvallis: Oregon State University Press, 2015), 211.

16 Ibid., 217.

17 "Blacks in Oregon," https://oregonencyclopedia.org/articles/blacks_in_ oregon/#.WBedPdxuTE9 (accessed October 31, 2016).

18 Nell Irvin Painter uses the term *enlargements* to describe various historical phases in which more people were given access to the category of whiteness. Nell Irvin Painter, *The History of White People* (W. W. Norton & Company, 2011).' an idea as dangerous as it is seductive."—Boston Globe Telling perhaps the most important forgotten story in American history, eminent historian Nell Irvin Painter guides us through more than two thousand years of Western civilization, illuminating not only the invention of race but also the frequent praise of "whiteness" for economic, scientific, and political ends. A story filled with towering historical figures, The History of White People closes a huge gap in literature that has long focused on the non-white and forcefully reminds us that the concept of "race" is an all-too-human invention whose meaning, importance, and reality have changed as it has been driven by a long and rich history of events.

19 Leanne C. Serbulo and Karen J. Gibson, "Black and Blue: Police-Community Relations in Portland's Albina District, 1964–1985," *Oregon Historical Quarterly* 114, no. 1 (April 1, 2013): 6–37; Ellen Stroud, "Troubled Waters in Ecotopia: Environmental Racism in Portland, Oregon," *Radical History Review*, no. 74 (March 20, 1999): 65–95; Ethan Johnson and Felicia Williams, "Desegregation and Multiculturalism in the Portland Public Schools," *Oregon Historical Quarterly* 111, no. 1 (2010): 6–37.

20 Serbulo and Gibson, "Black and Blue," 8.

21 Ibid.

22 Johnson and Williams, "Desegregation and Multiculturalism in the Portland Public Schools," 26–33; Serbulo and Gibson, "Black and Blue," 21–23.

23 Casey Parks, "After Gentrification: America's Whitest Big City? Sure, but a Thriving Black Community, Too," *The Oregonian*, August 19, 2016.

Bibliography

PRIMARY SOURCES AND GOVERNMENT DOCUMENTS

"Alexander Lattie's Fort George Journal, 1846." *Oregon Historical Quarterly* 64, no. 3 (September 1, 1963): 197–245.

"An Address Delivered By Daniel Webster." *Granite Monthly: A New Hampshire Magazine* 5 (October 1881).

Article 4, Section 2, Clause 3: Missouri Constitution of 1820. http://press-pubs. uchicago.edu/founders/documents/a4_2_3s12.html (accessed March 28, 2016).

Barnard, Edward C. *Naked and a Prisoner: Captain Edward C. Barnard's Narrative of Shipwreck in Palau, 1832–1833*. Sharon, MA: Kendall Whaling Museum, 1980.

Blanchet, Francis Norbert. *Historical Sketches of the Catholic Church in Oregon, During the Past Forty Years*. Portland, OR, 1878.

Burnett, Peter Hardeman. *Recollections and Opinions of an Old Pioneer*. New York: D. Appleton, 1880.

———. "Letter from Peter H. Burnett, Esq." *Quarterly of the Oregon Historical Society* 24, no. 1 (1923): 105–108.

Carey, Charles Henry. "Diary of Rev. George Gary." *Quarterly of the Oregon Historical Society* 24, no. 1 (1923): 68–105.

Clarke, Samuel Asahel. *Pioneer Days of Oregon History*. Portland, OR: J. K. Gill Company, 1905.

Colvocoresses, George Musalas. *Four Years in the Government Exploring Expedition: Commanded by Captain Charles Wilkes, to the Island of Madeira, Cape Verd Island, Brazil*. New York: J. M. Fairchild, 1855.

Dally, Henry J., E. F. Murray, and Hubert Howe Bancroft. *Narrative of His Life, and Events in Cal. since 1843: By Henry J. Dally*. Manuscript, Bancroft Collection, University of California, Berkeley.

Dana, Richard Henry. *Two Years Before the Mast: A Personal Narrative*. New York: Houghton Mifflin, 1911.

"Documents," *Oregon Historical Quarterly*, 4, no. 4 (December 1903): 394–409.

"Elijah White's 1842 Oregon Census," 1842. MSS 1. Oregon Historical Society, Portland, Microfilm.

Erskine, Charles. *Twenty Years Before the Mast: With the More Thrilling Scenes and Incidents While Circumnavigating the Globe Under the Command of the Late Admiral Charles Wilkes, 1838–1842*. Chicago: Lakeside, 2006.

Forsyth, John, and William A. Slacum. "Slacum's Report on Oregon, 1836–7." *Quarterly of the Oregon Historical Society* 13, no. 2 (1912): 175–224.

Gray, William Henry. *A History of Oregon, 1792–1849 Drawn From Personal Observation and Authentic Information*. Portland, OR: Harris and Holman, 1870.

Grover, La Fayette. *The Oregon Archives: Including the Journals, Governors' Messages and Public Papers of Oregon, from the Earliest Attempt on the Part of the People to Form a Government, Down To, and Inclusive of the Session of the Territorial Legislature*. Salem, OR: Asahel Bush, public printer, 1853.

Hines, Gustavus. *Oregon, Its History, Condition and Prospects Containing a Description of the Geography, Climate and Productions, with Personal Adventures among the Indians during a Residence of the Author on the Plains Bordering the Pacific While Connected with the Oregon Mission*. New York: G. H. Derby, 1851.

Howison, Neil M. "Report of Lieutenant Neil M. Howison on Oregon, 1846: A Reprint." *Quarterly of the Oregon Historical Society* 14, no. 1 (March 1, 1913): 1–60.

Hudson, William L. "Journal of William L. Hudson, Comdg. U.S. Ship Peacock, on the Vessels Attached To the South Sea. Vol. Two." Microfilm Cabinet, drawer 1C—Q115.U46H83 1950. American Museum of Natural History Archives, New York, NY.

Jacobs, Harriet Ann, Lydia Maria Francis Child, and Jean Fagan Yellin. *Incidents in the Life of a Slave Girl: Written by Herself*. Cambridge, MA: Harvard University Press, 1987.

Jefferson, Thomas. *Notes on the State of Virginia*.1785; Richmond, VA: J. W. Randolph, 1853.

Lee, Daniel, and Joseph H. Frost. *10 Years in Oregon*. New York: J. Collard, 1844.

Lester, William Wharton. *Decisions of the Interior Department in Public Land Cases, And Land Laws Passed by the Congress of the United States; Together with the Regulations of the General Land Office*. Philadelphia: H. P. & R. H. Small, 1860.

Macy, William Hussey. *There She Blows! Or The Log of The Arethusa*. Boston: Lee & Shepard, 1877.

McKean, Samuel T. "Memoirs of Samuel T. McKean." *Cumtux: Clatsop County Historical Society Quarterly* 13, no. 1 (Winter 1992): 2–11.

Meany, Edmond S. "Diary of Wilkes in the Northwest." *Washington Historical Quarterly* 16, no. 1 (January 1, 1925): 49–61.

Nesmith, James W. "Diary of the Emigration of 1843." *Quarterly of the Oregon Historical Society* 7, no. 4 (December 1, 1906): 329–359.

O'Sullivan, John. *"Annexation." United States Magazine and Democratic Review* 17, no. 1 (August 1845): 5–10.

The Oregon Constitution and Proceedings and Debates of the Constitutional Convention of 1857. Salem, OR: State Printing Dept., 1926.

The Oregon Native Son, Volume 2. Portland, OR: Native Son Publishing, 1900.

Oregon Pioneer Association. *Transactions of the Eighth Annual Reunion of the Oregon Pioneer Association.* Salem, OR: E. M. Waite, 1881.

———— *Transactions of the Fifteenth Annual Reunion of the Oregon Pioneer Association.* Portland, OR: Press of Geo. H. Himes, 1887.

Paine, Thomas. *Collected Writings.* New York: Library of America, 1995.

Pickett, Charles Edward. *Address of Charles E. Pickett to the California Legislature upon the Government Fee in the Public Domain—Intercommunication and Land Monopolies and Correlative Topics.* Sacramento, CA: Public Domain, 1874.

————. *Address To The Veterans Of The Mexican War: Embodying A Historical Contrast Of The Two Great Political Parties Of The United States On Vital Issues.* San Francisco: Public Domain, 1880.

Portrait and Biographical Record of the Willamette Valley, Oregon: Containing Original Sketches of Many Well Known Citizens of the Past and Present. New York: Chapman Publishing, 1903.

Reynolds, William. *The Private Journal of William Reynolds: United States Exploring Expedition, 1838–1842.* New York: Penguin, 2004.

Schafer, Joseph. "Documents Relative to Warre and Vavasour's Military Reconnaissance in Oregon, 1845–6." *Quarterly of the Oregon Historical Society* 10, no. 1 (March 1, 1909): 1–99.

Simpson, George, Peter Skeen Ogden, Henry I. Warre, and M. Vavasour. "Secret Mission of Warre and Vavasour." *Washington Historical Quarterly* 3, no. 2 (April 1, 1912): 131–153.

Sketch of the Seminole War, and Sketches during a Campaign By a Lieutenant of the Left Wing. Charleston, SC: Dan J. Dowling, 1836.

Smith, Silas H. "Celebrations in Clatsop County." *Cumtux: Clatsop County Historical Society Quarterly* 24, no. 1 (Winter 2004): 37–42.

Statutes of a General Nature Passed by the Legislative Assembly of the Territory of Oregon: At the Second Session, Begun and Held at Oregon City, December 2, 1850. In the Seventy-Fifth Year of the Independence of the United States. Salem: OR: Asahel Bush, Territorial Printer, 1851.

Storke, Yda Addis. *A Memorial and Biographical History of the Counties of Santa Barbara, San Luis Obispo and Ventura, California.* Chicago: Lewis Publishing, 1891.

United States Office of Indian Affairs. *Annual Report of the Commissioner of Indian Affairs to the Secretary of the Interior for the Fiscal Year Ended 1851.* Washington, DC: US Government Printing Office, 1851.

"U.S., Atlantic Ports Seamen's Protection Certificates, 1792-1869" N.d. M2003, Roll 1. National Archives and Records Administration, Washington, DC.

U.S. Congress. *Congressional Globe.* 29th Cong., 1st Sess., 1846.

U.S. Congress. House. *Index to the Reports of Committees of the House of Representatives for the First and Second of the Forty-Fifth Congress 1877–1878.* 45th Cong., 2d Sess., 1878.

U.S. Congress. Senate, *Report of the Commissioner of Indian Affairs,* 28th Cong., 2d Sess., 1844. Vol. 1, S.Doc. 1, serial 449.

U.S. Congress. United States Office of Indian Affairs. *Annual Report of the Commissioner of Indian Affairs.* 29th Cong., 1st Sess., 1846.

White, Elijah. *Ten Years in Oregon: Travels and Adventures of Dr. E. White and Lady, West of the Rocky Mountains.* Ithaca, NY: Andrus, Gauntlett, & Co. 1850.

Wilkes, Charles. *Narrative of the United States Exploring Expedition: During the Years 1838, 1839, 1840, 1841, 1842.* Philadelphia: C. Sherman & Sons, 1858.

———. "Report on the Territory of Oregon." *Quarterly of the Oregon Historical Society* 12, no. 3 (September 1, 1911): 269–299.

Williams, George H. "The 'Free-State Letter' of Judge George H. Williams. Slavery in Oregon." *Quarterly of the Oregon Historical Society* 9, no. 3 (September 1, 1908): 254–273.

ARTICLES AND ANTHOLOGY BOOK CHAPTERS

Barry, J. Neilson. "Astorians Who Became Permanent Settlers." *Washington Historical Quarterly* 24, no. 3 (July 1, 1933): 221–231.

Bordwell, Constance. "Delay and Wreck of the Peacock: An Episode in the Wilkes Expedition." *Oregon Historical Quarterly* 92, no. 2 (July 1, 1991): 119–198.

Burnett, D. Graham. "Hydrographic Discipline among the Navigators: Charting an 'Empire of Commerce and Science' in the Nineteenth-Century Pacific." In *The Imperial Map: Cartography and the Mastery of Empire,* edited by James R. Akerman, 185–260. Chicago: University of Chicago Press, 2009.

Clayton, Daniel. "The Creation of Imperial Space in the Pacific Northwest." *Journal of Historical Geography* 26, no. 3 (July 1, 2000): 327–350.

Colbert, Mildred. "Naming and Early Settlement of Ilwaco, Washington." *Oregon Historical Quarterly* 47, no. 2 (June 1, 1946): 181–195.

Covington, James W. "The Armed Occupation Act of 1842." *Florida Historical Quarterly* 40, no. 1 (July 1, 1961): 41–52.

Dolin, Eric Jay. *Leviathan: The History of Whaling in America.* New York: W. W. Norton & Company, 2008.

Elliott, T. C. "Peter Skene Ogden, Fur Trader." *Quarterly of the Oregon Historical Society* 11, no. 3 (September 1, 1910): 229–278.

Gough, Barry M. "The Royal Navy and the Oregon Crisis, 1844–1846." *BC Studies: The British Columbian Quarterly,* no. 9 (1971): 15–37.

Harris, Cheryl I. "Whiteness as Property." *Harvard Law Review* 106, no. 8 (1993): 1707–1791.

Johnson, Ethan, and Felicia Williams. "Desegregation and Multiculturalism in the Portland Public Schools." *Oregon Historical Quarterly* 111, no. 1 (2010): 6–37.

Loewenberg, Robert J. "Creating a Provisional Government in Oregon: A Revision." *Pacific Northwest Quarterly* 68, no. 1 (January 1, 1977): 13–24.

McClintock, Thomas C. "James Saules, Peter Burnett, and the Oregon Black Exclusion Law of June 1844." *Pacific Northwest Quarterly* 86, no. 3 (July 1, 1995): 121–130.

Millner, Darrell. "Blacks in Oregon." The Oregon Encyclopedia. https://oregonencyclopedia.org/articles/blacks_in_oregon/#.WBedPdxuTE9 (accessed October 31, 2016).

Perry, Adele. "Reproducing Colonialism in British Columbia, 1849–1871." In *Bodies in Contact: Rethinking Colonial Encounters in World History*, edited by Antoinette Burton and Tony Ballantyne. 143–63. Durham, NC: Duke University Press Books, 2005.

Rolater, Fred S. "The American Indian and the Origin of the Second American Party System." *Wisconsin Magazine of History* 76, no. 3 (1993): 180–203.

Scammon, Charles Melville. "In and Around Astoria." *Overland Monthly and Out West* 3, no. 6 (December 1, 1869): 495–499.

———. "Pioneer Nig Saul." In *The Overland Monthly*, edited by Bret Harte, 273–76. San Francisco: A. Roman & Company, 1875.

Schafer, Joseph. "Jesse Applegate: Pioneer, Statesman and Philosopher." *Washington Historical Quarterly* 1, no. 4 (January 4, 2010): 217–233.

Schoeppner, Michael. "Peculiar Quarantines: The Seamen Acts and Regulatory Authority in the Antebellum South." *Law and History Review* 31, no. 3 (August 2013): 559–586.

Serbulo, Leanne C., and Karen J. Gibson. "Black and Blue: Police-Community Relations in Portland's Albina District, 1964–1985." *Oregon Historical Quarterly* 114, no. 1 (2013): 6–37.

Shine, Gregory Paynter. "'A Gallant Little Schooner': The U.S. Schooner Shark and the Oregon Country, 1846." *Oregon Historical Quarterly* 109, no. 4 (December 1, 2008): 536–565.

Smith, Stacey L. "Remaking Slavery in a Free State: Masters and Slaves in Gold Rush California." *Pacific Historical Review* 80, no. 1 (2011): 28–63.

Stroud, Ellen. "Troubled Waters in Ecotopia: Environmental Racism in Portland, Oregon." *Radical History Review*, no. 74 (March 20, 1999): 65–95.

Sylvester, Avery. "Voyages of the Pallas and Chenamus, 1843–45 (In Two Parts, Part II)." *Oregon Historical Quarterly* 34, no. 4 (December 1, 1933): 359–371.

Taylor, Quintard. "Slaves and Free Men: Blacks in the Oregon Country, 1840–1860." *Oregon Historical Quarterly* 83, no. 2 (July 1, 1982): 153–170.

Veracini, Lorenzo. "Introducing." *Settler Colonial Studies* 1, no. 1 (2011): 1–12.

———. "The Settler-Colonial Situation." *Native Studies Review* 19, no. 1 (July 2010): 101–118.

Wells, William Bittle, and Lute Pease. *Pacific Monthly*. Portland, OR: Pacific Monthly Pub. Co., 1900.

Wolfe, Patrick. "Race and Racialisation: Some Thoughts." *Postcolonial Studies* 5, no. 1 (2002): 51–62.

———. "Settler Colonialism and the Elimination of the Native." *Journal of Genocide Research* 8, no. 4 (2006): 387–409.

BOOKS AND UNPUBLISHED MANUSCRIPTS

Akerman, James R. *The Imperial Map: Cartography and the Mastery of Empire.* Chicago: University of Chicago Press, 2009.

Alexander, Michelle. *The New Jim Crow: Mass Incarceration in the Age of Colorblindness.* New York: New Press, 2010.

Anderson, Benedict. *Imagined Communities: Reflections on the Origin and Spread of Nationalism.* New York: Verso, 2006.

Applegate, Shannon. *Talking on Paper: An Anthology of Oregon Letters and Diaries.* Corvallis: Oregon State University Press, 1994.

Bancroft, Hubert Howe, and Frances Fuller Victor. *History of Oregon, Volume One.* San Francisco: The History Company, 1886.

———. *History of Oregon, Volume Two.* San Francisco: The History Company, 1888.

Bartlett, Ichabod Sargent. *History of Wyoming.* Chicago: S. J. Clarke Publishing, 1918.

Belich, James. *Replenishing the Earth: The Settler Revolution and the Rise of the Anglo World.* Oxford: Oxford University Press, 2011.

Berlin, Ira. *Generations of Captivity: A History of African-American Slaves.* Cambridge, MA: Harvard University Press, 2003.

———. *Slaves without Masters: The Free Negro in the Antebellum South.* New York: Pantheon, 1974.

Bhabha, Homi K. *The Location of Culture.* Abingdon, UK: Psychology Press, 1994.

Berwanger, Eugene H. *The Frontier against Slavery: Western Anti-Negro Prejudice and the Slavery Extension Controversy.* Champaign: University of Illinois Press, 2002.

Billington, Ray Allen, and Martin Ridge. *Westward Expansion: A History of the American Frontier.* Albuquerque: University of New Mexico Press, 2001.

Bolster, W. Jeffrey. *Black Jacks: African American Seamen in the Age of Sail.* Cambridge, MA: Harvard University Press, 1997.

Boyd, Robert T. *Chinookan Peoples of the Lower Columbia.* Seattle: University of Washington Press, 2013.

———. *The Coming of the Spirit of Pestilence: Introduced Infectious Diseases and Population Decline among Northwest Indians, 1774-1874.* Seattle: University of Washington Press, 1999.

Brosnan, Cornelius J. *Jason Lee, Prophet of the New Oregon.* Rutland, VT: Academy Books, 1985.

Brownell, Jean. *Negroes in Oregon Before the Civil War.* Oregon Historical Society, Portland. Unpublished Manuscript, 1962.

Chaffin, Tom. *Pathfinder: John Charles Frémont and the Course of American Empire.* London: Macmillan, 2004.

Colaiaco, James A. *Frederick Douglass and the Fourth of July.* London: Macmillan, 2015.

Dark, Russell. *Bar Sinister: The Story of the Columbia River Bar Pilots.* Clatsop County Historical Society, Astoria, OR: Unpublished Manuscript, n.d.

Dodds, Gordon B. *Oregon: A History.* New York: W. W. Norton, 1977.

Douthit, Nathan. *Uncertain Encounters: Indians and Whites at Peace and War in Southern Oregon, 1820s–1860s.* Corvallis: Oregon State University Press, 2002.

Dunbar-Ortiz, Roxanne. *An Indigenous Peoples' History of the United States.* Boston: Beacon Press, 2015.

Epstein, Dena J. *Sinful Tunes and Spirituals: Black Folk Music to the Civil War.* Chicago: University of Illinois Press, 2003.

Fanon, Frantz. *Black Skin, White Masks.* Translated by Richard Philcox. 1952; Rev ed. New York: Grove Press, 2008.

———. *The Wretched of the Earth.* Translated by Richard Philcox. 1961. Reprint, New York: Grove Press, 2005.

Faragher, John Mack. *Women and Men on the Overland Trail.* New Haven, CT: Yale University Press, 2001.

Franklin, John Hope. *The Free Negro in North Carolina, 1790–1860.* New York: W. W. Norton, 1971.

———, and Alfred A. Moss. *From Slavery to Freedom: A History of African-Americans.* 7th ed. New York: McGraw-Hill, 1994.

Galbraith, John S. *The Hudson's Bay Company as an Imperial Factor, 1821–1869.* Berkeley: University of California Press, 1957.

Gates, Paul W, Robert W Swenson. *History of Public Land Law Development.* Washington, DC: US Govt. Printing Office, 1968.

Gilroy, Paul. *The Black Atlantic: Modernity and Double Consciousness.* Cambridge, MA: Harvard University Press, 1993.

Guillaumin, Colette. *Racism, Sexism, Power and Ideology.* New York: Routledge, 2002.

Hixson, W. *American Settler Colonialism: A History.* New York, NY: Palgrave Macmillan, 2013.

Horne, Gerald. *Negro Comrades of the Crown: African Americans and the British Empire Fight the U.S. Before Emancipation.* New York: NYU Press, 2013.

Horsman, Reginald. *Race and Manifest Destiny: The Origins of American Racial Anglo-Saxonism.* Cambridge, MA: Harvard University Press, 1981.

Horton, James Oliver, and Lois E. Horton. *In Hope of Liberty: Culture, Community and Protest among Northern Free Blacks, 1700–1860.* New York: Oxford University Press, 1998.

Howe, Daniel Walker. *What Hath God Wrought: The Transformation of America, 1815–1848.* New York: Oxford University Press, 2009.

Hunt, Herbert, and Floyd C. Kaylor. *Washington, West of the Cascades: Historical and Descriptive; the Explorers, the Indians, the Pioneers, the Modern.* Chicago: S. J. Clarke Publishing, 1917.

Jacobs, Margaret D. *White Mother to a Dark Race: Settler Colonialism, Maternalism, and the Removal of Indigenous Children in the American West and Australia, 1880–1940.* Lincoln: University of Nebraska Press, 2011.

Jetté, Melinda Marie. *At the Hearth of the Crossed Races: A French-Indian Community in Nineteenth-Century Oregon, 1812–1859.* Corvallis: Oregon State University Press, 2015.

Jeynes, William. *American Educational History: School, Society, and the Common Good.* Thousand Oaks, CA: SAGE Publications, 2007.

Johnson, David Alan. *Founding the Far West: California, Oregon, and Nevada, 1840-1890.* Berkeley: University of California Press, 1992.

Johnson, Stephen, ed. *Burnt Cork: Traditions and Legacies of Blackface Minstrelsy.* Amherst: University of Massachusetts Press, 2012.

Josephy Jr., Alvin M. *The Nez Perce Indians and the Opening of the Northwest.* Boston: Mariner Books, 1997.

Joyner, Charles W. *Shared Traditions: Southern History and Folk Culture.* Chicago: University of Illinois Press, 1999.

Lavender, David. *Westward Vision: The Story of the Oregon Trail.* Lincoln: University of Nebraska Press, 1985.

Linebaugh, Peter, and Marcus Rediker. *The Many-Headed Hydra: Sailors, Slaves, Commoners, and the Hidden History of the Revolutionary Atlantic.* Boston: Beacon Press, 2000.

Lott, Eric. *Love and Theft: Blackface Minstrelsy and the American Working Class.* New York: Oxford University Press, 1993.

Malloy, Mary. *African Americans in the Maritime Trades: A Guide to Resources in New England.* Sharon, MA.: Kendall Whaling Museum, 1991.

McDonald, Lucile Saunders. *Coast Country: A History of Southwest Washington.* Portland, OR: Binfords & Mort, 1966.

McKinney, Sam. *Reach of Tide, Ring of History: A Columbia River Voyage.* Portland: Oregon Historical Society Press, 1987.

McLagan, Elizabeth, and Oregon Black History Project. *A Peculiar Paradise: A History of Blacks in Oregon, 1778-1940.* Athens, GA: Georgian Press, 1980.

Melville, Herman. *Moby Dick.* New York: Bantam Books, 1981.

Missall, John, and Mary Lou Missall. *The Seminole Wars: America's Longest Indian Conflict.* Gainesville: University Press of Florida, 2004.

Morgan, Ted. *Shovel of Stars: The Making of the American West 1800 to the Present.* New York: Simon and Schuster, 1996.

Morrison, Dorothy Nafus. *Outpost: John McLoughlin & the Far Northwest.* Portland: Oregon Historical Society Press, 1999.

Morrissey, Katherine G. *Mental Territories: Mapping the Inland Empire.* Ithaca, NY: Cornell University Press, 1997.

Nokes, R. Gregory. *Breaking Chains: Slavery on Trial in the Oregon Territory.* Corvallis: Oregon State University Press, 2013.

Noll, Mark A. *The Rise of Evangelicalism: The Age of Edwards, Whitefield and the Wesleys.* Downer's Grove, IL: InterVarsity Press, 2010.

Normen, Elizabeth J. *African American Connecticut Explored.* Middletown, CT: Wesleyan University Press, 2014.

Omi, Michael, and Howard Winant. *Racial Formation in the United States: From the 1960s to the 1990s.* New York: Psychology Press, 1994.

Painter, Nell Irvin. *The History of White People.* New York: W. W. Norton, 2011.

Philbrick, Nathaniel. *Sea of Glory: America's Voyage of Discovery: The U.S. Exploring Expedition, 1838–1842.* New York: Penguin, 2004.

Pomeroy, Earl Spencer. *The Pacific Slope: A History of California, Oregon, Washington, Idaho, Utah, and Nevada.* Reno: University of Nevada Press, 1965.

Powell, Lawrence Clark. *Philosopher Pickett: The Life and Writings of Charles Edward Pickett, Esq., of Virginia.* Berkeley: University of California Press, 1942.

Raboteau, Albert J. *Slave Religion: The Invisible Institution in the Antebellum South.* New York: Oxford University Press, 2004.

Robbins, William G. *Landscapes of Promise: The Oregon Story, 1800–1940.* Seattle: University of Washington Press, 1999.

———. *Oregon: This Storied Land.* Portland: Oregon Historical Society Press, 2005.

Roediger, David R. *How Race Survived US History: From Settlement and Slavery to the Obama Phenomenon.* New York: Verso, 2008.

———. *The Wages of Whiteness: Race and the Making of the American Working Class.* New York: Verso, 1999.

Rohrbough, Malcolm J. *The Land Office Business: The Settlement and Administration of American Public Lands, 1789–1837.* New York: Oxford University Press, 1968.

Ruby, Robert H., and John A. Brown. *Indians of the Pacific Northwest: A History.* Norman: University of Oklahoma Press, 1988.

Schwantes, Carlos Arnaldo. *The Pacific Northwest: An Interpretive History.* 1996; Rev. ed. Lincoln: University of Nebraska Press, 2000.

Snay, Mitchell. *Gospel of Disunion: Religion and Separatism in the Antebellum South.* Chapel Hill: University North Carolina Press, 2014.

Stanton, William Ragan. *The Great United States Exploring Expedition of 1838–1842.* Berkeley: University of California Press, 1975.

Starbuck, Alexander. *History of the American Whale Fishery.* New York: Castle, 1989.

Strong, Thomas Nelson. *Cathlamet on the Columbia: Recollections of the Indian People and Short Stories of Early Pioneer Days in the Valley of the Lower Columbia River.* Portland: The Holly Press, 1906.

Stern, Theodore. *Chiefs and Change in the Oregon Country: Indian Relations at Fort Nez Percés, 1818–1855.* Vol. 2. Corvallis: Oregon State University Press, 1996.

Taylor, Quintard. *In Search of the Racial Frontier: African Americans in the American West, 1528–1990*. New York: W. W. Norton, 1999.

de Tocqueville, Alexis. *Democracy in America*, vol. 1, *The Henry Reeve Text*. New York: Knopf, 1945.

Tomblin, Barbara. *Bluejackets and Contrabands: African Americans and the Union Navy*. Lexington: University Press of Kentucky, 2009.

Unruh, John D. *The Plains Across: The Overland Emigrants and the Trans-Mississippi West, 1840–60*. Champaign: University of Illinois Press, 1993.

Veracini, Lorenzo. *The Settler Colonial Present*. New York: Palgrave Macmillan, 2015.

———. *Settler Colonialism: A Theoretical Overview*. Cambridge Imperial and Post-Colonial Studies Series. Basingstoke, UK: Palgrave Macmillan, 2010.

Viola, Herman Joseph, and Carolyn Margolis. *Magnificent Voyagers: The U.S. Exploring Expedition, 1838–1842*. Washington DC: Smithsonian, 1985.

Warner, Robert Austin. *New Haven Negroes: A Social History*. New York: Arno Press, 1969.

Watson, Bruce McIntyre. "Lives Lived West of the Divide: A Biographical Dictionary of Fur Traders Working West of the Rockies, 1793–1858." http://www.lulu.com/shop/bruce-mcintyre-watson/lives-lived-west-of-the-divide-a-biographical-dictionary-of-fur-traders-working-west-of-the-rockies-1793-1858/ebook/product-20951764.html;jsessionid=A6B2B4ABA128846DBE5D81F1E3BBD496 (accessed September 29, 2013).

West, Elliott. *The Last Indian War: The Nez Perce Story*. New York: Oxford University Press, 2011.

Whaley, Gray H. *Oregon and the Collapse of Illahee: U.S. Empire and the Transformation of an Indigenous World, 1792–1859*. Chapel Hill: University of North Carolina Press, 2010.

White, Richard. *The Middle Ground: Indians, Empires, and Republics in the Great Lakes Region, 1650–1815*. Cambridge: Cambridge University Press, 2011.

———. *The Roots of Dependency: Subsistence, Environment, and Social Change among the Choctaws, Pawnees, and Navajos*. Lincoln: University of Nebraska Press, 1988.

Wolf, Eva Sheppard. *Race and Liberty in the New Nation: Emancipation in Virginia from the Revolution to Nat Turner's Rebellion*. Baton Rouge: Louisiana State University Press, 2006.

Wolfe, Patrick. *Settler Colonialism*. London: Continuum, 1998.

———. *Traces of History: Elementary Structures of Race*. New York: Verso Books, 2016.

Wright, E. W. *Lewis & Dryden's Marine History of the Pacific Northwest: An Illustrated Review of the Growth and Development of the Maritime Industry, from the Advent of the Earliest Navigators to the Present Time, with Sketches and Portraits of a Number of Well Known Marine Men*. Portland: Lewis & Dryden, 1895.

Index